MW01290295

ORA'S BOY

ORA'S BOY

JAMES NOVAK

© 2011 by James Novak. All rights reserved.

No part of this book may be reproduced, stored in a retrieval system, or transmitted by any means without the written permission of the author.

Names and identifying details of some of the people mentioned in this book have been changed.

ISBN: 978-1-4699-0736-9

Library of Congress Control Number: 2011961437

Printed in the United States of America

Any people depicted in stock imagery provided by Thinkstock are models, and such images are being used for illustrative purposes only.
Certain stock imagery © Thinkstock.

This book is printed on acid-free paper.

Because of the dynamic nature of the Internet, any web addresses or links contained in this book may have changed since publication and may no longer be valid. The views expressed in this work are solely those of the author and do not necessarily reflect the views of the publisher, and the publisher hereby disclaims any responsibility for them.

DEDICATION

This book is dedicated to my sisters, Lorraine Benoit and Claudette Saunders, who shared the journey with me during those difficult years and who were instrumental in recalling the memories of our youth.

And to my wife, Denise Novak, who stood by me, encouraged me, and made this book possible through her constructive reviews, suggested changes, and tireless effort in editing my manuscript. Thank you, sweetheart . . . You're the best!

CONTENTS

CHAPTER 1

GOD BLESS MRS. CAMIRE

On a cold, dreary November day back in 1939, I entered the world, the third child of Charles Arthur Virgin and Ora Marie Rose Virgin, so said my birth certificate. They were divorced one month later. That opened the floodgates for a life of shame, gossip, and misery, in the French Catholic immigrant neighborhood where I was born.

If you were downtrodden, an uneducated immigrant, spoke only French or broken English, and worked in the sweat shops of New England in the 1930s, gossip was your principal form of entertainment. To those poor souls whose everyday existence was relegated to rising at early dawn, working in the drudgery of the mills six and a half days a week, and honoring the traditions of their religion, Ora provided the fodder they sought after to delight their scornful tongues.

In the late 1930s, you were looked down upon if you married outside of your religion. Marriage vows were taken very seriously and divorce was extremely uncommon and disgraceful. It was understood that Catholics only married Catholics, Protestants only married Protestants, and Jews only married Jews. Whether you were happy or miserable was immaterial. You stood firmly by your marriage vows and stayed married for life . . . "til death do us part."

God forbid if you were Catholic and married someone from another religion or, worse yet, terminated your marriage by divorce. That would obviously indicate you were disrespectful of the tenets of your religion and were disavowed from ever receiving the sacraments. As a further consequence, you became the center of gossip and were disgraced by your very own family and neighbors.

In many families, women had no rights. They were expected to do as their husbands demanded.

If a woman divorced her husband, she was thought to be weak of character, mentally unstable, possibly promiscuous, and deemed to be an utter failure. Now, if you happen to be a Catholic and married outside of the church and got divorced, you were doomed to go to hell and be forever chastised by the church! Divorce is a mortal sin. You disgraced yourself in the eyes of the church.

It was even more difficult to bear if you lived in a French Catholic community in a small New England town in the late 1930s. Back then, you were really ostracized and scorned in your community. You were particularly scorned by those self-righteous neighbors who exalted themselves by preying on your failure.

How do I know that? Well, you see, my mother, Ora, a Catholic, married my Episcopalian father, Charles, outside of the Catholic Church and divorced him in December 1939. Shame on Ora.

From birth, I was burdened with the name, Lucien Roger Virgin. The most unfitting name imaginable. I was given a name that subjected me to derisive chiding and made me the butt of cruel and insensitive jokes.

Back where I was born, in the small New England mill town of Laconia, New Hampshire, I was embarrassed by my name and was reluctant to introduce myself to people for fear of their anticipated smirks. If I was embarrassed, I can only imagine the ridicule my mother sustained from her pious neighbors, whose daily prayers were addressed to the Blessed Virgin, Mary. In their minds, Ora was anything but a Virgin, and would have been more appropriately named, Ora Harlot. I was stuck with the last name of my father, who I only saw once in my life when I was six years old.

As for my first name, Lucien, my mother confessed to me that my grandmother begged her to name me Lucien after her son, Lucien, who died at an early age. That was not the name my mother would have chosen for me. My mother reluctantly acceded to my grandmother's desire. She always yearned for her mother's acceptance and approval and that was just another way of submitting to her wishes.

The name Roger derived from my uncle Roger, my grandmother's little pet son who beat his wife and spent all her hard-earned money on liquor, while his wife and children lived in squalor. That was my beginning. That's how I was branded with my unwanted name.

Why were my parents divorced just one month after I was born? The question begs an answer. Well, it seems their marriage disintegrated before I was born. According to my older sisters, Charlie wasn't a bad father. He appeared to love his two daughters and never struck his wife. However, the story has it that he was a womanizer and carouser, which left very little money for the family to live by on a painter's salary.

One evening, before I was born, my mother, father, five-year-old sister Lorraine, and two-year-old sister Claudie, gathered in the living room. Right then and there, those two little girls were asked to decide which parent they wanted to live with. No explanation given.

Instinctively, Claudie went to her crying mother's side. Perhaps out of sympathy, for she saw the tear running down the side of her mother's face. Lorraine began to walk toward her father, but, suddenly turned, and went to stand beside her little sister. Her move to Ora's side was done to unify with her little sister; not because she favored her mother over her father. What a terrible decision to force upon two little girls.

It was a bitter divorce. In court, Charlie claimed that Ora was an unfit mother. He fought to gain custody of the girls, even took them away from their mother and brought them to stay with his parents, Grandma Bessie and Grandpa Jim, in Tilton, New Hampshire. Charlie was so spiteful and so determined to bring pain and suffering to Ora, he did everything he could to hurt her. One day, he took the girls to a park to play. After they laughed and played on the swings, he pointed to a building and asked them, "Do you girls want to live in that building over there so you can be right next to the park?"

At their tender young age, they sensed there was something peculiar about the ominous looking building where Daddy pointed his finger.

Lorraine responded, "No, Daddy, that's a scary building. We don't like it."

As simply as that, they rejected his offer. They had no idea that building happened to be the Daniel Webster home in Franklin,

New Hampshire, where children without parents were placed for adoption.

He selfishly chose to abandon his two lovely daughters, simply to inflict pain on his wife. That may have well happened had not Grandma Bessie intervened. Grandma Bessie, in her infinite wisdom, knew the girls would be better off living with their mother. She became exasperated with her son, booted him out of her house, and testified in court on Ora's behalf so she could gain full custody of her children. With the divorce out of the way, Ora was entrusted with three young children to support, without any financial help from Charlie or any other source.

In recounting those early years, we initially lived in an apartment on Church Street in Laconia. In the 1940s, Laconia was a mill town, like many of the other town's in the state. Unique to Laconia, was the large influx of French Canadians who migrated there to work in the mills. My mother was a proud, feisty, hard working, frail French Canadian who was forced to quit school after the eighth grade to work in the mills and pay room and board to my Grandmother. To say she had a difficult childhood would be an understatement.

Soon after I was born, she was down to her last five dollars, with no food in the house to feed her three children. One cold winter day, she took Lorraine by the hand and walked to the nearby market. She ordered hamburger meat and put her five-dollar bill on the meat counter. While the butcher ground the meat, she went to pick up a loaf of bread. When she returned to pick up the ground meat, he asked her for her money.

"Ora, I've got your meat ready here. That comes to $1.79," he told her.

She was dumbfounded. Her five dollar bill was not on the counter. She distinctly remembered leaving the five dollar bill there.

Her argument was futile. "I know I left it . . . right there," she pleaded, as she pointed at the exact spot where she left the money.

He simply denied he ever saw it. There she stood, Lorraine in hand, tears streaming down her face, totally defenseless. She couldn't prove he took the money. However, out of the "graciousness of his heart," he extended her credit so she could feed her children. That was a turning point in my mother's life. As they made their way

4

through the snow covered sidewalk, she revealed to my big sister that from that day on, she would never, ever, be broke again.

In recalling my early years, I've relied a great deal on my sisters' recollections since they have a better recall of events that took place when I was an infant. Through our conversations, I discovered a whole new life I didn't even know existed. For instance, I didn't know I was boarded out most of the time when we lived off and on in Laconia the first four years of my life. What a revelation!

*   *   *

While she worked in the factories somewhere, she boarded us out to live full time with the Camire family. I swear Mrs. Camire was sent by God to look out after me. In my world, she was the most loving, caring surrogate mother I could have asked for. On the other hand, this blessed, kind woman bore the cross of being married to the meanest, most evil man the devil ever put on the face of this earth. There wasn't one ounce of goodness in that man.

The Camire's had six children who lived in constant fear of the next outburst and beating by their father. When he was drunk, which was often, everyone stayed as far away from him as possible. Without provocation, he would go after his children with a leather strap. The oldest, Theresa, was the main focus of his wrath. Everyone lived in fear of this lunatic. For the most part, he didn't have much to do with my sisters or me; however, we were nevertheless exposed to his insane rages and were scared to death of that despicable man.

Poor Mrs. Camire, she lived a life of hell on earth. She was a devout Catholic and would suffer at his hands rather than divorce him or even disclose the punishment she endured to a priest.

I am told, Mrs. Camire, whom my sisters called "*Matante*," which is a loving colloquial term meaning "my aunt," absolutely loved me. She was paid some pittance by my mother to take care of the three of us. The woman was a saint. She was a loving soul, and as good a mother as she could be to her six children and the three little Virgin toddlers she had in her stead. She would do everything in her power to protect us.

My mother dropped by occasionally to pay Mrs. Camire for sheltering us. However, she always had something to do and didn't stay around very long. Lorraine recalls *Matante* scolding my mother for not coming by to visit her children more often. I am sure my sisters felt abandoned and neglected during this time. Fortunately, I was too young to know.

One time, in a drunken stupor, Mr. Camire picked up my sister Claudie by the neck and raised her off the floor. Mrs. Camire was out of the room at the time. Big sister Lorraine, who was all of five or six, walked right up to that filthy slob, looked him right in the eye, and demanded he put Claudie down immediately. Lorraine was our guardian and wasn't afraid of anything.

Staring right into his eyes, in her cool, calm manner, she sternly told him; "Put . . . Her . . . Down . . . Now."

They stared at each other for a moment, which may have seemed like an eternity, and then he cowered and let Claudie drop to the floor. He never laid a hand on her again.

Not the case with me. He resented me because Mrs. Camire showered me with affection. I was her baby. There were several times when he lifted me from the floor by my right ear and dangled me in the air, much like holding a dead rabbit. While still dangling by my ear, he would threaten to put me in the burning wood stove in the kitchen. I cried and screamed while he laughed aloud and rejoiced in the attention he commanded.

As a consequence of his cruelty, my right ear was larger than my left ear and was so noticeable, my classmates called me "Dumbo" or "Elephant Ears" when I was old enough to go to school. I had horrible earaches and was hospitalized a few times, which I am sure was a result of his brutality. Ironically, my sisters never ever saw him pick me up by my ear. He was a coward. He wouldn't dare do that to me in front of Lorraine.

Some people never learn from their mistakes. My mother belonged in that category. She desperately craved male attention. Now, to my way of thinking, it would seem quite difficult for a divorcee with three children to find a man willing to marry her. Apparently that wasn't a problem for Ora. Somewhere along the line, and none of us three kids know when, she managed to snatch up and marry her second husband. She may have shed the name, Virgin, but a second marriage to a non-Catholic, only fueled the flames of gossip.

We never went to her wedding. All we know is that she married Harold Manson while we were living at the Camire's and they went to the St. Regis hotel in New York for their honeymoon. Later, Lorraine learned Harold's uncle was the Manager at the St. Regis.

Soon after they were married, we moved to East Hartford, Connecticut. As far as we could determine, they planned their moves around Lorraine's school schedule. The same day Lorraine finished the first grade at Saint Joseph's school, we were on our way to Hartford. If Ora and Harold had a plan for us, we were never told.

CHAPTER 2

World War II

We moved to East Hartford in 1942, smack dab in the middle of World War II. Aircraft companies couldn't build planes fast enough to support the war effort. Furthermore, the pay for aerospace workers was far better than the pay for factory workers in Laconia. Since many of the young men were drafted or volunteered to join the service, Harold had no problem landing a good paying job at Pratt & Whitney Aircraft Company in Hartford.

The draft was enacted by President Roosevelt in 1940 and all men between the ages of 18 to 65 had to register for the draft. From 1940 to 1947, over 10,000,000 men were inducted into the military. However, not all men whose number was called had to serve. Thirty percent of the draftees were rejected for physical reasons and were classified 4-F. The 4-F classification was given primarily for muscular and bone malformations, hearing or circulatory ailments, mental deficiency or disease, or even syphilis. There were ramifications when a man got that classification. You might as well have been classified as a leper. Nobody wanted to date those boys who didn't pass their physicals.

Dad #2 was a 4-Fer. We don't know what physical disability plagued Harold, but he certainly had to live with the contempt and animosity of his neighbors whose loved ones were killed or away in a foreign land fighting for their country. We suspect he was classified 4-F because of back problems. He stood very rigid and stiff, and although he never complained to us, he lacked flexibility of motion because of the stiffness in his back.

Our recently remarried mother constantly belittled and badgered Harold. The euphoria of their recent wedding soon disintegrated. The only common threads in their marriage were work, drink, and fight. Looking back on it, our mother was definitely bipolar. She had a Jekyll and Hyde personality. One minute she was loving and sweet and the next she demonstrated her violent temper and went into fits of rage, screaming and throwing whatever was in her path.

We learned at a very early age to stay away from her when she was angry. When Harold came home late, usually after drinking, there would always be a bitter quarrel. Mom would completely lose it. Instead of going into another room to calm down, she chose to immediately attack and belittle him, which often escalated into a fist fight, with the two of them throwing punches at one another. In a rage, she often picked up a pan of food from the stove and threw it at Harold. Lorraine and Claudie would run to their room and I would join them and hide in the closet. I sat in the corner of the closet, my hands shaking nervously, tears running down my face, until a door was slammed and silence returned to the house. Sometimes, I stayed in the solitude of the closet for hours. Oh, how we feared those encounters. My sisters would even pray to God that it would end. And it did . . . until the next time.

Looking back on it, Harold was a pretty good guy. He would have made a better father had my mother given him half a chance. Ora was extremely controlling. In her mind, it was her and her three children pitted against the world. In her subconscious, she believed she was protecting her children, when in reality she was letting Harold know she wore the pants in our family. She would only allow him to act like our father when it was convenient for her to do so.

We lived in an older two story colonial style Victorian house in East Hartford, close to the Pratt & Whitney plant. Harold worked the day shift and Ora worked the night shift. That left Harold to care for us at night. Lorraine recalls that every evening after supper, Harold gave us each a penny to go to the grocery store at the end of the street to buy a piece of candy. Without her around, he behaved like the father he wanted to be.

Lorraine was going through a period of sleepwalking when she was around seven years old. One night, she actually walked right out the front door and was walking down the street before Harold caught up with her. Even when we were sleeping, Harold diligently checked our rooms at night. He obviously panicked when Lorraine wasn't in her bed. Yet, he never showed his inner-fear as he ran

9

down the street after her. When he reached her, he softly clasped her hand and told her, "Don't you think its cold out here? Let's go back and get in your nice, warm bed." She obligingly turned around, as he assured her that everything was fine. Much relieved, he slowly walked her back to her bedroom.

Life during World War II is difficult to visualize. You had to have been there and lived it. There was a sense of national pride and unity in America that would never be duplicated in the history of the United States. To put it in perspective, you have to realize we were attacked by another foreign country on our very own soil when the Japanese bombed Pearl Harbor in 1941. Thus, the threat was ever-present that they would attack the mainland if they had the chance. Even in the safe harbor of our home, we feared the Japanese.

Patriotism flourished after the attack on Pearl Harbor. It went way beyond placing a flag outside in a flag holder. Everyone proudly and unselfishly made the necessary sacrifices to support the war effort. We had to adapt to many changes. Everything, including food, gas, tires, cotton, and clothing was rationed. Families were issued ration books, with stamps, to buy everyday commodities. Bartering for wanted goods became a common practice between families. Ration stamps were even traded for cash. People collected and donated the aluminum foil from the inside of cigarette packages. The aluminum foil was deposited in bins scattered about town. Many of the neighborhood cars were mounted on wooden crates because of a drastic shortage of rubber. It was virtually impossible to obtain replacement tires. Once you ran out of stamps, you were out of luck. Of course, there was a black market and ways to barter for everything. My mother was a master at bartering and we always managed to have enough gas for our car.

We had blackout shades in our house in East Hartford. So, you might ask, "What are blackout shades?" Since we lived close to the Pratt & Whitney plant, we were required to take special precautions for fear of an enemy attack. Consequently, all our pull-down blinds were made of a thick heavy canvas material and painted black on the outside to prevent any light from showing through. Often, at night, emergency sirens signaled the alarm and everyone immediately turned off all their lights and pulled down their blackout shades.

My mother was a bit paranoid and extremely frightened by the possibility of a Japanese attack. She even went so far as to place us near the kitchen stove when the siren blasted and told us she would turn on the gas and die right there, rather than allow us to be captured and murdered by the Japanese. As eerie as that may sound, she really meant it.

That was just a sampling of life in WW-II. Because of the scarcity of food during that time, people with enough land planted gardens. I don't recall if we had a garden, but there was a garden behind our house. Claudie recalled the day she went out there to pet two little gray kittens she saw running through the cornfield. My mother saw her chasing the cats and stopped her just before they entered the garage. Fortunately for her: Claudie's two gray cats were, in fact, two large rats!

Even though we were only renting the house in East Hartford, my mother couldn't resist the opportunity to make an extra dollar. She had no qualms about disrupting our family and renting out rooms to complete strangers. That said, she rented one of our bedrooms to an elderly man while we lived there. That began a trend that continued forever after.

*   *   *

Earlier, I alluded to the other trend that emerged. As soon a Lorraine finished the second grade in East Hartford, we moved back to Laconia. To this day, we never knew why they left two good paying jobs after only one year to move back to New Hampshire. Again, there was no explanation given. It just defied logic.

Mom went back to work in the needle shop and Harold worked at Moody's garage across from the high school. Lorraine was back at the French school, St. Joseph's, and Claudie entered kindergarten there also.

For me, it was back to the Camire's. I was three years old and no longer in diapers. And, I learned that if I needed to go to the bathroom, I had to go outside and use the outhouse. That's correct. They didn't have a toilet in the house. That's just the way it was. Naturally, it stunk in the outhouse, but my biggest fear was that I would fall through the hole. That was not beyond the realm of possibility. I dreaded that. Worse yet, in the winter, if any of the nine of us living there had to "do our business," we literally went into a large pot they kept inside the house. I can still recall my little butt touching the edge of that cold, stinking pot. At the end of the day, poor Lucien Camire had to carry that pot full of accumulated human excrement to the outhouse to be discarded.

I hardly recall living with my family after we returned to Laconia because I didn't see them that often. By then, I was nicknamed "Sonny." But, nobody knew where Sonny was. Mysteriously, I was kept away from my sisters. It's as though I was kept in hiding from someone.

As sweet as Mrs. Camire might have been, I certainly didn't want to be around her insane husband. Without my sisters there to defend me, I was more vulnerable to Edmund Camire's cruel antics. Mrs. Camire could only do so much to protect me. Why was I there? Why were we even in Laconia again? Why were they living on Court Street? Why wasn't I allowed to live with my family? So many questions were never answered.

Court Street was at least two miles from school. Harold took his car to work. My mother car-pooled to work, but my sisters had to walk the two miles to and from the French school every day. Winters in New Hampshire can be brutally cold. Both sisters often stopped at the top of Union Avenue hill, where the needle shop was located, and went inside to warm their hands and feet before continuing the long walk to school. Again, it defied logic. There was a good public school only a couple blocks away from where they lived on Court Street, yet, my mother insisted my sisters attend the French Catholic School.

What did she gain by that? Was she really concerned about the quality of their education? Was she trying to gain some sort of acceptance from the Catholic Church? Or, was she again trying to please her mother? It may have been a combination of the above. For whatever reason they chose to move back there, they settled into a pattern. Ora was secure in her job at Laconia Needle. Harold was well established at Moody's Auto & Body shop. Lorraine and Claudie made new friends and adjusted to the routines of the French school. I, in turn, was cloistered away in familiar surroundings at the Camire's.

Spring finally arrived, the snow eventually melted, the rivers swelled, and the lilacs and daffodils bloomed again, signaling the end of another harsh winter. June marked the conclusion of another school year for Lorraine. She just completed the third grade when you can guess what happened next? Yes, we were uprooted again. We were beginning to feel like a tennis ball at Wimbledon. Back and forth. Back and forth. Like a bunch of gypsies, all we ever seemed to do was move. We moved back to Connecticut again.

CHAPTER 3

END OF THE WAR

This time we moved to a house in a sprawling new development called Silver Lane Homes in Manchester, Connecticut. Housing construction was booming in the area to support the large influx of workers who relocated to work at Pratt & Whitney. To me, all the houses looked alike in Silver Lane. It was more akin to a subsidized housing complex. All the houses were painted in a bluish gray hue. They all seemed to be the same size, the same look, and the same gray color. I was actually scared to roam too far from home for fear I wouldn't be able to find my way back.

I don't know why we moved to Connecticut again. For that matter, I'll never know why we left in the first place. It had to be Ora's idea. She ruled the roost and Harold followed her lead, except when he had too much to drink. Then the tiger came out of his cage! I can only imagine they were lured back by the pursuit of high paying jobs. The plant was working three shifts and couldn't produce planes fast enough. Because of their previous experience, they were in demand. There was definitely a shortage of male workers and my mother was reputed to be an excellent worker. At least in Connecticut, everyone assumed Harold was our biological father, and besides, people there couldn't care less about our religion or our nationality.

Ora and Harold worked different shifts again. Supposedly, one of them would always be home to look out after us. Oddly, though, I don't recall seeing them that often. They didn't have the time or the inclination to shop for food or they chose to barter their food rations for other things. There was never enough to eat. Knowing my mother, their main focus was on making money, not on eating. With her, the means to the end always revolved around the pursuit of the almighty dollar. That's difficult for someone to understand, unless you lived during the great depression of the 1930s. In my youth, I couldn't appreciate the hard times she must have lived through. Apparently, the Depression affected her more than other people.

By the time she was nine, big sister Lorraine took on the role of surrogate mother. There was no Mrs. Camire in Connecticut. Even though she was barely nine, Lorraine was always there to comfort Claudie and me and to crank out those peanut butter and jelly sandwiches, which seemed to be our everyday staple of subsistence.

Butter was a scarce commodity during the war. In its place we ate a concoction called Nucoa that was basically lard with a red powder stirred in it to make it turn yellow. Try it once; you'll pass on it forever.

Claudie and I were so malnourished; we constantly had large boils, reeking with puss, on our elbows and knees. They were very painful. We'd yell out when my mother placed pads, immersed in boiling water, on the boils to make them burst open. Oddly enough, Lorraine didn't have any boils. She must have skipped the peanut butter.

Since I was the runt of the litter, I pretty much played whatever my sisters chose to play. Lorraine was very creative and we wiled away the days playing girlie things like make believe house, or make believe afternoon tea, or make believe school, or whatever fantasy she concocted at the time. She was totally intrigued by the medical profession, so she would be the doctor, Claudie the nurse and, of course, I had to be the patient if I wanted to play with them.

I loved my sisters and sensed they would always protect me; however, being the youngest, they rejoiced in playing mind games at my expense. I was their scapegoat and gave in without much resistance. One of their favorite pastimes was to pretend I didn't exist. Lorraine would ask, "Have you seen Sonny?"

Claudie would respond, "No, I don't know where he is."

This would go on for about fifteen minutes while I screamed at the top of my lungs, "I'm here!" "I'm here!" I would sometimes work myself up in such a frenzy over that tease; they would end up hugging me and assuring me that they knew I was in the room. Still, I fell for it every time.

I'll never forget the time my sisters let me join them on a little journey down to the end of the subdivision and across the road where there was a wooded area and a creek bed. At the creek, one of the neighborhood kids coaxed me into stepping into the water, with promises that it would soothe my feet.

"Oh, get in there, Sonny. It'll make you feeeeel soooo goood," he convincingly told me. Of course, he didn't tell me I was stepping in quicksand. As I slowly began to sink into the murky water, all the kids panicked, ran, and left me to wonder if I would be totally swallowed in the sinking mud.

With sheer desperation, and a shocked look on their faces, Lorraine and Claudie tugged and pulled until they successfully managed to free me out of the muck.

All the while, Lorraine was saying things like, "Don't tell Mom. She'll be mad at you. You're not supposed to be here." Good reverse psychology. She tried to convince me that 'I' was the one that was in trouble. To settle the doubt in her mind, she let me know that if I told anyone what happened, 'I' would suffer dire consequences. That day, 'I' learned the code: "Hear no evil. See no evil. Speak no evil." That proved to be a very practical lesson in honing my survival skills.

When I wasn't with my sisters, for the most part, I played alone. There were other boys in the neighborhood, but I was younger and smaller than most boys, so I knew I wouldn't be bullied if I stayed home and played by myself. A tricycle, an imagination, and some Popsicle sticks; what more did a boy need! However, just because I didn't want to play with boys, didn't mean I was averse to playing with girls. In fact, my best friend was my gal pal, Gayle. Even in those pre-adolescent years, I recognized that Gayle was a little doll. She would have won a Shirley Temple look-alike contest in a heartbeat. Her blonde hair was fashioned in ringlets, much like Shirley Temple. I confess, I had a crush on this little Princess of the Projects. Lorraine and Claudie found it to be rather charming when I serenaded her with a song I improvised, by substituting her name, Gayle, for the word "gal" in the song Judy Garland popularized in 1943 from the movie with the same name, titled, *"For me and my Gal."*

"The bells are ringing, for me and my Gayle,
The birds are singing, for me and my Gayle,
Everybody's been knowing, to a wedding they're going . . ."

Since Lorraine was ten and Claudie was seven at the time, they were allowed to go to the movies on Saturday afternoon, with the stipulation they had to drag me along. Horror movies were just coming into vogue and they knew how impressionable I was. For their pleasure and enjoyment, at my expense, they took me to see, "The Mummy's Curse."

Oh my God, I was scared out of my wits. I trembled as the Mummy, wrapped in gauze, emerged from his tomb in the dead of night. Dragging his right foot through the swamp, he slowly approached his next victim. I was petrified; they were ecstatic! Yet, I knew they were just as frightened of the Mummy as I was.

We all slept together, covered under blankets, in Lorraine's bed that first night after seeing the movie. From that day on, I refused to go down into the cellar of our house. For weeks, I stayed awake at night and prayed that the Mummy wouldn't come to our house—from the creek with the quicksand across the road.

No more code of honor. If they scared me like that again, I threatened to tell my mother.

*　　*　　*

In the fall of 1944, I turned five and attended kindergarten at St. James parochial school in downtown Manchester. Claudie should have been in the second grade but somehow skipped a grade and entered the third grade at St. James. Lorraine went away that year to live with Aunt Mildred and Uncle Cecil on their farm in Standish, Maine.

Lorraine actually attended school in a little one-room schoolhouse in the bucolic town of Standish. I vaguely recall the farm. It was so different from life in the big city of Manchester, Connecticut. It contrasted the simplicity and serenity of the simple life in rural Maine with the crowding and hectic lifestyle that prevailed in the growing metropolis of Manchester.

We went to Standish to visit Harold's sister, Aunt Mildred, in the summer of 44.' What I remember most was how calm and peaceful it was up there in the middle of nowhere. I totally forgot about the war and the constant bickering between my mother and Harold. They were on their best behavior when we were in Maine.

Their house was way out in the country, within view of only one neighbor. He was an old man who lived alone in a small shack across the road. As you looked down the road, as far as the eye could see there were rock walls bordering both sides of the road. I assumed that was to keep the cattle from straying from your property.

I don't know how many acres Uncle Cecil owned, but he wasn't a cattle farmer. Oh, they had pigs and chickens and a little bull terrier dog named Rixie. Most of all, they had two huge gardens on their farm. One was on the west side of the house near the barn and the other was in the field behind the house. There was no scarcity of food. Up the road was a large dairy farm where they got all the dairy products they could ever want. This was the simple life in its purest form.

They had a hand pump in the kitchen sink where they pumped clear fresh water from the well. The first time we visited them, there wasn't even a toilet in the house. Since it was summer, we certainly didn't mind going to the little three-seat outhouse that set in a corner of the barn. The girls and I played in the fields and went down to the pig pen in the back pasture to visit the pigs. We enjoyed every moment of the brief time we spent in Maine. Uncle Cecil and Harold even took me fishing in one of the nearby lakes. I was so excited when I caught my first hornpout, I didn't even mind its horn sticking me in my hand.

Aunt Mildred was the quintessential classic, stoic, cultured lady of her time. She was extremely poised, well read, and sophisticated. Yet, blended with that poise and elegance was a warm heart and loving soul. She was especially fond of Lorraine and offered to have her live with them the next school year. That was God sent for Lorraine. She loved Aunt Mildred and Uncle Cecil and had the best year of her childhood the year she stayed with them. They were kind and caring to my big sister and contributed immensely to her future development in so many ways.

It was just before Christmas in 1944 when Harold took me to the Elks Club annual Christmas party for children. I suspect my mother made him take me. She didn't go with us. Perhaps she was working. The big party was held at night and the auditorium was full of bug-eyed children waiting to see Santa Claus, with his long white beard, dressed in his red velvet suit. It was one of those evenings a boy never forgets. When it was my turn to meet Santa, he reached in his bag and handed me a painted wooden toy train with an engine and caboose. At that moment, I cried with tears of joy. I am sure I beamed from ear to ear when I looked at Harold to show him my Christmas present from Santa. I couldn't help but notice the smile on his face, as he looked every bit as happy as I did. For a rare moment, I felt like I was bonding with my Dad.

*   *   *

1945 was a special year for many reasons. Least of which was that everyone, regardless of their age, witnessed the end of World War II unfolding right before their eyes. Every warm-blooded American was impacted in some way by the war. The events of that historical tragedy were followed daily at home on the radio and weekly on movie screens across the country. Every Saturday, before the main matinee, theatres flashed highlights from the battlefront from the week before. We watched with a mixture of pride and horror as the American P-38 Lightning, P-51 Mustangs, B-17 Flying Fortress, and the B-29 Super Fortress, demonstrated America's flying superiority over the enemy forces.

Unfortunately, we were also exposed to the dark side of combat when we witnessed the hundreds upon hundreds of young American soldiers being gunned down on foreign soils from the far reaches of Normandy, France, to enemy territories in Guam, Japan, and the Philippines. We were living history.

In my kindergarten days at St. James School, we practiced bombing drills by crouching in the classroom with our hands over our heads until the siren ended. It didn't matter if we were in the schoolyard, the cafeteria, or the classroom. We were taught to rush to our classroom, kneel on the floor in the corner farthest away from the windows, place our hands over our head, and stay in that silent crouch until the nuns told us it was safe to stand up again.

In my early boyhood, I followed the war on the radio and watched it on the big screen at the Saturday matinee. Americans shared the pride and joy of victory as the allied forces advanced toward the ultimate surrender of the Japanese on VJ Day, August 15, 1945.

While historians may argue as to the exact date the war ended, nobody will ever disagree with the horror of the impact of August 6, 1945, when Colonel Paul Tibbets flew a B-29 Super Fortress over the Japanese city of Hiroshima and released the most destructive explosion in modern history, dubbed "Little Boy." That moment changed the world we live in forever.

Later that day, President Truman informed the world that we had just released the atomic bomb on Hiroshima, to be followed three days later with another atomic bomb being dropped over the city of Nagasaki. The war certainly ended with that devastating blow to the Japanese forces, which was quickly followed by Japanese emperor, Showa Hirohito's public broadcast of his intent to surrender on August 14, 1945. For all practical purposes, the war was over.

After five long years of tragedy and human sacrifice, it was finally over. Mothers, fathers, wives, girlfriends, brothers, and sisters, shouted the praises of victory outside their homes for all to hear. They shed tears of joy and banged on pots and pans with sticks and spoons for their neighbors to share their ecstasy.

For me, the most unforgettable moment of all happened on a late August evening when Mom and Harold took me and Claudie to the city square near the park in downtown Manchester. We watched the soldiers come marching home to a heroes welcome before the throng of well-wishers and loved ones. People stood five deep on the sidewalks throughout the parade route. I was hoisted on Harold's shoulders, dressed in my little Navy outfit, waving my hand held American flag. What a euphoric moment. One that would be indelibly stamped in my mind forever.

Shortly after the end of the war, we moved again. I don't know if there was a big layoff at the plant or if my mother sold our house to a returning G.I. for a handsome profit, but, some magical magnet pulled us back to Laconia, New Hampshire, to begin the next chapter in my life. What was an ending became a new beginning.

46 Winter Street

CHAPTER 4

46 WINTER STREET

It's remarkable how life changed after the war. It was as though a dam overflowed and all the pent up demand from the sacrifices made the previous five years came pouring over. The G.I.'s returned home with hoards of money saved while in combat. Many went to college under the G.I. bill. Others bought homes with their savings and adjusted back into civilian life. It seemed like everyone was buying a new car. Likewise, housewives and newlyweds were busily buying shoes, dresses, hosiery, and all the finer things in life they didn't have access to during the war. Ration cards, which were so much a part of the American way of life, suddenly vanished into oblivion. All this pent up demand and spending signaled a new era of prosperity.

It soon became obvious that my mother and Harold also managed to save a considerable amount of money while working in Connecticut. Shortly after we returned to Laconia, they bought a new Chevrolet and a nice two story duplex right in the heart of the French community.

Laconia was made up of six distinct wards. Although French Canadians were scattered about everywhere, Ward 2 was predominantly populated by French speaking Catholics. Not only did our house sit in the middle of Ward 2, our back yard abutted the French school and parish property.

We literally lived a stone's throw from school. Besides owning the two story duplex, Ora and Harold owned the adjacent lot next to the house, which had seven garages at the rear of the property. They rented those out for added income. We also had a two-car garage beside our house. When we first moved there, the Paris's lived on the right side of the duplex. They had rented there for several years before my mother bought the place.

It didn't take the Mrs. Manson money machine very long to figure out that she could convert their side into two apartments and increase her revenue. Unfortunately, with little regard for the Paris's, she booted them out as soon as she began the conversion.

We lived on the left side of the duplex. The upper floor had three bedrooms and a bathroom. From time to time, I had my very own bedroom at the far end of the left side. Lorraine and Claudie shared a large bedroom on the right side next to the bathroom. So, who occupied the third bedroom? The answer: Any renter who responded to the "Room for Rent" sign my mother placed in the lower front window. Needless to say, we had a menagerie of houseguests over the years.

The one renter I recall above all was Sergeant Page. Mom and Harold called him "Pagey," but I always addressed him as Sergeant Page. I could tell by the spark in his eyes that he preferred to be identified by his military rank. Most people tried to forget World War II after it ended, but Sergeant Page wouldn't let it be forgotten. His crowning achievement in life was being a sergeant in the U.S. Army. That was his identity, his life, and he didn't know how to let it die. He had few clothes, other than his military uniforms, which he wore practically every day. He walked the streets of Laconia, in his uniform, in search of a salute of gratitude or a free beer at Freddy's Café. In time, he was ridiculed for still wearing his uniform, as he staggered back to his room from Freddy's to spit-shine his shoes to prepare for the next day. I believe alcohol finally got the best of the old Serge and he moved away to enter the V.A. hospital.

There we were, a family of five, having to share our one bathroom with complete strangers. So much for privacy. In Ora's world, privacy took a back seat to her relentless pursuit of the almighty dollar.

Downstairs, the living room was immediately on your left. The kitchen was at the end of the hall. Mom and Harold entered their bedroom from either the double French doors in the living room or from the kitchen. A door at the rear of the kitchen led to an enclosed back porch. The glassed-in porch was delightful in the summer, but far too cold to sit in during the winter. That became my bedroom whenever my room was rented out.

The basement area was huge. It was accessed by two separate doors at the rear of the house. Shortly after we moved in, my mother had an oil-burning furnace installed on our side. We even had a root cellar in the basement where my mother stored homegrown canned goods, potatoes, and apples, to carry us through the long winter months. At that, we still had room to roller skate around the furnace.

The tenant's side was heated by a coal furnace. Coal was stored in a large coal bin and Harold shoveled it into the furnace every day. We weren't allowed on their side, for the simple reason that if anything was missing from their storage areas we wouldn't be blamed. That was fine by me. That side of the cellar gave me the creeps. I fearfully imagined a robber entering through an unlocked cellar door and torturing us. That's how my mind worked at the impressionable age of six.

Below our back porch, was an enclosed storage area where we kept our icebox, bicycles, ladders, paint, and such.

Our back yard covered over a half an acre. Even in the dead of winter, Mom preferred to hang her washing out on the clothesline in the fresh air. When she took the sheets off the clothesline, they stood upright like a cardboard wall. Beyond the clotheslines, we grew a garden, which went clear to the fence separating our property from the French school skating rink. Our other lot was a popular shortcut to the French school. We didn't mind the school kids walking through our lot on their way to school. They certainly didn't harm the property or even step on the grass.

However, once they stepped off our lot, there was a small strip of land that actually touched our neighbor's property line. To call it a "backyard" would be an overstatement. From the rear of her house, her property extended almost to the skating rink. Her lot hadn't been maintained for years. It was literally a weed patch. Weeds stood at least four feet high. Mrs. Lafrabois was typical of many of the older Canadian immigrants who settled in Laconia. She had nothing better to do with her life than constantly find things to complain about. Complaining was how she spent her day. She spent most of her day peering out her rear window to spot some poor kid walking on the beaten down path that barely touched a corner of her property.

She was quick to open her rear door and yell, "Get off my property" or "That's private property." Everyone ignored her and proceeded on their way to school.

I supposed some people were just born with a mean temperament and nothing would change them. Like everyone else, I just let her rant and rave and ignored her complaining. More importantly, we were finally together as a family in a place we could call home. That was my favorite house when I was growing up.

Lorraine returned to the new house on Winter Street from her year in Standish, Maine, just before the beginning of the next school year. While she was away, Claudie and I whiled away the summer roaming around our new surroundings. We had a whole new neighborhood to explore. Claudie was pretty much a tomboy and closer in age to me so we enjoyed playing the same games. Rather than playing with dolls and girlie things, we were more into Cowboys and Indians, climbing trees, and playing catch with a baseball. We tied pillows to saw horses and rode into the sunset chasing the bad Indians away from our imaginary camp.

Cowboy movies were popular in the mid-1940s, and occasionally my mother gave us the twelve cent fare to go to the old Garden theatre on Saturday afternoon to watch our singing heroes, Roy Rodgers and Dale Evans, Gene Autry, Tom Mix, and, of course, the Lone Ranger and his pal Tonto.

At night, I lulled myself to sleep pretending I was sitting around the campfire with Gene and the boys after a hard day riding our horses out on the range.

On Sunday evening at five o'clock, we huddled around the radio and scared the dickens out of ourselves listening to "The Shadow." The show began with an ominous deep voice announcing: "Who knows what evil lurks in the hearts of men? (Pause) The Shadow knows!" That kept us glued to the radio for the next half hour.

Ora and Harold both worked days. Claudie and I were told to stay home while they were at work. For the most part we did. We waited for the ice truck to come up the street so we could put the ice my mother ordered into the icebox in the storage shed. While the iceman placed a block of ice on our porch, we scurried to the back of the ice truck to grab a chunk of ice to lick across our waiting lips. Even though we lived in a modern house with plumbing and electricity, we didn't have a refrigerator the first year we lived there.

We also waited for the LaBonte Farms milk truck to deliver our bottles of milk, which they set on the front porch. We then put it in the icebox so it wouldn't spoil. In the winter, we brought the milk into the house before it froze. Otherwise, the cream at the top would spill over and empty onto the side of the glass quart bottles. Yes, life was different in the 40s'. Yet, it was orderly and uncomplicated.

* * *

If you were born and raised in New England, you were born and raised to be a Boston Red Sox fan. You were born with Red Sox blood, and the slightest indication that you might favor the dreaded evil New York Yankees branded you a disloyal traitor. It was a great rivalry. I recall many a day sitting on the stoop by the front porch next to the Fournier's candy store in the summer of 46,' listening to the Red Sox play ball.

What an exciting season. The Sox had a completely new lineup that year. Players like Bobby Doer, Johnny Pesky, Rip Russell, Pinky Higgins, Dom DiMaggio, and, of course, the venerable Ted Williams, were penned into the starting lineup. We beat the Yankees for the pennant and played our hearts out only to be defeated in the seventh game of the World Series by the St. Louis Cardinals.

Who could forget. The game was tied going into the eighth inning. The Cardinals had Mr. Hustle, Enos Slaughter, on first base. At the crack of Harry Walker's bat, Slaughter ran with all his might and never stopped until he slid into home plate. Unfortunately, Johnny Pesky delayed the relay throw to home plate and Slaughter was safe. Game over.

We hadn't won the World Series since 1918, the year the Red Sox traded Babe Ruth to the Yankees. Our losses became known as "the Curse of the Bambino." And, like all good Red Sox fans, I learned to say the mantra, "Wait til next year."

The Fournier's lived in a two story house next to their little candy store, which was squeezed in between another two story house. The candy store couldn't have been more than 15 feet wide by 30 feet long. The Fournier's were old and probably retired. I can't imagine they made a living selling penny candy and soda pop.

As you entered the store, on the right side stood an enclosed glass case, with a large variety of candies. Most of the candies sold for a penny apiece. Further down the aisle were the soda bins, full of various flavors of chilled soda bottles. Or, as we called it in New Hampshire, "tonic." They didn't have soda in cans back then. On the other side of the narrow aisle was a pinball machine, and beyond that, stood stacked cases of soda bottles, waiting for their place in the chilled water. That was it.

That pinball machine became a close friend of mine the six years we lived on Winter Street. On cold winter days I huddled with friends by the warmth of the pot-bellied stove and watched the silver ball being maneuvered by the skilled dexterity of enthusiastic players. After countless hours observing the talented players, I too honed my skills on that magical machine, and eventually became a feared competitor for those who dared gamble their abilities against mine.

Our mother rarely gave us money, so Claudie and I learned to improvise. Fortunately, there was always an ample supply of empty beer bottles in the cellar that we turned in at Morin's supermarket for cash. We were paid two cents each for the 12-ounce bottles and a nickel for the quart size. The secret was to take only a few bottles at a time. We waited until after the weekend was over to deplete their stash and never took more than a few bottles at a time. Just enough to buy a few pieces of candy at Fournier's to munch on while I watched the older boys play the pinball machine or listened to my beloved Red Sox compete in the game of summer.

*   *   *

The end of summer signaled the beginning of another school year. Finally, all three of us would be attending the same school. It was time for me to make new friendships that would last a lifetime. I would be in the same class, with the same boys and girls, for at least the next eight years. However, I was still the new kid on the block and had to earn the respect of my classmates. And, as narrow-minded and hateful as it may sound, I am sure that some of the mothers of my fellow classmates told their sons and daughters that I was the little boy whose mother had been married twice to men who weren't Catholics.

Like it or not, that's the stigma my sisters and I had to live with. I couldn't change that. I was part of the fabric of my mother's past. At least most young kids didn't carry the biases and prejudices of their parents and, in time, I was accepted for myself, despite my mother's immoral reputation.

At St. Joseph's, the girls wore blue one piece dresses with hard white plastic collars that snapped onto their uniform, much like the clips on a binder. The boys only had to wear a shirt and tie to school. Through the first four grades, the boys were separated from the girls. Boys attended classes with boys, and girls only with other girls. We weren't even allowed to mingle outside during recess.

It was widely held that if you wanted your children to have a good education, you sent them to a Catholic school. The nuns had a reputation for being very strict and didn't condone misbehaving in the classroom. This was a French speaking school; consequently, French was the primary language and English was our secondary language. We had a strict curriculum of French, Catechism, Penmanship, Geography, English, and Math. There was absolutely no tolerance for nonsense. God forbid if you failed to do your homework or fell behind in your learning. However, you always knew what was expected of you.

If you failed to answer the teacher correctly, often you had to stand by your desk or in the back of the room for the rest of the period. If you were caught passing notes or otherwise goofing off, the teacher ordered you to stand in the dark coat closet in the back of the room. Above all, under no circumstances did you ever want to have to go to the office of Sister Superior. That was a guaranteed phone call to your parents.

Our teachers were nuns from the order of the Sisters of the Assumption. It was known to be a very strict order. The nuns observed the three vows of chastity, poverty, and obedience. This particular segment of the order was devoted to educational work. They wore full-length black tunics with a black veil over their heads. Their hair was completely shaved off and their head was wrapped in white gauze like material. A white cloth covered their forehead and they wore stiff white bib collars that extended from shoulder to shoulder in a semi-circle pattern in the front of their habit. It didn't take us little wise guys long to refer to them as "penguins."

They had to be born with the patience of Job to put up with some of our shenanigans. Some of the boys . . . not me, of course, knew just how to push their patience to the limit. Watch out if you crossed the line. It was not uncommon to be slapped across the face or to have your fingers whacked by a ruler for misbehaving. You got what you deserved, and sometimes more than you bargained for. I recall Sister Rudolph striking Eddie Martel so hard she broke his nose. Eddie didn't return to St. Joe's after that. They dished out a lot, but in their defense, they put up with a lot. You were there to learn; they were there to teach. Looking back on it, they did an excellent job.

*   *   *

Three events stand out in my mind from that first year at St. Joe's. The first event happened on a cold November night in 1945. There was a knock on the door and when Lorraine opened it, there stood a tall man, dressed in a black and red wool shirt and matching hat. Deer hunting season began November 1 and this man appeared in full hunting garb. Claudie and Lorraine immediately recognized the man and began calling out "Daddy, Daddy."

As he stooped down to hug them and wrap my sisters in his arms, I noticed his eyes were bloodshot and he smelled like beer. I stood back about ten feet and silently observed. I waited for him to call my name or step forward to hug me. That never happened. Strangely, he never made eye contact with me or even acknowledged that I was there. It's as though I didn't exist.

I had this strange feeling that if I took a step forward, he would take a step back. I was aware that this stranger I had never seen was supposed to be my father. Yet, I knew at that moment that he didn't want to have anything to do with me. I felt embarrassed and abandoned. I didn't say a word. I just stood there staring at him. So, this was Charles Arthur Virgin. As quickly as he came, he was gone. My mother didn't say anything, although she witnessed his complete rejection of me.

The next day, he came by early and took my sisters shopping. I wasn't invited. He bought them shoes for school. I didn't mind.

I was glad my sisters were getting much-needed new shoes. My mother didn't spend money on us unless it was absolutely necessary. She believed that as long as there wasn't a hole in the bottom of the sole, you didn't need new shoes. Whether they fit or not didn't concern her. I never saw Charlie Virgin again. That was my one encounter with the man whose name I was burdened to carry.

The next big event was when I made my first Communion. That's a big deal in the Catholic religion. It's preceded by going to holy confession to rid yourself of all your sins in order to receive the sacrament of the body of Christ.

I was all for receiving the body of Christ, but, I must admit, I had trouble believing in confession. We were taught that priests were apostles of Jesus and somehow magically represented God on earth. I accepted they were the leaders of the church; however, I believed only God could forgive my sins and that was a personal matter between me and God. I kept that to myself and went through the right of passage with the other boys and girls who made their first Communion that year. That was one of the few times my parents actually came to watch me perform something. One good thing about it was that they bought me new clothes for the special occasion.

The final event was a mind-blower. Remember poor Mrs. Camire? Oddly enough, my mother didn't send me back to live with the Camire's when we returned to Laconia in the summer of 45.' As the story goes, Mr. Camire had become even more violent and threatened to kill his wife. Even to the point that the older children took her away from the house on Pine Street so he wouldn't hit her anymore. Her face was swollen so badly, she looked like a black and blue punching bag. The man was unbelievably cruel and insane.

On a warm summer day, for the only time in his entire life, he gave young Pauline and her sister Doris seventy-five cents apiece so they could go downtown to the roller skating rink on a Saturday afternoon. When they returned home, nobody was in the house. After searching around, they heard the car running in the closed garage. They opened the garage door to find Edmund Camire had hooked a hose onto the exhaust pipe of his car and ran it through the side window. He committed suicide by carbon monoxide poisoning. It was all over. They were free of him at last. Who knows what evil lurks in the hearts of men?

CHAPTER 5

ST. VINCENT DE PAUL

It was the summer of 1946. I had just completed the first grade at St. Joseph's school. Lorraine returned from another brief summer vacation with Aunt Mildred and Uncle Cecil in Maine. She turned twelve that summer and was responsible for taking care of Claudie and me while our mother worked at Laconia Shoe Company. Harold was well established in his job at Moody's Auto & Body shop.

Lorraine essentially became our surrogate mother. She took on that responsibility with pride and honor. To cut right to the chase, our big sister was more maternal than our own mother.

I was at that age where I began to observe how other families functioned. It didn't matter whether they were wealthy or poor. I saw families go to church together on Sunday morning. I saw classmates shopping with their parents or going to Keller's Soda Shop for an ice cream cone. I saw parents with their children playing on the swings and enjoying a day together at Opechee Park. They took family vacations when the factories shut down for two weeks in the summer. I was already questioning why we didn't function like other families. Yes, I was jealous of those other families. I was envious. Yet, in a strange way, that only served to draw Lorraine, Claudie, and I closer together.

It wasn't as though we were poor. My mother had plenty of money. Unfortunately, she was obsessed with money. She was working at a decent job at Laconia Shoe. She made more than the average worker because she worked at a piece rate, rather than an hourly wage. Harold had a good job. She received a good income from the two apartments she rented. She also made money renting out rooms in our house. Besides that, she made money renting out the seven garages on our adjacent lot. As if that wasn't enough, she washed and ironed curtains on Friday nights and Saturday mornings for the wealthy people in town. It's no wonder she was always too tired and stressed out to do anything with her children.

I always felt she was obsessed with money simply so she could show the people who scorned her for her moral indiscretions that she could possess more material things than they did. However, in retrospect, her value system was flawed. Perhaps she could have earned the respect of her contemporaries by being a more caring and loving mother. I regret she had a hard life and didn't have mothering skills; however, Lorraine took on her responsibility as a mother and developed those maternal skills. So, why couldn't she? Oh, that's not to say I don't think our mother didn't love us. I believe she did . . . . as long as it didn't involve time or money.

When she and Harold did take the time to "unwind," it wasn't by doing things with her children. Ora had this dual personality. During the week, she was all work and no play. But on the weekends, when she wasn't working, she consumed her life with drink and party. She lived to go to the Rod & Gun Club on Saturday night to dance and drink the night away. There, she lived in her fantasy world. It's as though she entered another universe, while we were left at home to fend for ourselves.

More often than not, she brought home strangers they called their "new friends" they met at the Rod & Gun. Every now and then, in her drunken stupor, she would wake us up and parade us down to the kitchen in our pajamas to show us off to these drunken strangers. For the most part, these "new friends" were not local people, but were visiting the area on vacation. My mother rejoiced in the role of being the life of the party.

We saw Harold in a different way. Oh, no doubt he liked to drink. Unfortunately, he had a nasty disposition when he drank too much. I think they refer to that as a "mean drunk." Yet, if the truth were known, Harold wasn't a party animal like my mother. He was more grounded and would have been content to drink at home on Saturday night. In discussing Harold with my sisters, we agreed he could have been a very good father had my mother allowed him to fill that role. We honestly believe all Harold wanted was to be loved by my mother and to be a good family man. It's sad. She never ever let him be the man he wanted to be. We were not his children by birthright, so Ora denied him that opportunity.

With all her money, she never gave us an allowance or even a penny or two for candy. We were only provided the bare necessities. At that, my mother sewed most of my sisters' clothes to save money. That didn't matter so much when they were younger, but Lorraine was about to enter the seventh grade and was embarrassed to wear the bonnets and childish clothes my mother made for her. She just wanted a few things like the other girls her age were wearing. She was at that age where she felt she needed a training bra. Despite her pleas, my mother wouldn't even buy her a decent dress for school.

One day that summer, Lorraine finally took it upon herself to buy what she so rewardingly deserved. She had had enough of Ora's penny pinching. So, one day, she boldly opened the hidden metal box in my mother's room and took out a twenty-dollar bill. She was determined to get that training bra at all costs. It was a bold move to say the least. She must have been very desperate.

With money in hand, she took Claudie with her and went on her little shopping spree at Clear Weave women's store on Main Street. As the story goes, they didn't have any training bras, but she bought a much-needed dress and a pair of shoes. She also offered to buy Claudie clothes, but Claudie was too frightened to accept her offer. After she paid for her purchases and the girls left the store, the clerk immediately picked up the phone and called my mother to be sure she approved of the purchases.

My mother was livid. Taking her money was a worse crime than burning down her house! When my mother lost her temper, all hell broke loose. As Lorraine walked up Winter Street with her new dress and shoes in hand, Harold came down the street to meet her and warn her of Ora's violent outburst at the house.

First, he asked her, "Lorraine, did you take some money from your mother's metal box?" She knew it was wrong to take the money and began to cry as she answered his question.

"Yes, I did," she replied, as the tears came streaming down her face. "The other kids make fun of me because of my clothes. I just wanted a dress from Clear Weave's," she went on to say. "And my shoes don't fit anymore."

Harold looked into her sad eyes and tenderly squeezed her hand to let her know he understood her dilemma. But, he was helpless. There wasn't anything he could do to help her. Had he given her the money, Ora would have screamed at him. Eventually, Harold, Claudie, and Lorraine, entered the house through the rear cellar door to be greeted by my waiting mother's wrath.

Her eyes were burning with hatred as she yelled at Lorraine, "You're going to hell for this. Don't you ever steal one cent from me again. Do you hear me?"

How could she not hear her. The entire neighborhood heard her yelling at her daughter. She told Lorraine, in no uncertain terms, she would pay back every penny of the money she stole . . . and then some. For the next two years, Lorraine had to hand over the money she earned babysitting, which far exceeded the twenty dollars. If that weren't enough punishment, my mother found her a job scrubbing one of the tenant's floors. She had to hand over that money too.

If only my mother could have realized how desperate Lorraine had become to have to resort to stealing money to buy a dress and a pair of shoes. She couldn't even see that she had three excellent children that loved her unconditionally despite the chasm that was separating her from us.

*   *   *

Ora operated in a shroud of secrecy. She kept everything to herself. She never shared what she was up to until that very last moment when she finally had to tell us what was coming next. Like, we never knew when we were moving to Connecticut or when we were moving back to Laconia, and so forth. Thus, it came as a big surprise to me, as well as my sisters, when she told me I was going away to school for the second grade.

First, she told my sisters the doctor told her it would be better for her health if I went away to school for awhile. Her health? Other than yelling all the time and fighting with Harold, we weren't even aware that she had been to see a doctor. Then, she approached me privately and told me the news that I wouldn't be going to St. Joseph's in the fall. I didn't understand what was happening.

She softened the blow by telling me, "It's a nice school, Sonny. You're going to like it there. And your sisters are going to be right there with you. You'll see them every day."

I was six years old. I didn't understand why we had to go away to school. If I was going to see them everyday, as she said, then why couldn't we stay at home?

I didn't like the fact that I was changing schools for the third straight year. I didn't want to go to a private school fifty miles away from home. But, on that fateful day in early September, my mother drove my sisters and me to our new school in Manchester, New Hampshire.

The car pulled up in front of the dark blue clapboard three storied building on Lake Avenue. My mother took my small suitcase out of the trunk, told my sisters to wait in the car, and walked with me up the steep concrete steps to the entrance of this ominous looking building. I looked back at my sisters, as my mother rang the old-fashioned cranking bell. Overhead, in gold trim on a black background read the sign: "*Saint Vincent de Paul School.*"

An old nun answered the ring and swiftly escorted us to the main parlor. My mother kissed me on my forehead, turned, and quickly darted out the front door.

I cried out, "Mom, where are you going? Where's Claudie and Lorraine? Don't leave me. Please, please, don't leave me here." Tears were streaming down my face.

She was gone. Nobody but the old nun was there to hear my pleas. I could only wonder, what was happening to me. Where were my sisters? I was confused and abandoned. What was I doing there? At that very moment, I was scared out of my wits. The place was eerie. I stood there alone. Silently stood there, knowing full well that I was on my own. That I had to carefully avoid any dangers in my new surrounding at this place called *St. Vincent de Paul.*

My very own mother lied to me. She brought my sisters along so I would think they'd be with me. That was never her plan. Lorraine immediately realized this was not the type of private school she was led to believe.

When she returned to the car, Lorraine pleaded with my mother, "Mom, this is a scary place. You can't leave Sonny there. Go back and get him." That fell on deaf ears.

35

I'll never know the real reason she sent me there, but I'll always remember it as the most traumatic experience in my young life. What had I done to deserve this punishment? It's cruel to deceive a child; it's even crueler to be deceived by your very own mother.

The nun took my hand and walked me down a long narrow hall to what would become my home for the next school year. We went to another building, attached to the rear of the long hallway. There, she walked me up a flight of stairs to a room full of neatly arranged metal cots. There were three rows of cots in that room. We walked through that room to a smaller room, where there were some eight or ten more metal cots. She pointed to one of them and told me, "That's your bed." While I slid my little suitcase under the cot, she began to tell me my new daily routine.

We woke up to a loud bell and the overhead lights were turned on at 5:00 a.m. We then proceeded to the bathroom at the end of the larger room. We only had a short time to make our beds, dress in our school uniform, and line up for early mass or prayer in the chapel. After morning religious service, we quietly marched, in pairs, to the cellar for our breakfast meal. We sat at long tables that filled the room and a nun monitored us during meals. We couldn't speak to anyone the entire time. That was supposedly some sacrifice we made to God to become better Catholics.

These new rules happened so fast I didn't have time to react. I just followed the other boys to the evening meal. It was there, I noticed that I was probably the smallest boy in the school. There weren't any girls there. For the most part, these boys were ruffians and had a pack mentality about them. They didn't come from loving, caring homes. They were mostly the abandoned children of French Canadian factory workers who slaved in the hosiery mills in Manchester. They were not like my classmates at St. Joseph's. They stared at me as if I were some kind of prey. That first night, I crawled into my cot, pulled the brown wool blanket over my head, and cried as softly as I could so none of the other boys would hear me.

What I soon learned is that St. Vincent's was actually an orphanage. It was the 83rd institution founded by the Sisters of Providence, whose motherhouse was located in Montreal, Canada. The house opened their doors to 12 orphans (7 boys and 5 girls) on December 19, 1882. It was the main depository in the state of New

Hampshire for French Catholic children, abandoned by their parents. Most of the boys came from Manchester. That was the largest city in the state, with a population of around 50,000. Forty percent, some 23,000 residents of Manchester were French speaking Canadians.

In my suitcase was a school uniform. We wore black wool blazers with black matching short length pants. We also wore long light brown full-length stockings, held up by garters attached to the front and back of our underwear. Under our blazer, we wore a white shirt and black tie. We wore that outfit every day.

The second day, I watched the other boys dress and immediately followed their lead. I don't even recall being introduced in class. There were some thirty boys at the orphanage and we gathered in two classrooms. For all I know, I may have been in a classroom with sixth graders. That didn't matter. I found refuge in burying myself in learning. It didn't take much effort to excel in the classroom. These boys were like zombies in class and didn't care if they learned anything. I had to be careful not to act too smart even though I was by far the smartest boy in the class.

At around three in the afternoon, we went outside to play in the schoolyard. I simply followed the bigger boys out there. There wasn't any grass, swings, or anything to play on. It was a big empty concrete yard, enclosed by a six-foot tall wooden fence. There was no way to escape. I was alone in a corner when I heard a boy call out, "Hey, there's the new kid. Let's get him." The next thing I knew, five or six boys formed a circle around me and began taunting me for no reason.

A big kid punched me and said, "C'mon, put em' up sissy. Whatsa matter? You afraid to fight?"

I wasn't a fighter. That angered them even more. Suddenly, I felt a sharp pain across my nose and blood poured freely from my nostrils. Then, they hit my face and body with more blows, coming from all directions. After I was down, they kicked me in the abdomen. I had no choice but to take the blows. As more boys gathered, that must have drawn the attention of one of the nuns inside. My head was spinning as I heard the whistle and saw the nun coming to my rescue.

When she asked me who hit me, I suddenly became aware of the jungle I was in. I didn't even know these kids, so how could I even point them out? Nobody was reprimanded and I was brought inside to be cleaned up. I passed the first test of survival at St. Vincent de Paul: *Don't squeal on anybody.* From that day on, I dreaded going out to the schoolyard in the afternoon. I was the new kid on the block. Consequently, I didn't have any friends. I didn't speak to anyone and nobody spoke to me. I simply stayed as close to the door as I could and apprehensively waited for the next attack.

The bigger boys constantly threatened me. I lived a life of fear. Every night I imagined the big boys holding me down in bed and beating me up. They were capable of beating me up without the nuns ever knowing they did.

One night, I was constipated and had to go to the bathroom to relieve myself. However, I was too scared to walk down the dark hall to the toilet. I couldn't restrain myself any longer. So, I emptied my bowel in my hand and quietly wiped it on the underside of the metal frame of my cot. I closed my filthy hand and stayed awake until the next morning when I could wash it away.

It was a cold October evening when my mother and Harold suddenly appeared at St. Vincent's. They came to check on me. You would have thought I'd be happy to see them and greet them with open arms. That's probably what they expected. The reception was quite different. They never bothered to ask how I was feeling. I actually didn't care they were there. I had become cold and unwanted like the other boys in the orphanage. How could I trust her again after she had deceived and abandoned me?

My mother tried to act sweet when she took me outside the building. She smiled at me as if that would make everything better and asked, "Do you want anything, honey?"

I thought for a brief moment, and then replied, "Ya, I want to see my sisters." She didn't answer.

They took me across the street to a corner variety store and bought me a cheap cloth Halloween mask. I didn't even choose it. I didn't even want it. I knew the big boys would take it away from me as soon as they left. I probably would even be called a sissy because they showed up. They had no idea the pain and sorrow I was suffering. I was no longer the little boy from Laconia they abandoned six weeks earlier.

I quickly adapted to the routine at St. Vincent's and became a model student. Somehow, in the back of my mind, I knew that Lorraine wouldn't abandon me and one day would come and take me away from that awful place. Every morning, I prayed to God to watch over me and take me to a better place, wherever that might be.

I will never forget my Christmas at St. Vincent's. I don't know where all the boys were. It was so peaceful. I was the only boy left at the orphanage. I suspect many of them were boarders, like myself, and were home with their families for the holidays, while others were taken in by strangers.

I was with the nuns. There were five nuns in total, counting Sister Superior. Generally, on Saturdays, two nuns gave us a bath. That day was special for me. All five nuns gave me a bath. Suddenly, they weren't the stern, rigid nuns I knew. They all giggled, smiled, and took turns rubbing my body. My God, I was the center of attention! I actually relished the moment.

On Christmas morning, they let me join them in the parlor and even bought me a Christmas present. It was a box full of play money of different denominations. The nuns took a vow of poverty, so I was touched that they took money from their meager earnings to buy me a present. I knew I was different from the other boys and sensed the nuns really liked me. Of course, they couldn't show favoritism when the other boys returned. It was just nice to know that somebody cared for me when I was left all alone in that scary building.

As the winter passed and the snow piled higher, the big boys shoveled it toward the fence on Lake Avenue. After awhile, it was piled so high that for recreation they stood at the top of a mountain of snow and threw snowballs at the people passing by. It got dark early in the winter months. One evening, a boy threw a snowball and hit none other than Bishop Brady, who happened to be walking down the street. You might as well have shot the Pope. He was the leading Catholic figure in the entire state. I recall praying before him on Sundays at St. Joseph's Cathedral on Beech Street.

You could see the rage on Sister Superior's face, as she marched us all into the house and demanded, "Which one of you animals hit Bishop Brady?"

Whether they did it or not, all the boys ducked their heads as though they were in deep prayer. Again, she asked, "O.K., which one of you ruffians did this terrible thing?" "Come on, point him out." Silence.

Then, one of the bullies pointed at me and said, "He threw the snowball that hit the Bishop."

I stood there silently. I didn't say a word. The other boys were confused by my reaction. I was sure they expected me to frantically deny it. Frankly, I wasn't even near the fence and didn't see the boy throw the snowball.

The old nun sent everyone to the sleeping quarters, but kept me behind. She knew I didn't do it. However, she questioned me at no end to confess who did. It's as thought I would go to hell if I didn't squeal. She finally accepted my explanation that I didn't see it happen.

Well, not all bad comes from bad deeds. From that day on, I was accepted by the big bullies for not squealing. I was an O.K. kid after all. No longer was I shoved, punched, or pushed by the other boys.

By the end of March, the snow was almost gone, the days were becoming longer, and the smells of spring were in the air. Somehow, I knew my mother and Harold were coming for a visit because the nuns were at their best behavior and even took me for a haircut at the barbershop at the bottom of Lake Avenue. It wasn't the haircut I remember that day. It was what the barber kept in the glass case by his mirror. There, before my very eyes, was a large revolver. My, what thoughts can go through the mind of a seven-year-old boy. Why would a barber keep a gun in open view? What would I do if a robber came in the door? If everyone in Manchester carried a pistol, what kind of danger was I in? I certainly was relieved when the two nuns returned to the barbershop to take me back to the orphanage.

Ora and Harold came to visit me the Saturday after I got the haircut. Frankly, it was awkward. They didn't know what to do with me and I didn't know what to do with them. They were the adults and should have had a plan.

My mother asked me, "What do want to do, Sonny?"

I should have said, "Get me to hell out of here." Instead, I answered with the usual, "I don't know."

How was I supposed to know where kids went to have fun in Manchester? All I knew was St. Vincent's. You would have thought they could have at least checked to see if there was a zoo or kid's park somewhere in the city. I watched her hands fidget around in her coat pocket. Then, the dialogue went like this:

Mother: "Do you want to go somewhere?"

Me: (Silence)

Mother: "Nice weather we've been having, huh?"

Me: (Silence)

Mother: "Do you want to go to a park?"

Me: "Where?" I put the ball in her court.

We ended up in a park on Elm Street. That's what it was. Just a park. It didn't have any swings, teeter board, merry-go-round, or anything. Just some walking paths and a statue of some 18th century figure with his right hand covering his heart. You can only stare at a statue for so long. I sensed they were getting restless and wanted to get a beer. Sure enough, they suggested we go to lunch. I wasn't even hungry. I just wanted them to dump me back at the orphanage and be on their way.

If I seemed cynical to them, I was. I wasn't about to let my mother make false promises and disappoint me again. In my year at St. Vincent's, I had become street smart and skeptical of adults, way beyond my young years. I had witnessed boys pulled from the classroom, never to be seen again. If I had been a big, stocky boy someone could use on a farm, I may have been adopted too. I was hardened. I didn't trust adults. Having been deceived, I certainly didn't trust my mother and knew Harold lacked the intestinal fortitude to stand up to her. The only people I trusted were my sisters. And I didn't even know where they were.

When the school year ended in June of 1947, my mother came to get me to return to Laconia. I didn't question her health. After all, isn't that why she sent me away? No, I was just glad the nightmare was over and that I would be reunited with my sisters. I didn't know what the future held for me. However, I knew one thing. I would run away from home before I ever went back to St. Vincent de Paul's.

CHAPTER 6

LACONIA

$\mathbf{A}$ few years back, I worked as a ski guide in Colorado when a man in a group I guided noticed my nametag showed that I hailed from Laconia, N.H. He quickly pointed out that he was also from Laconia. What a small world. Then, he said something that really made me think about my childhood. He said, "Wasn't that a great place to grow up as a kid."

I didn't have the heart to tell him that depended on what side of the tracks you came from. Obviously, his childhood experiences were dramatically different from mine. He came from an affluent, solid family environment that showered him with love and affection and nurtured his growth to a future life of prosperity. Conversely, I came from an environment of hostility and chaos, where the pursuit of happiness was totally obfuscated by a psychologically damaged mother whose concept of family evolved solely around the pursuit of her happiness, much to the detriment of her children.

In the final analysis, it wasn't Laconia that brought on a childhood of misery. It was the result of the dysfunctional family that I came from. Laconia could have been a wonderful place to be raised had the circumstances been different.

Laconia is located in the heart of the Lakes Region. It is one of the most picturesque places on the face of this earth. Situated near the shores of Lake Winnipesaukee, in the central part of New Hampshire, it is totally surrounded by lakes and mountains. In fact, some 23% of the 26 square miles of the city is covered by water.

Lake Winnipesaukee, located northeast of the city, is the largest lake in New Hampshire. It encompasses 182 miles of shore around the lake and 72 miles of water surface. No small lake by any standards, the lake with the odd name, is 21 miles long and 9 miles wide.

The hub of social activity around the lake took place along the shore of The Weirs, which is actually a village that is part of Laconia. From there, heading south along Route 3 toward Laconia, the road follows along Paugus Bay, which flows over the Lakeport dam, then forms into Lake Opechee. Lake Opechee is virtually right on the edge of the city. I have many fond memories of summer days spent at Opechee. That's where I learned to swim.

The mass of water then flows right through the center of town where it becomes the Winnipesaukee River. The river eventually flows into another large lake, by the name of Lake Winnisquam, on the southwest edge of the city. Lake Winnisquam is actually the fourth largest lake in the state. It is 10 miles long and 1 ½ miles wide. Like Lake Opechee, it's right on the edge of town. Many of the homes in Laconia sit on the shores of Lake Winnisquam.

If you like fishing, swimming, or boating, this is definitely the ideal place to come. And they do. Laconia's population has averaged around 15,000 permanent residents for as long as I can remember. In the summer, the population in the Lakes Region Area, which encompasses all the lakes and surrounding small towns, swells to some 250,000. The area comes alive and bursts with activity. It's one of the most favored vacation areas in the Northeast.

If that's not enough, tourists came from all over New England to ski in the winter at Belknap Mountain, located in Gilford, a mere 6 miles east of the city.

When I returned to Laconia in the summer of 1947, the town was flourishing. There were plenty of jobs available in the mills for anyone wanting to work. The largest factory in town was Scott & Williams, with a plant that took up an entire block in the Normandin Square area and another plant, equally as large, situated next to the Lakeport dam. Scott's, as we locals called it, was a leading manufacturer of knitting machinery sold all over the world. They also made carburetors for tanks during World War II.

At one time or another, the mills and factories in Laconia also produced lumber, textiles, hosiery, stockings, shoes, skis, and even the needles that were used in the knitting machines. For the most part, the mills were located by the Winnipesaukee River and drew electric power from the strong flow of the nearby river.

Main Street was the quintessential New England Main Street. Every store imaginable, and then some, was located there. If you needed anything, you headed to Main Street. This was long before the advent of malls. The street was lined with clothing stores, hardware stores, restaurants, banks, furniture stores, department stores, flower shops, and more taverns than a town this size would ever need. My grandfather, Joe Garneau, even had his barbershop on Main Street. The venerable Laconia Tavern Hotel, where President Eisenhower once stayed, is still standing at the north end of Main Street.

If you were looking for something to do, Main Street housed the Colonial movie theatre, the city bowling alley, and a pool hall on one of the nearby side streets. The roller skating rink was on Court Street, right around the south corner of Main Street. It's no small wonder everyone gathered downtown on Friday night and Saturday to shop, eat, or just plain visit with old friends.

One of the most prestigious clothing stores in all of New Hampshire, O'Shea's, is firmly woven in the fabric of Laconia's history. For many years, spring marked the end of the log drive and the lumberjacks came roaring out of the North Country to board the train headed to Laconia. With the lonely hard days in the woods behind them and a pocket bulging with back pay, they came to Laconia to whoop it up. Many of them left a few dollars with Dennis O'Shea before heading for the fleshpots and saloons on Mill Street. A few days later, the weary lumberjacks would show up at O'Shea's again, haggard with hangovers, sporting bruised knuckles and bloodshot eyes, to claim their money and spend it on clothing needed for the long months ahead.

One of the unique features in O'Shea's was the method used for handling customer transactions. There weren't any cash registers on the floor. The sales clerk would write up your purchase and place a copy of the sales slip, with your payment, into a round metal canister. The canister was placed on a track and traveled along a network of overhead cables, much like a railroad track, to the open office on the balcony above. In the office, another clerk took your money, inserted your change into another canister, and sent it on its way down the cable line back to the sales clerk.

At O'Shea's there was always an undercurrent of mischievousness flowing quietly under the circumspect exterior. Perhaps that was because the store had a fine reputation for the way it treated its employees. It was said that once you went to work at O'Shea's, you had a job for life.

The pneumatic cash system was always good for a prank. It was not uncommon for a feather from a feather duster to be carefully placed in the canister, so when it was opened it would spring out at a startled cashier. The surprise scream would sometimes make customers forget what they came to buy. This stunt could be duplicated by filling the canister with cigarette smoke. A dead spider or insect were also known to have taken the ride.

I don't know of any other towns the size of Laconia that can claim some of the prominent events that continue to be held there to this day. When I was a boy, there were three renowned motorcycle races in the entire country. The 200-mile championship was held in Daytona, Florida. The next major race was held in Langhorne, Pennsylvania, and the 100-mile national championship was held every June in Laconia. The race was a big draw back then, but more importantly, it was the annual pilgrimage for thousands of motorcycle riders that came there from all over the east coast.

Motorcycle week is now a ten day event that begins a week before Father's day and culminates with the race on the following Sunday afternoon. This event has gone on for over eighty-eight years and has drawn as many as 300,000 bikers participating in this gargantuan rally. Try to visualize 300,000 crazy bikers roaring night and day through a small town of 15,000 people. The stories and memories could fill the pages of this book.

Back in the old days, it wasn't uncommon to see some crazy rider buzzing down Church Street or Union Avenue with a stuffed bear, he confiscated from a motel, tied to his rear seat. Before the police clamped down, it was worth the trip down Winter Street to Busy Corner to watch the topless biker ladies flashing their bare breasts for all us good Catholic boys to enjoy.

There were many street fights among the bikers back in the good old days. The locals pretty much stayed out of their way and let them take over the town for a week. Who can forget the time the Hell's Angels gang came to town and burned down the boardwalk at The Weirs. It's a shame that 99% of them gave the rest of the riders such a bad name!

The venue has calmed down and even respectable people ride $25,000 motorcycles these days. They no longer camp on the high school lawn or pee on the grounds at the library. Now, they bring their wives or girl friends and make motel reservations well in advance of the big week. The hub of activity is pretty much isolated six miles north of town at the Weirs. Cars are not allowed near the Weirs during Bike Week.

Laconia also hosts an International Sled Dog race in the winter. That doesn't draw the crowds like Bike Week; nevertheless, it is a recognized International race and sled dog racers come from as far away as Alaska to compete.

They don't hold this event anymore, but back in the 40s' and 50s,' they held the 60-meter national ski jump championships at Belknap Mountain. I never missed it. I was awed watching those brave men, flying like birds in the sky. The jumpers tucked their arms right by their side until the very last second before landing near the flat part at the bottom of the steep hill. What a demonstration of courage. I'll never forget the amazing jumping Dion's. They were the local ski jumping favorites, coming from Lebanon, New Hampshire. There was Bernie Dion, and his cousins Roger and Doug. Their sons, Ray, Ernie, and Leon followed them. They were the best in the East. Several of them skied for the U.S. Olympic teams. Tragically, Bernie broke his neck while ski jumping.

One year it was extremely cold and windy on the day of the meet. They should have cancelled it, but they didn't. One of the jumpers was so light, the wind blew him off the course and into the nearby woods. Shortly after that, they cancelled the meet.

I would be remiss if I didn't mention The Weirs, and particularly Irwin's Winnipesaukee Gardens. It was there I have my fondest memories of growing up in Laconia. I loved The Weirs. After you crossed the bridge on Route 3 and headed down Lakeside Avenue, you couldn't help but feel a tingle of excitement as you approached the bells and clanging sounds emanating from the numerous arcades along the boardwalk. It was hard to resist the sweet smells of grilled hot dogs, freshly baked pizza, and caramel corn, made before your very eyes at the Korner Kubbard on the boardwalk.

To your right was Endicott Rock and the Weirs beach, where tourists came from all over to enjoy a day in the sun and swim in the clear water of Lake Winnipesaukee. Further down from the beach on the boardwalk was the train station where they sold refreshments and tickets to enjoy a beautiful two and a half hour cruise around the lake on the 205 foot M/S Mount Washington. Beyond the railroad station, you could see the fabulous and famous Winnipesaukee Gardens, the creation of Jim Irwin, the most visionary entrepreneur I have ever known. That man did more to shape the history and character of the Weirs than any other person did before or since his time.

It was Jim Irwin, while playing the trumpet in Murphy's band out of Boston that saw Lake Winnipesaukee as an area ripe with possibilities. He was a great promoter. In 1922, he arranged for what was probably the first ski train in history to bring skiers to the Weirs for a winter carnival. To attract a crowd, he had a ski jump built right in the middle of Tower Street. He also brought radio to the Lakes Region, establishing radio station WKAV in 1922, which was the first commercial radio station north of Boston.

By and large, his most prized legacy was the giant dance hall he built right over his boat livery. It became the biggest drawing card in the history of the Weirs. It was the most popular attraction ever built on Lake Winnipesaukee and the liveliest nightspot in the state for many decades. Irwin's Winnipesaukee Gardens was the place where, on virtually any summer night, people could listen and dance to the best music in America, performed by the greatest musicians of the Golden Age.

He fashioned his dance hall after a dance hall, known as The Pier, he had seen in Miami while touring with his band on a swing through Florida. It was immediately successful, from the day it opened its doors. At one time or another just about all the big bands in the country played at the Gardens. There was Glen Miller, Count Basie, Harry James, Paul Whiteman, Louie Armstrong, Les Elgart, Fats Waller, and Duke Ellington, to name a few. The Gardens provided a venue for the top bands touring the country to play in an ideal lakeside setting that was perfect for a summer night.

Tuesdays and Thursdays were Big Band nights. That's when the big bands touring the country played at the Gardens. They had house bands play on the other nights throughout the summer. These bands actually lived there in the summer and headed to Florida to play their music in the winter. The most popular house band I recall was Tony Brown and his "Band of Renown." The Big Band sounds came to your home, live from the Gardens, right over radio station WKAV. The 40s and 50s were an era of dancing. On the weekends, it wasn't uncommon to fill the dance hall with up to 2,000 people, swinging and swaying to the sweet sounds of summer.

Jim Irwin didn't rest on his laurels with his famous Winnipesaukee Gardens. No, he was not one to miss a golden opportunity. On the weekends, he brought speedboat races to the Weirs. Right below the dance hall, he ran a fleet of seven triple cockpit Chris-Craft speedboats, carrying the name, "Miss Winnipesaukee," that provided twenty minute high speed rides that started at 9:00 a.m. and ran until dusk.

The man never missed an opportunity to put the Weirs on the map. He even capitalized on the bathing beauty phenomena that started at the Miss America pageant in Atlantic City, by creating the Miss Winnipesaukee pageant the very same year the Gardens opened. Moreover, there's not a person who ever launched a boat on Lake Winnipesaukee that isn't familiar with Irwin's Marine in Lakeport, which is likely the largest boat dealer in New England.

People from all over the world come to New England in the fall to view the magnificent fall foliage. The bright hues of red and gold glistening in the fall sunlight is a sight to never be forgotten, but also a harbinger of the hard, cold winter that lies ahead for those who live there. In that part of the country, seasons weren't counted in the traditional sense of winter, spring, summer, and fall. Instead, they were referred to as maple syrup season in the winter, lilac season in the spring, blueberry-picking season in the summer, and finally apple or cider season in the fall. Those were some of my memories as a boy growing up in Laconia. What fond memories. The skier I met in Colorado had it right; Laconia was "a great place to grow up as a kid."

CHAPTER 7

RETURN TO LACONIA

I returned to Laconia after I finished the school year at St. Vincent's. It was great to be reunited with my sisters. We picked up where we left off. Well, sort of. Perhaps it was my imagination, but I felt Lorraine and Claudie were being especially nice to me that summer. Maybe they missed me while I was away. On the other hand, perhaps they felt a bit guilty because they didn't have to go to St. Vincent's. I'm not sure. We never talked about it. However, one thing did change. I was much more cautious around adults. I didn't trust them. Above all, I knew I could only depend on myself.

With Lorraine in charge, my mother packed us a lunch of sandwiches and a mayonnaise jar full of Kool-Aid and sent us off in the morning to Opechee Park to spend the day at the beach. We went there practically every day. It was about a mile walk each way to and from Lake Opechee. As soon as we arrived, we spread our beach towels out at our special spot on the bank overlooking the beach. We stayed at Opechee from early morning until late afternoon.

I am sure we looked like three little ragamuffins, walking hand-in-hand, as we made our way down the beaten path past the large gas storage tank near the railroad tracks on our way to the park. Lorraine always insisted we walk closely together and let her know where we were going at all times. She didn't do that to control us; she did that because she cared for us.

I learned to swim at Opechee. The city ran the park and gave free swimming classes in the morning. Lorraine was generally content to sit on the bank and watch over us, while Claudie and I preferred to be in the water. I looked up to Claudie and always tried to keep up with her. There were two rafts in the lake, referred to as the little raft and the big raft. The initial goal was to swim well enough to swim beyond the buoys to the little raft. Having mastered that, the next big test was to swim from the little raft, some fifty yards or so further out, to the big raft. Hey, if Claudie could do it, then I could do it. Midway through the summer, I proudly made it to the little raft. Finally, by the end of summer, I was determined to reach the big raft to show my sisters I could do it too.

On that eventful day in late August, I dove in the water from the little raft and swam underwater as far as I could. When I emerged, I flailed my small arms into some sort of overhand stroke, and finished off dog paddling my way to the big raft. I was thrilled. I made it! Only to be greeted by Claudie saying, "What are you doing here?"

While gasping for air, I responded, "I made it! I made it!" I'm sure I was grinning from ear to ear. I just accomplished another step in the process of growing up. Claudie swam beside me all the way back to shore to be sure I made it back safely. Lorraine wasn't as thrilled with my latest accomplishment as I was.

Toward the end of summer, we were tired of eating the same old sponge wet sandwiches. They became so soggy from the sweat coming off the old Kool-Aid jar, they fell apart before you could put a bite into your mouth. You have to realize this was before they had sandwich bags or Saran wrap to wrap them in. We never had fruit or cookies packed in our lunch. Just a plain old sandwich and the jar of Kool-Aid we shared. We didn't complain. Lake Opechee was our escape, and even wet soggy sandwiches and warm Kool-Aid was better than nothing at all.

I still stopped by Fournier's candy store to check on the latest Red Sox score on my way home. When the baseball season ended that year, my beloved Red Sox finished in third place in the American league, behind the Detroit Tigers and those damn New York Yankees again. Worse yet, the Yankees beat the Brooklyn Dodgers and won the World Series in seven games.

It's funny how we go through phases and stages in life. At nearly eight years old, I was going through a period where I imagined there were burglars breaking into the house at night. I was deathly scared to go to bed. Yet, I was afraid to tell anyone about my fears. To make matters worse, my mother rented out my upstairs bedroom, so I had to sleep on the porch over the storage shed.

There was a side entrance door to the porch. A rumor was going around that a peeping-tom was spotted looking in the neighborhood windows at night. Before I went to bed, I made up excuses to go down to the cellar to make certain both rear doors were locked. I also checked the porch door to be sure it was locked.

When I lay in bed, I was sure I saw the curtains moving. I felt the presence of someone in the room. I was literally frightened out of my wits every night. How did I overcome this fear? Well, I imagined my old pals, who sat around the campfire in those cowboy movies I saw at the Gardens Theater, were right beside me, ready to pounce on anyone that dared to come near me. That, and with the help of a lot of prayers, I finally lulled myself to sleep. This fright of the night must have lasted about a year . . . until I got my old bedroom back.

*   *   *

I was glad to be back at St. Joseph's with my old classmates from the first grade. Ironically, I already knew practically everything the nuns were teaching in the third grade. I had learned it at St. Vincent's. However, I wisely kept that to myself and pretended I was learning like the rest of my classmates. Quite naturally, for a boy of seven, my favorite subjects were recess and daydreaming. While the rest of the class was struggling with multiplications and catechism, I was preoccupied planning my more important after school activities.

We weren't allowed to have anyone at our house, so I took it upon myself to play at my friend's houses. There was Bobby Morin, who was Mr. & Mrs. Fournier's grandson, and Mike Ouellette, whose parents owned Mike's Diner on the corner of Main Street and Union Avenue. Mike was an only child and his parents showered him with every toy imaginable. He even had his own horse.

Then there was also Roland "Fats" Boudreau. His father owned the auto dealership across from the school and Sacred Heart church. "Fats" was kind of a bully. He was one of those kids that had no enemies, but was intently disliked by his friends. Of course, I got along with Fats. He always seemed to have money and willingly bought my friendship.

When I returned to St. Joseph's, I had some catching up to do. Most of the boys in my class were already in Cub Scouts. They didn't have anything like that at St. Vincent's. No small wonder. Would you expect the nun that beat you over the head with a ruler to be your den mother in the afternoon? Or, who did you expect would buy you a Cub Scout uniform in an orphanage? So, while Bobby Morin was coercing me to join Pack 62 with the rest of my classmates, I was reluctant to join.

I had already matured to the point I knew better than to ask my mother for anything. That was out of the question. On the other hand, I really did want to join Cub Scouts. However, I didn't want to be ridiculed because I didn't have a uniform. What was my alternative? Well, let's see, there was my rich grandparents, the Garneau's, who were highly regarded in the French Catholic community. Certainly, they would help their grandson out?

Grampy Garneau owned a thriving barbershop and they also owned a nice eight-unit apartment house on Church Street. I never asked them for anything before. I hoped they would see fit to help their grandson out a bit. Maybe we could start off with a Cub Scout shirt and kerchief?

I mustered up the courage, went to their house, and asked my grandmother, "Grammy, can you buy me a Cub Scout kerchief so I can be in Cub Scouts?"

She pondered the question for a minute, then lashed out at me in her broken English, "No, No, Sonny. You know that's not me to do dat. Your mudder, she has to buy you dat. You don't ask me, you ask your mother for dat," she said. Then, she gave me that consoling fake smile only a grandmother can give.

Now I know where my mother got it! You would have thought I was asking her to put me through college. She handled that like a traffic cop giving directions. Didn't I know better than to prevail upon them? She would have to straighten out my mother about such matters.

For the time being, I had to tell Bobby Morin that Cub Scouts didn't really interest me. However, I was not opposed to going over to his house after school and tossing around his football and rough housing with him. I didn't mind that at all. You see, Bobby was smaller than I was, so I could run over him when we played football in his yard.

My friend Mike was another story. Mike skipped a grade and was younger than everyone else in the third grade. Actually, he shouldn't have skipped a grade. That entire year, Mike struggled to keep up with the class academically. I know he was embarrassed and spoke with a stutter. Above all, Mike was a sweet, sensitive boy. We had a lot of fun together. He was often alone because both his parents worked in their busy restaurant. We had the run of his house after school. Hey, and if we were hungry, we only had to walk down his driveway to the diner. His mother would gladly fix us a sandwich or grill us a hamburger. And, if we wanted to go to a movie on Saturday afternoon? No questions asked. Mike knew I didn't have any money, so he willingly paid my way. The real point was that we enjoyed being together and money was never an issue in our friendship.

Then there was Fats. He just wasn't well liked. One on one, he really wasn't a bad kid. However, when he was with a group of boys, he turned into a real jerk. He wasn't called "Fats" for nothing. He was by far the biggest boy in class. He outweighed me by about fifty pounds and was always bullying the smaller boys. He constantly bragged about all the things his parents bought him and flashed money around in front of the other kids in school.

I really didn't pick him for a friend. He picked me. He would come to me and say, "Let's do this, or let's do that." Most likely because I lived the closest to him, he was always inviting me over to his house or he would come to my house, even though he knew he couldn't come inside. Mainly, we were friends because I tolerated him. Besides that, the schoolyard and skating rink was virtually in my backyard. I couldn't help but see him there.

I'll never forget the time Fats took me to his father's warehouse past the Scott & Williams's parking lot, about a block from his house. This building was hardly noticeable and set back in an inconspicuous corner behind the parking lot, partly hidden by overgrown shrubs and tall grass. Instead of entering through the main door, he led me around the back of the building to another small door that had obviously been broken into. Heck, it was hanging on a hinge.

Once inside, I was shocked. Before my eyes were two large U.S. Army tanks. What was I to think? I certainly wasn't thinking his father owned two U.S. Army tanks!

Now, what to did he get me into? Fats Boudreau was such a damn liar. He just wanted me along so he'd have someone to share the blame if we were caught in there. My curiosity got the best of me. As I walked around inside what appeared to be an abandoned building, I noticed rows of file cabinets stuffed with documents. There was even a set of golf clubs in there. Then, as I turned to my left, I noticed huge stacks of glass doors and windows leaning on their side. There must have been at least a hundred of them.

Without any notice, Fats launched a brick at a glass window resting on the floor. In that instant, you could hear an echo in the building as the brick smashed into the large plate glass window. He looked at me with a stupid smile on his face. I was dumbfounded. All I could think of was the police coming after me, as I quickly ran out the broken door and never stopped running until I arrived home.

I guess Fats didn't learn to be a good citizen in Cub Scouts. Fortunately for me, God and my mythical cowboys heard my prayers and the police didn't come by and haul me off to jail over that incident.

* * *

That Halloween, my mother allowed me to go to the children's Halloween party at the Opechee Park clubhouse. It was a very cold night and I wore my new Navy pea coat she bought me for winter. I remember having a good time at the party. Unlike most of the other children, my parents were not there to give me a ride home when it was over. When it was time to leave, all the kids were scurrying about, grabbing their coats and jackets, and rushing out the door to the awaiting cars to take them home.

I vaguely remembered where I left my coat; however, as I looked up and down the coat rack for it, it just wasn't there. I panicked and reported my coat missing to one of the chaperones. She looked for it with me. It just wasn't there. Someone had stolen my new coat. I probably was the last one to leave the building. None of the adults offered me a ride home.

As I walked home alone on that cold Halloween night, tears began to run down my face. Not so much because someone stole my winter coat, but more so because I knew the relentless verbal thrashing that awaited me when I got home.

There was no hiding it. I took my punishment like a man. There was no reasoning with my mother.

After she told me how incompetent, irresponsible, and careless I was, she just had to add, "I hope you had a good time. That's the last party you'll ever go to."

Furthermore, she wasn't about to buy me another coat. I was in for a long, cold winter. I looked at Harold in the corner of the room and could tell he understood and felt sorry for me. If he had his way, he would have bought me another coat. That wasn't to be.

Three weeks later, it was Thanksgiving. We ate the big feast at my Uncle Roger's house. My mother always seemed to look up to her brother and sought his approval, just as she did with Grammy Garneau. After an afternoon of drinking, the adults left me with my cousins to fend for ourselves, while they went out to continue their party at the Elks.

That was the only night I ever spent at my cousin's house. It was disgusting. Their bedroom smelled from the stench of urine. There were no sheets or pillowcases to sleep on. Their blankets and mattresses were filthy and soiled. What was once white was gray from never having been cleaned. My body yielded to the will of bed bugs and I inherited a head full of crawling cooties in their bug infested bed. I felt sorry for my cousins, but promised myself I would never sleep at their house again.

My Aunt Evie was a good woman, but like all good Catholics, she endured a life of punishment and misery with a drunken, worthless husband, for the sake of keeping the family together and honoring the sacrament of marriage.

I suspected that misery was handed down from generation to generation. One thing for sure, I knew that someday I would break that chain and move as far away as possible.

A few days before Christmas, we began our Christmas break from school. I was looking forward to the break even though I had no idea what I was going to do. I joyfully accepted the mesh stocking with the peppermint candy and orange in it that some benevolent parishioner gave to all the kids. I also received a nice pair of wool stockings from Cormier's Hosiery Mill, for which I was also grateful. I didn't know what to expect for a gift from Harold and my mother, although I was hoping for a pair of ice skates. The city pumped water from the nearby brook and flooded the ball field right behind our yard and, voila, we had a skating rink. Oh, how badly I wanted to be out there skating with the other kids.

What really made this a special Christmas was that Uncle Cecil and Aunt Mildred were coming to be with us. We were excited to see them again.

On Christmas day, in the first box I opened were the ice skates I wanted so badly. That wasn't all I got. In another box was a new winter coat. Now, that was something I really needed. It was tan colored with a nice brown furry collar. I looked very chic in it. Just when I thought all the presents were opened, Harold told me I had another package under the Christmas tree. I couldn't believe it. Inside the box was a full Cub Scout uniform! That was the happiest Christmas of my life. While beaming from ear to ear, Lorraine took my picture in my new Cub Scout uniform.

My Cub Scout Uniform, Christmas 1947

I don't know who bought me my new uniform. Somehow, I don't think it would have happened without Uncle Cecil and Aunt Mildred. Besides, since they were there, very little alcohol was consumed and it was just a wonderful, merry Christmas.

I soon told Bobby Morin, "I changed my mind and decided to join Cub Scouts after all."

The euphoria of the holiday season quickly vanished and life returned to normal. That meant Harold and my mother were constantly fighting again. It was getting ugly. Lorraine, Claudie, and I, spent every afternoon and evening ice-skating at the French school rink to be away from our mother's constant badgering.

The girls had figure skates and Lorraine envisioned herself as the next Sonja Henie. Claudie was more aggressive and could be seen playing "snap the whip" on the ice with the boys. I was content to awkwardly circle the rink, with my arms reaching for the sky to hold onto, while I learned to master my over-sized skates. We put our skates on and headed for the rink as soon as we got home from school. We only took them off to catch a quick bite to eat at supper. Then, it was back to the rink until it closed for the night.

We had a television at home, but that was just for show. We were only allowed in the front room when my mother gave us permission. I suspect the television was just there to show her friends she owned the biggest television set in Laconia. It was a huge Stromberg-Carlson console set. To compliment that, they bought the tallest outside antenna in the city. It looked like someone placed a stand-alone TV tower on top of our house. Wires were tied down in every direction to keep it propped up. Now, that would get the neighbors attention!

The antenna even had a rotor feature. Poor Mom. She just had to show her mother and the neighbors she could afford just as much, if not more, than they could. I never did understand the business with the rotor antenna. It rotated 360 degrees, but that didn't change the fuzzy screen one iota. The only TV station we received clearly was WMUR in Manchester and that was due south. To me, it only made sense to point the antenna in that direction and let it be. Oh well, if it made her happy and made her feel important, then good for her.

*   *   *

We dreaded Saturdays. My mother would take off shopping with her friend, Marie Clavette. She'd return home, with liquor on her breath, right before Harold arrived home from work. That is, when Harold came directly home.

It was a Saturday night ritual to have beans and frankfurters for supper. Simple enough to fix. Open a can of beans, throw a few cold franks in a fry pan and ten minutes later, dinner is served. If Harold came in late from drinking at Freddie's Cafe, Ora would invariably begin her nagging ritual.

Their voices got louder and their language got stronger, as tempers flared. Then, it would get out of hand. They would grab each other and before long fists were flying. Often, my mother would fall down on the kitchen floor. But, as soon as she could gather herself together again, she stood up and continued punching away.

One time, Harold almost broke my mother's arm. It was getting so bad, we did everything we could to avoid being in the house on Saturday afternoon.

I would scream at them to stop fighting. "Stop it, please stop it," I pleaded. They didn't hear me. It was like two gladiators in a pit, ready to tear each other apart.

Once, my sister Claudie was so scared, she called the police to come to the house and stop the fight. They came and took Harold to jail for the night.

The worst that I remember happened on another occasion. My mother threw the hot fry pan full of beans at Harold. Beans were flying everywhere. They were on the table. They were on the kitchen chairs. They were all over the floor. The fry pan barely missed Harold and ended up in the corner of the room. He lunged after her and threw her down by the stairs at the top of the basement.

I snapped. It happened so quickly. I came to my mother's rescue. Everything was a blur. I lunged in the air, tackled him, and knocked him down. The next thing I knew, Harold, my mother, and I, rolled down the stairs and landed on the cement floor in the basement. We laid there in a daze. I was confused. I wondered what had just happened. Harold was embarrassed. My mother was embarrassed. The fight was over. However, the scars remain with me to this day.

Something happened that day that changed me forever. It was even tested later in my life. I go berserk if I see a man put a hand on a woman. I can't explain it, nor can I control it, but heaven forbid if I ever see a man strike a woman.

It was difficult leading a dual life. Not just for me, but for my sisters as well. We put on the best front we could. We were embarrassed, but we hid it well. Just because we lived in a nice house with a big rotor TV antenna on the roof, people falsely assumed we lived in a "normal" family environment. We kept our despair to ourselves. Our mother just didn't have it in her to acknowledge the good things we did. Like love-starved children, we just continued to try harder and harder to get her approval. Even a "thank you" would have been nice once in awhile. It just wasn't in Ora's vocabulary. No, she was the martyr and we were her cross to bear.

Claudie spent hours every Saturday cleaning the bathroom. She scrubbed the floor on her hands and knees until it sparkled, while my mother was out "shopping" with her friend, Marie. Not once did she ever acknowledge that Claudie did a good job. Not even a thank you. I don't think you ever forget the pain of a broken heart. That pain lingers with Claudie to this day.

The week before Lent, the Sacred Heart church always held a big winter carnival in the parish hall. The women sold baked goods to raise money for the parish. The hall was lined with games of chance, where you threw darts or rings in hopes of winning a prize. Before the carnival, the nuns coerced the students to sell raffle tickets on various prizes. The student who sold the most tickets was recognized in a classroom ceremony and given some sort of token prize, like a statue of the Virgin Mary or something like that.

That's when I first learned I possibly would grow up to be an overachiever. That can be both a blessing and a curse. That year, I was the number #1 seller of those raffle tickets in the entire school. Maybe that wasn't important to anyone else, but it sure was important to me. I craved that recognition.

What was my secret? That was simple: I just worked longer and harder than anyone else did. I scoured the non-Catholic neighborhoods in the city. I stopped people shopping on Main Street to sell them tickets. I walked right into the restaurants and sold them to people dining, until I was kicked out. My best secret weapon was to catch the drinkers in the bars after they were juiced up on Saturday afternoon. That's when they were the most vulnerable. I don't know how many times I heard in French: *"C'est le petit garcon au Aurore."* Translated, *"That's Ora's little boy."* Say what you want, I was a winner! I knew then, I could sell anything.

I did join Cub Scouts in the winter of 1948. Ironically, Bobby Morin's mother was my den mother. Our den meetings were held at Bobby's house on Wednesday afternoon. Mostly, we played, read from the Cub Scout manual, and did artsy craftsy things. I sure enjoyed the social interaction and being part of an organization. Even though the other boys had been in Cub Scouts for over a year, in no time at all, I learned the Cub Scout motto, the Cub Scout promise, and the Law of the Pack. I was now a proud member of Pack 62.

I missed a few Cub Scout meetings that winter. In late January, I was stricken with a non-suppurated enlargement of one of my parotid glands. I had contacted that acute infectious disease, commonly known as the mumps. It was very contagious that year and just about everyone I knew had it. Being the generous soul I am, I passed it on to my sister, Claudie. We were both isolated in my mother's downstairs bedroom for two weeks, until the swelling went down and the fever went away. Nobody was allowed near us and my sister accused me of driving her insane with my non-stop jabbering.

Lorraine took every precaution imaginable to avoid contracting the disease. At about the time Claudie and I began to recover from our fever, guess who came down with the worst case of mumps in the family? Lorraine had the mumps so badly, she had to go to the hospital. Even one of Marie Clavette's mystical voodoo cures couldn't cure her. Poor thing. The doctor's had to insert a tube near her throat and drain the poison from her. She was so ill, even the contemptible Sister Rudolph and another nun went to visit her in the hospital. There she laid, blood oozing down the side of her neck onto a sterile white sheet, wondering if they had come to give her the Last Rites. The one who tried the most to prevent it, turned out to be the one who had it the worst. Fortunately, my sisters and I survived the year of the mumps. Never would we have to deal with that again.

*   *   *

So many new and exciting experiences unfold in the canvas of your life when you are in your early adolescent years. Like, I had never seen a dead person lying in a coffin before. That year, I had that opportunity. My great-grandmother, on my mother's side, Mrs. Croteau, died. They held a vigil and a wake at her house.

I soon learned what a wake was. It's where a bunch of adults eat and drink and renew old acquaintances and gab the night away in the kitchen, while some poor old dead body lay silently, and hopefully, at peace in a casket in another room to be mourned by an occasional passerby. What's there for kids to do at a wake? Nothing. They're forgotten. They don't exist. I couldn't help but observe that my sisters went up and touched my old great-grandmother's dead body, as if it were some sort of daring feat, then proceeded to run out of the room.

I happened to have my own brand of curiosity brewing. With nobody in the room, I quietly knelt down on the kneeling pad beside the coffin, and mumbled some sort of prayer. I carefully looked around and made sure nobody else was in the room. When I was certain that Great Grammy Croteau and I were the only ones in there, I reached out with my left hand and touched the silver hair on her head. My eyes popped wide-open as I looked at the clump of hair gathered in my left hand. Oh my God, what had I done? I quickly looked at her to be sure there wasn't a noticeable clump of hair missing. There was. I swiftly placed the hand full of hair in my left pocket. I didn't dare tell anyone, not even my sisters.

I couldn't get home fast enough. Oh God, please help me. Do I put the hair in the garbage can? No, I thought that would be sacrilegious. Do I put it in my dresser drawer to haunt me for eternity? What's a boy to do? I eventually decided just to leave it in my coat pocket. After all, it's just a dress coat. I rarely wore and it would be stored in my mother's closet away from me. Besides, maybe Great Grammy Croteau wanted me to keep it to remember her by.

I remembered all right. That night I remembered the Mummy's Curse crawling out of the swamp in the dead of night to come and retrieve that clump of hair. The next day, it found its way to the garbage can.

Later that winter, Mrs. Ouellette paid my mother to take care of my friend Mike for two weeks while they went to Florida for a vacation. Mike and I slept on the porch. Somehow, it wasn't cold out there anymore and I overcame my fear of ghosts and robbers coming to get me when Mike stayed with us. Mom and Harold were civil for a change and didn't fight in front of him.

Mrs. "O" was so nice. She called Mike from Florida all the time, and even spoke with me. Before I knew it, their vacation was over and they were back from Florida. They brought my family a whole sack of fresh navel oranges. They also bought Mike and me beautiful matching wool sweaters with a reindeer woven in the middle of the pattern. We looked like little twin brothers in our new matching sweaters. Mrs. "O" was an angel. I sure wished she had been my mother.

Soon after the Ouellette's returned from their vacation, the ice melted on the skating rink. The daffodils began to sprout in the flower garden in the vacant lot by our house. The lilac trees near our garage blossomed to fill the air with the sweet scent of lilac perfume. Another spring arrived in all its glory. Before long, we were taking a family photo by the huge spruce tree in the vacant lot. There stood Harold in his medium blue suit. My mother wore a flashy new red dress. Claudie stood taller than her older sister. I wore the nice sweater Mrs. Ouellette gave me. Lorraine smiled, beaming in her graduation cap and gown. My big sister graduated from St. Joseph's school that June.

Lorraine graduates from 8th grade - June 1948

CHAPTER 8

GOODBYE HAROLD

Immediately after Lorraine graduated from the eighth grade, my mother practically demanded she abandon her foolish idea of attending high school and work at the shoe factory instead. Lorraine became completely agitated by our mother's constant insistence and badgering. All summer, it was a tug-of-war between the two of them. From my mother's standpoint, if she allowed Lorraine to go to high school, that would set a precedence for Claudie and myself. She kept telling Lorraine that going to high school was a waste of time. Back in the 40s, you didn't have to stay in school until you were sixteen. She persisted with the argument that Lorraine could earn good money working at Laconia Shoe. To support her argument, she'd point out how well she did with only an eighth grade education. We knew better. She really wanted Lorraine to quit school and start paying room and board, like she had to do when she finished the eighth grade.

She totally misunderstood and underestimated my sister. Lorraine knew that not only was her education at stake, but that she was also fighting to set the precedent for Claudie and myself. Besides, Lorraine had loftier goals than just completing high school. From her early childhood, she dreamt and aspired to be a doctor. That's all she ever wanted to be. Perhaps that was out of the realm of possibility, but she certainly was entitled to try to live her dream. In the end, my mother begrudgingly relented. However, she sternly informed Lorraine, she would not contribute one red cent toward her books, clothing, school meals, and any extracurricular activities. From that day on, Lorraine was on her own. Ora was determined to hoard her money one way or another.

As if that wasn't stressful enough for Lorraine, Mom took her by the hand and brought her to Foster's Dairy Bar, on the way to the Weirs, to try to get her a job there. True, Mr. Foster advertised for summer help in the Laconia Citizen; however, quite naturally, he was seeking college students on summer break or, at a minimum, kids that were at least sixteen years old. It was a rather awkward situation. Mr. Foster diplomatically tried to tell my mother Lorraine was not quite what they were looking for.

My mother ignored him and persisted. She told Mr. Foster, "Look, Mr. Foster, I know she's young and small for her age, but you've got to believe me when I tell you she can do anything you need done in here." She was literally begging him to give Lorraine a job.

Lorraine was so embarrassed; she wanted to crawl under a table.

Finally, Mr. Foster graciously told Ora, "I believe you Mrs. Manson, but I don't have an opening for her now. If something comes up I'll let you know." Judging by the look on his face, he hoped that was the end of the discussion.

Without even thanking him for taking the time to talk with her, she grabbed Lorraine by the hand and hastily stormed out of Foster's Dairy Bar.

That summer, Loraine did get a summer job as a chambermaid at the Handy Landing Inn near the Weirs Bridge. If anything, we all inherited our mother's work ethic. At only thirteen, she worked diligently and conscientiously in her new summer job. The owner, Mr.Bennett, was pleased with her work; however, an incident at the Inn caused Lorraine to quit.

Some older men staying at the Inn on vacation made inappropriate advances at my sister. She was frightened and reported their behavior to Mr. Bennett. After that incident, she decided she would be safer if she found a job closer to home.

She finished the summer working for the Stein family in Laconia as a housekeeper and babysitter for their two children. For working six days a week, they paid her a whopping $10 weekly. The Stein's were nice people; however, Mrs. Stein had this uncanny ability to find more work for Lorraine to do than she could accomplish in an eight-hour day. Poor Lorraine. She put up with Mrs. Stein for the rest of the summer. She really didn't have a choice. She had to scrape up what money she could earn to buy her clothes and pay her way through her first year in high school. This was to be the precedent established for Claudie and me as well.

Claudie took over Lorraine's old job babysitting on Saturdays for the Sawyer's. They paid her twenty-five cents an hour to take care of their two children. Likewise, Claudie had to save her babysitting money to buy new clothes for her next year at St. Joseph's.

As if that weren't bad enough, to add to her woes, Claudie had to give her mother half of her babysitting earnings. It didn't stop there. Claudie also had to help her wash and hang curtains on Friday nights. By then, my mother's little side business was doing quite well. She even invested in some special made adjustable forms to lay the curtains on to dry.

The curtains were carefully laid flat over a bed of needles and the racks were adjusted in both directions to keep the curtains taut while they dried. It was a rather labor intensive task and worked best with two people to stretch the curtains on the rack. For helping her, Claudie didn't receive one penny. After all, we were constantly reminded by our mother that she worked very hard to buy the food we put in our mouths and to keep a roof over our head.

I was only eight years old that summer, so I wasn't expected to support myself . . . yet. I knew my day would come soon enough. With Lorraine working full time, Claudie and I didn't go to Opechee Park as often. That didn't matter; I was content to play with the boys in the neighborhood. I especially wanted to be near our house around five o'clock in the afternoon.

It was about that time every afternoon that Theresa St.Jacques walked up the street to the apartment she shared with her brother, Rudy. They rented an apartment across the street in the Cote's house. Her brother, Rudy, was a giant of a man. I don't know what happened to their parents, but it was Theresa's responsibility to care for Rudy. I admired her even more for that. In my view, Theresa St. Jacques was the most beautiful woman in the world. She was always immaculately dressed. Generally, she wore two-piece outfits, with matching high heel shoes. Theresa was tall and statuesque, and looked like a movie star to me.

My eyes were glued on her, as she gracefully walked up Winter Street on her way home from work. I even noticed the firmness of her calves with each step she took. Why, she was Ingrid Bergman and Grace Kelly all wrapped into one. There was no comparison between Theresa and all the unkempt, haggard women who lived on Winter Street. To me, it didn't matter that she was probably in her late twenties and that I was only nine. Better yet, she didn't even see me gazing at her like a hapless soul. That was my first infatuation. And she didn't even know it.

*   *   *

Clang . . . . clang . . . . clang rang the hand held bell to signal the beginning of another school year. The children immediately lined up in pairs, by class, and silently marched to their respective classrooms. Our new fourth grade teacher, Sister Lucille de Jesus, smiled as each student went to their assigned seat. Then, in a soft-spoken voice, she asked the students to tell her their name and briefly describe what they did last summer.

In that instant moment when you size up a person for the very first time, I immediately liked Sister Lucille. I instinctively knew this would be a good year.

I was actually shy and self-conscious in class and looked at the ceiling when I stood up to speak. Sister Lucille noticed and asked me to repeat what I said. This time she said, "I want you to look at me when you speak."

I couldn't conceal my shyness. I was so self-conscious, I completely forgot what I said and stopped speaking after I told her my name. I gazed up at the ceiling. Softly, she told me to sit down.

That was probably my best year at St. Joseph's. All the students liked Sister Lucille. She was a smart, friendly, down to earth, unpretentious nun who instinctively knew how to arouse an interest in learning. Why, we could even talk about sports with her in class. She didn't pontificate over us as though she was some saint sent down to earth by God almighty to educate a band of illiterate ruffians. To the contrary, she treated us as equals and created an atmosphere conducive to learning.

It was my opinion that Catholic schools tended to over dramatize anything that could possibly pose a threat to the tenets of the Catholic religion. That year it was Joseph Stalin. To hear Sister Lucille tell it, if Stalin wasn't stopped soon, he would leave Moscow, descend on Rome, and murder the Pope. Then, there would be nothing to stop him from crossing the ocean and entering the fourth grade at St. Joseph's Catholic school.

Having learned what Hitler did to over 6,000,000 Jews in Europe, it wasn't beyond my imagination to reckon that something like that could happen. After all, we were taught that Stalin succeeded Lenin and was one of the most murderous dictators in history. Besides, you didn't mix Catholics and communists in the same cocktail. Of course, we learned the best way to keep Stalin away from St. Joseph's was to convert the entire world to Catholicism. So, if we prayed for peace and donated money to the poor Catholic missionaries scattered throughout the world, we would win the cold war with Russia and communism and bring everlasting peace to the world. I am surprised she didn't bring a white dove to class to fly over the classroom.

I took Sister Lucille's word as gospel and soon signed on to be an altar boy at the Sacred Heart church to better prepare myself to go to heaven. Well, that and the fact that Bobby Morin, Fats Boudreau, and several other boys in our class also signed up to serve at the altar of God. I was also hoping that would make my mother proud of me too.

Soon after the school year began, Sister Lucille and I were discussing the possibility of the Red Sox winning the pennant that year. She was also an ardent Sox fan. That made her human in my world. What a race it was. At the end of the year, the Red Sox and Cleveland Indians were tied for the lead after an entire season of baseball.

They held a one game playoff on October 4th, 1948. Winner take all. Joe McCarthy pitched Denny Galenhouse in that final rubber match and the Sox lost the game 8-3. From that day on, I knew the Red Sox wouldn't win anything as long as McCarthy was their manager. I was convinced he had to go. We'll get them next year.

One of my favorite memories about St. Joseph's was the movies that were shown at the parish hall. We knew well in advance when a movie was coming. It was well publicized to be sure we brought the necessary ten or twelve cent fare to school that day. As embarrassing as it was, I often didn't have the money to go to the movie. Sister Lucille would graciously tell me, "That's O.K., you can pay for it later."

So, I was permitted to walk hand in hand with Bobby Morin down Union Avenue to the parish hall to view some of the most inspiring movies of our time.

Who could forget "The Bells of St. Mary's," starring Bing Crosby and Ingrid Bergman. She also starred in the 1948 movie, "Joan of Arc," which endeared me to her forever. Then, we saw the classic, "Father Flanagan's Boys Town," starring Spencer Tracy and Mickey Rooney. I'll always remember the famous line, *"He ain't heavy, Father . . . . he's my brother."* It really had an impact on me. Why couldn't I have gone to Boys Town in Omaha instead of St. Vincent's? After watching the movie, I often wondered if I would have been happy there.

One of my all time favorite movies was, "Knute Rockne—All American." Forever embedded in my mind would be Coach Rockne in the locker room at Notre Dame telling the team to *"Win one for the Gipper."* That movie earned Ronald Reagan the nickname, "The Gipper." It also made me a lifetime fan of the Notre Dame football team. If I were ever given a choice of where to go to college, it would always be Notre Dame.

As Christmas approached, one day after school Sister Lucille took me aside and said to me, "Do you know you have a beautiful voice?"

I didn't know how to take a compliment. I just blushed and replied, "Nope."

Earlier that day, we had been singing Christmas carols in class. I truly enjoyed singing, but never was told I had a beautiful voice. I enjoyed singing Latin prayers at mass with the priests. To me, the sounds from my voice came from my heart and my soul as well as my voice. Singing was a way for me to express my feelings with melody. I didn't even look up at the ceiling when I sang in class. With her encouragement, I joined the church choir. Shortly after that, I was singing in the chorus at the high mass on Sunday mornings.

I don't recall what I got for a Christmas present that year. Perhaps it was a run down pair of used skis. I do remember skiing with some of my classmates at Smith's hill on the way to Gilford on Saturday afternoons. Smith's hill was a wide-open field where we had to walk to the top of the hill. Then, we would glide down on our skis to the bottom.

My first pair of skis was definitely "hand-me-downs." They were an old pair of oversized Northland skis. I cut out inner tube strips and fabricated them into bindings. You could glide down the hill, but don't ever even try to turn those big boards. The ski would go straight and your foot would come completely off the ski and head in another direction. It was much better to point those babies straight down the hill. I enjoyed the exhilarating feeling as I gained momentum and speed on my way down the slope. The best way to stop was to fall to the ground and slide on your butt in the snow until you came to a complete stop.

Once we mastered that, we built a jump near the bottom of the hill and competed to see who could fly in the air the farthest. I took to skiing like a duck to water. It didn't take long before I was searching for bigger mountains to conquer. And now that my ice skates fit better, I was showing marked improvement at the skating rink behind our house.

I just didn't understand why adults always seemed to complain about the long, cold winters in New Hampshire. I looked forward to the days when school was cancelled because of a snowstorm. That was my opportunity to take a shovel from the storage shed under the porch and head out to Pleasant Street where the rich folks lived. I shoveled walkways and porches for twenty-five cents a house. I could stretch a couple of dollars a long way. Besides, then I could pay Sister Lucille the money she loaned me to go to the movies.

By February 1949, I had mixed feelings about the upcoming Sacred Heart Winter Carnival. It signaled the beginning of Lent. Sister Lucille placed a large cardboard chart in the front of the classroom with our names and dates on it. Each student would receive a gold or silver star for every day they attended morning mass. I was very competitive, but that's not one of the contests I particularly cared to win. I didn't want to go to mass every morning before school. On the other hand, I didn't want to be singled out as a pagan for not going to mass every lousy morning. I was really having trouble coming to grips with this dilemma when God must have come to my rescue.

One morning in class, I suddenly began to have severe stomach pains. The pains became excruciating as the hours passed. I finally had to tell Sister Lucille I was having terrible stomach cramps. Back then, they didn't have school nurses or would even think of calling a doctor or an ambulance. The solution was to get you off school property as soon as possible by sending you home. Fortunately, I didn't have far to walk.

I was doubled over and in tears by the time I reached the house. Nobody was home. I was reluctant to do it, but I had no choice. I called my mother at the shoe factory and she immediately came home. I was rushed to Laconia Hospital. I arrived just in the nick of time to have my appendix removed. After a few days in the hospital, I was sent home to recuperate before returning to school. I relished the pity and attention showered upon me by my family and classmates. More than that, I was overjoyed with the outcome that I was unable to compete for the most stars in Sister Lucille's sublime contest of faith.

*   *   *

How is it that we have this innate ability to sense when something isn't right? Perhaps, it's because my mother and Harold weren't fighting as much. There was a sort of a subdued calmness in the house that alerted me to some impending disaster. My mother wasn't ranting and raving all the time and was spending more time at home on Saturday nights. What I didn't know then was that she had met another man. She was having a secret relationship on the side. If Harold knew, he never let on that he did.

Ironically, Lorraine knew of Ora's secret affair. In many ways, Lorraine was the adult and Ora was the child. My mother often confided with her and sought her advice on numerous matters. It's no wonder, Lorraine was loyal and possessed the good common sense my mother lacked. I suspect my mother was a romanticist and imagined that a knight in shining armor would enter into her life and sweep her off her feet. Then, she would live happily ever after.

Unfortunately, that knight was not poor Harold. It's sad. Within Harold, there were a lot of qualities that could have made him an excellent husband and father. The truth, as I saw it, was that she never loved Harold and only married him as a means to provide security for her and her three children. In time, she must have felt like he was preventing her from fulfilling her dreams and finally told him they had grown too far apart and she wanted out of the marriage.

What was he to do? He couldn't change the fact she didn't love him. Conversely, she had little regard for how damaging her actions were to her reputation or the impact her decisions had on the lives of her children. I doubt she even cared.

For some time, this mystery man would telephone Ora at the house. My mother coerced Lorraine to answer the phone. If Harold was at home, she pretended it was one of her classmates. She would tell the other party some excuse like, "Gee, I'm sorry I'm busy doing my homework right now. Can I call you later?"

Lying was not Lorraine's forte. That sort of chicanery made her sick to her stomach. Finally, Lorraine told her mother she no longer would be a party to her deceitful way. It was up to Ora to take responsibility for her actions.

One day in the spring of 1949, I came home from school to an empty house. Harold was gone. His clothes were gone. His car was gone. He never even said goodbye. It was such a sad time. Soon after that, it was entered in the Belknap County court documents: Harold Manson and Ora Manson were officially divorced. She was free to fly like a bird again. He, in turn, withered away like a wounded duck. I missed him . . . . a lot.

It was on a Sunday that spring that my mother took Claudie and me to Tilton to spend an afternoon at Grandma Bessie and Grandpa Jim's. It's the only time in my life I ever saw them. They were very old, very poor, and lived in a run down two-story house, very much in need of repair. What they lacked in money, they made up for in heart. They were a gentle, loving old couple.

In the few hours that Claudie and I were there, they were extremely gracious to us. I was quite comfortable with them and didn't understand why Charlie or one of their other children didn't help them out. Certainly, my father, who was a painter, could have put a coat of paint on that old dilapidating house.

Grandpa Jim set me on his lap and read to me and Grandma Bessie served us ice tea. I couldn't help but think these sweet people were the parents of my father who had divorced my mother nine years before. Yet, they were treating us as though nothing had ever happened between them. To me, it was a bit strange. I was confused. Why hadn't I ever seen these people before? Why didn't my mother stay there and visit Grandma Bessie and Grandpa Jim with us?

It was late that Sunday afternoon when our mother finally returned to pick us up. When she entered their humble home, she had an unforgettable glow about her. She was beaming. She was smiling. She was the happiest I had ever seen her. What a transformation.

All too often, we had seen her crying in a deep depressive state as if she couldn't handle the struggles of her life any longer. That's how we knew her best. Somehow, we sympathized with her and bonded with her to help her through her struggles. There is no doubt in my mind she suffered from a bipolar disorder. On that day, I witnessed the total other end of the spectrum of her dual personality. I curiously wondered what made her so happy.

That Sunday, she dumped us off at Grandma Bessie's and Grandpa Jim's so she could prevail upon them to look after us while she went off to rendezvous with her boyfriend at the Franklin VFW, a mere three miles away.

That's her business. That's her life. Nevertheless, I felt badly that she took advantage of her first husband's parents that way. I later learned that the man she went to see at the VFW was the same man who had been calling our house while she and Harold were still married.

*   *   *

Ora carefully orchestrated the day we met the new love of her life. We were invited to Easter dinner at his mother's house in Franklin. That year, Easter Sunday fell on April 17th, a day before Mom's 39th birthday. We were told beforehand that Ben Novak was younger than she was. The fact is she was quite self-conscious of that. She wanted to mask it from Ben's mother so she wouldn't think any less of her. Nor did she want Mrs. Bourgeois to know she had any children. What was she thinking?

Our dear mother concocted this wild scheme where we were to pretend to be her younger sisters and brother. I guess so! After all, Lorraine was 13, Claudie was 12, and I was 9. We were told be sure to call her Ora whenever we addressed her and to not make the mistake of calling her "Mom."

There is nothing I could possibly say to add to this preposterously absurd scheme. She was so determined to make a good impression on Ben's mother she even bought us new Easter outfits to wear for the occasion. I could only imagine that Ben must be very wealthy. I envisioned his parents living in a gorgeous mansion, high on a cliff overlooking the town of Franklin.

Reality quickly set in as we drove into the gravel driveway at 142 Chestnut Street. It was high on a hill all right, but set on a rural farm with cackling chickens running about, an outhouse, and, the mansion turned out to be a very small, two-bedroom home. You practically had to duck your head as you entered the house from the side entrance.

Lena Bourgeois was a huge Polish woman. She greeted us with her hair pulled back tightly in a bun, wore no lipstick, and was wearing an old faded apron. Her cotton flowered dress went down to slightly above her ankles. I could see she rolled her nylons clear down to her mud stained black shoes.

I whispered to Claudie, "And this is the woman we came here to impress?"

Mrs. Bourgeois greeted us with a nervous handshake and escorted us into her tiny living room to meet her husband, Frank, and their son Eddie. Frank sat silently in the corner of the room sucking on his empty pipe. I don't think he said two words all day. For some unknown reason, I liked Frank. Eddie must have been about fifteen and struck me as a bully. It was obvious he thought Lorraine was just going to fall head over heels for him. That would be a cold day in hell.

I could tell Mrs. Bourgeois was nervous and not accustomed to having visitors, let alone her oldest son's new girlfriend and her young sisters and brother. I certainly didn't want to be the culprit that screwed up my mother's little scheme, so I was determined to keep my mouth shut. I was content to stare at Frank Bourgeois since he didn't talk. He reminded me of one of those old Indians that you see on a postcard sitting in front of a General store in Arizona or someplace like that. I liked him.

Lena Bourgeois must have been hard of hearing. She bellowed out her words in broken English and we could hardly understand what she was trying to say. It seemed like she began each sentence with the work, "ach." As in, "ach you do this," or "ach you sit there." She babbled away incessantly without saying anything meaningful. She could have said something about our nice Easter clothes or asked us if we went to Easter mass that morning. No. She asked dumb questions like, "Ach you find the house all right?" and "Ach you live in Laconia?" "That be far from here, huh?" This was not the home of Albert Einstein.

My mother looked regal compared to her. She sat quietly smiling at Lena Bourgeois and let her "young sister," Lorraine, answer all of Lena's inspiring questions. Ora was definitely on her best behavior.

One thing that cannot be denied, Mrs. Bourgeois was one heck of a good cook. She put out a wonderful Easter dinner. She even made the dinner rolls from scratch. Everything was going just dandy until Claudie reached out to the middle of the table with her hands to pick up the slice of ham that had fallen from the serving fork. My mother was mortified. You could feel her eyes gazing down at Claudette.

Claudie felt the cold stare and asked, "What's wrong Maaaa (pause) Ora." Well, if that didn't let the cat out of the bag, I don't know what would. Game over.

Lena Bourgeois gave my mother that knowing look. Of course, my mother acted like nothing happened. Nothing was said. Mrs. Bourgeois might have been a country bumpkin, but even an idiot would have seen through our mother's stupid scheme.

I haven't mentioned anything about our mother's new boyfriend, Ben, because there isn't much to say. He was a rather obscure figure at the gathering. He didn't really speak to us. It's as though he was embarrassed about his family meeting us, yet, he wanted his mother to approve of his new girlfriend. I think she couldn't care less. If I sized her up right, she just wanted him to move out of their cramped little house. Any girlfriend would do.

He was eight years younger than my mother. I wasn't impressed by that. I failed to see what made him so special. Perhaps time would tell. I thanked Mrs. Bourgeois and gave her a hug on my way out the door. I waved goodbye to Frank. He smiled and waved back.

CHAPTER 9

PERCEPTIONS

Is perception reality? It was apparent by the summer of 1949 that Ben Novak had my mother totally spellbound. Why, she was as giddy as a young teenage girl in love with her first boyfriend. She so desperately wanted to love and be loved by this man. She was oblivious to his true character. If love is blind, then she was truly in love. Even though we saw Ben differently, we were glad to finally see her happy.

Personally, I didn't dislike Ben. I just didn't like him. I saw him quite differently than my mother did. Having already witnessed the failure of her marriage with Harold, I was naturally concerned for her. I was apprehensive of this man's real intentions. After all, here was a man eight years younger than her, who fancied himself as "a real catch." What ulterior motive did he have dating an older woman with three kids? The more I observed him, the more skeptical I became.

Ben worked in Franklin and came to Laconia to date Ora on the weekends. He'd appear fancifully dressed in brown gabardine slacks and a light tan sport coat, with a color coordinated sport shirt underneath. Even though I was only nine, I couldn't help but notice he always wore the same coat and pants, but wore a different colored sport shirt every time. I came to believe that was his only outfit. Maybe my mother didn't notice. Besides, he did look quite dapper and I could understand how that would impress her. He would also show up wearing dark, oversized sunglasses. He thought he was real cool; I thought he was real cocky.

Unfortunately, when he opened his mouth, it became obvious to me and my sisters that he wasn't the brightest bulb on the chandelier. Ben suffered from foot in mouth disease. He would use big words in a sentence that didn't make any sense. Like the time he told me, "I saw the car cross the medina." Huh? He meant the median.

The classic was the time he and my mother were entertaining friends and they got into a discussion about dogs. Ben blurted out, "My neighbor in Franklin has a douche hound." My mother looked curiously at Lorraine for clarification.

Lorraine didn't want to embarrass Ben. She politely said she thought he meant, a "dachshund." He was never known to use a word that might send the reader to the dictionary. Worse yet, he was too self-enamored to see the error of his ways.

It didn't take Ben very long to let me know he was a brave soldier in the big war. When my curiosity got the best of me, he'd give me that combat-scarred look of his and tell me he "didn't want to talk about it." Yet, he was quick to let me know he was a real card shark and spent a lot of his time at the racetrack at Rockingham Park betting on the horse races. He was definitely a braggart, but struck me as being all fluff and of little substance. This may sound like a harsh assessment of my mother's boy friend, but that's exactly how I sized him up.

I thought if he were thinking of marrying my mother, he would show some interest in me. Not once did he ever ask me, "What do you like to do? Do you like baseball? How do you like school? Do you like going to the movies?" Nothing. It was always about him. I had every right to be concerned. Not so much for me, but for my mother. He brought nothing to the table that I could see, except his perceived good looks in exchange for her hard-earned assets. I wasn't alone in feeling that way either.

My mother was totally smitten. There was nothing we could say to change her mind. She even confided in Lorraine and asked her what she thought of him. Lorraine was tactful, but not one to beat around the bush. She flat out told her mother she was concerned that Ben was only after her money.

With that sound advice, my mother proceeded to announce they were to be married in the Sacred Heart Church on September 3, 1949. The announcement of their impending wedding didn't surprise me, but I certainly was knocked over when she said they were getting married in the Catholic Church. How could she possibly be married in the Catholic Church when this would be her third marriage? That contradicted everything I had learned about Catholic marriage. After all, marriage is a sacrament. Something just didn't seem right.

One day that summer, I questioned my mother about that in front of Ben. She proudly let me know they were so intent on having their marriage blessed by the church; she paid $1,000 to obtain a special dispensation from the church hierarchy. I was dumbfounded. In 1949, you could buy a brand new car for less than $1,000. And my sisters were working for peanuts just to buy their own clothes and lunches at school. Obviously, she didn't care what the church thought about that. Ben was also quite proud of the large sum Ora doled out to get permission to marry at Sacred Heart. Why not? It wasn't his money. She was living in a Pollyanna world. Frankly, I was dismayed by the whole situation. Was her perception, in fact, a deception?

The more I learned about him, the more I became concerned. I learned Mr. Flash drove a bread truck for a living. That paid about $35 a week. More disturbingly, I learned he had some serious gambling debts he needed to pay off. It really disturbed me to learn that my mother was paying off his gambling bills to save him from physical repercussions by some tough hoods. Besides, his days living on Chestnut Street with his mother were numbered. This was not a pretty picture. Nobody could talk any sense into my mother. She was determined to make this marriage work. More often than not, what you see is what you get.

*   *   *

Despite all the drama surrounding our little household, we managed to stay very busy that summer. Motorcycle Week signaled the beginning of another beautiful summer in the Lakes Region. With that, came a new task levied upon me by my mother. She sent me to the Railroad Station, where many of the motorcyclists gathered, to find boarders looking for a room to rent. Most kids would have been embarrassed to approach the cyclists to peddle rooms. I wasn't. If that put me in my mother's good graces, then I would do it.

In no time at all, I was riding on the back of a motorcycle with a couple of riders that were looking for a place to stay. It was no secret these poor cyclists were gouged by the locals during motorcycle week. I suspect my mother made as much money in three days as she normally would in a month. You only had to keep an eye out so they wouldn't leave in the middle of the night with blankets and pillows in hand. Not to worry, Ben was there to keep a watchful eye on everything.

I was pretty much on my own that summer. Lorraine was hired as an usher at the Colonial Theater and worked as often as they'd allow. At only thirteen, Claudie landed a job at Ferland's Fur Shop. She had a neat job. Basically, she answered the phone. Good work if you can find it. Her real *raison de existence* was to notify Mr. Peron should his wife leave the shop during operating hours. Apparently, Mrs. Peron, (formerly Mrs. Ferland), enjoyed the flavors of liquor whenever the opportunity presented itself, so Claudie was tasked to call him if his wife left the building. As the summer went on, Mrs. Peron taught Claudie how to make repairs to fur coats, so it wasn't all lost in vain.

Then there was my mother. Besides stitching soles at Laconia Shoe Company, she still worked Friday nights cleaning curtains and added another job to her endless resume. That summer, she took on an additional job cleaning cabins at Little Cape Cod cabins on the way to the Weirs on weekends. Little Cape Cod was regarded as one of the more upscale cabin colonies in the Weirs area. Mom was a heck of a hard worker. They were grateful to have her help. They even allowed her to take me to work with her so I could swim in Paugus Bay and play on their private raft. I only went there a couple of times. There really wasn't much for me to do there and I wasn't allowed to fraternize with the guests. I had much more fun playing with my friends at Opechee Park.

The Laconia Elks club held the biggest summer carnival in the area. Probably, the biggest in the state. They held it behind the Elks club on South Main Street. It brought in an avalanche of tourists every year. Besides booths of scrumptious food and games of chance, the highlight was the daredevil high wire trapeze act the Elks brought in every year. People stayed there until after midnight every night of the weeklong carnival just to watch that show.

My grandfather, Joe Garneau, was supposedly a big shot in the Elks and I always went over to say hello to him. Grampy never bought me anything though. The carnival culminated with the raffle drawing for the new car they raffled off every year that was the highlight of the carnival. That was always followed by the moans and groans of the locals, who were miffed that the eventual winner always came from somewhere in Massachusetts.

Before I entered the fifth grade, there was one more little thing that had to be done. On 3 September 1949, my mother walked down the aisle at Sacred Heart Catholic Church to be married to Mr. Ben Novak of Franklin, New Hampshire. She looked great in her new two-piece outfit. He looked quite dapper in his new pale blue suit. It was a small wedding, attended by his family and our immediate family. His brother, Adam, and his wife, and his sister, Melanie, and her husband, were also there from his side. I was so occupied at the time, I didn't realize that my Grandfather and Grandmother Garneau weren't there. I don't think they had any love for Ben and frankly they were probably disgusted with the fact my mother was being married for the third time, in the Catholic Church no less. My grandmother didn't want any part of her flighty daughter's wanton ways. That would not be well received by their circle of friends in the Sacred Heart parish. I assumed that. Nobody discussed such matters with a nine year old boy. After all, what did I know about anything.

The wedding was followed by a sit down dinner at the Laconia Tavern hotel. After pictures were taken on the steps of the Tavern, I was told I would be staying with my new grandparents for a few days while my mother and Ben went on a brief honeymoon to Boston. That was fine by me, as long as it was only for a few days. I didn't like to stray too far from my sisters. I couldn't help it. I was wary of adults. I guess, subconsciously, I feared they might be scheming to take me back to St. Vincent's.

When I arrived at Grammy Bourgeois, I was tired from all the excitement of the day and asked if I could take a nap. She showed me where I'd be sleeping, in the tiny bedroom at the top of the stairs. There were two beds in the room. I assumed one was Ben's ex-bed and the other was her son, Eddie's.

I had never seen Polish pillows before. They were huge. Soon I was sound asleep, swallowed up in one of the Polish pillows. I didn't wake up until after five o'clock that afternoon to the sweet aroma of fried chicken. They didn't have any toys to play with or a television to watch, so after supper I sat outside in the backyard and gazed at the stars. I wondered what my mother and Ben were doing, what Lorraine and Claudie were doing, and, more importantly, what would I be doing the rest of the time I was there.

The next morning, after consuming the best flapjacks I ever ate in my entire life, Frank handed me a small pail and led me by the hand to the woods and fields beyond the barn. We picked blueberries for most of the morning until our pails were full. It's strange. It was one of those rare moments in your life you never forget. Frank hardly spoke, but somehow I knew I was his friend. I knew he'd watch over me. And, I soon learned I needed to be protected.

My gut instinct told me to watch out for Eddie. Eddie was a big, stocky farm boy that seized the opportunity to tease me whenever he could. He jabbed me when I walked past him if nobody was looking. And, in his bedroom, he piled on top of me and suffocated me with one of those humongous Polish pillows. I didn't want him to know I was afraid of him. That would only incite him more. So, that afternoon when he invited me to go swimming with him and his friends, I couldn't back down.

The outing began pleasantly enough; however, I became increasingly worried as the big boys paddled out in a rowboat to the middle of the huge pond. Once we reached the middle, they dared me to jump into the water. I was frightened. I had never been there before. They told me the water from the pond flowed over a dam into the Merrimack River. Before I could hold back the tears, they tossed me overboard and began rowing away from me, laughing all the while.

I cried, screamed, and panicked, in fear of going over the dam. At the very last moment, when I was only about ten feet from the edge of the dam, one of the bullies grabbed my flailing arm and pulled me back into the boat. I was gasping for air and shaking all over. Eddie and his gang of thugs were still laughing at me.

One of his friends uttered something like, "We'll show those Laconia boys not to mess with Franklin."

When we reached shore, Eddie warned me if I breathed a word of what happened that day, he would really hurt me.

I told him I would keep my mouth shut this time; however, if he ever laid a hand on me again, I would tell Ben and even report him to the police. He knew I meant every word I said. I even thought of recruiting some of the older boys in Laconia to bring to Franklin to settle this score.

*   *   *

The following week, we were back in school. We already heard all the rumors about my 5th grade teacher, Sister Leo, more appropriately known as, Leo the Lion. She and Sister Rudolph must have been roommates at the convent. They were made from the same mold. They even looked like sisters. No pun intended. Short, squat, tough as nails. It had been rumored that in the past, some classes were so out of control, the students brought certain teachers to tears right in the classroom. It was rumored some of them even had a nervous breakdown.

Sister Leo was not about to be victimized in her classroom. She could make Stalin look like a Boy Scout. I think she spent her sleeping hours dreaming about which boy she was going to whack the next day. I, for one, was not about to be a cutesy wise-ass in her class. Much easier to be a model student. Besides, I might learn something. She definitely kept me on my toes that year.

Sister Leo never gave me any trouble. I liked to think I was on her "good boy" list. After all, I was doing all the right things. Altar boy, singing in the church choir, and moving up the ranks in Cub Scouts. To add to my repertoire that year, I even played basketball for St. Joseph's in the intramural league on Saturday mornings.

Now that I was in the 5th grade, the boys in Cub Scouts were allowed to join the Boy Scouts in Troop 62 on the annual parish paper drive. That turned out to be one of the most fun times I ever had. The Boy Scout paper drive was well publicized and even advertised in the Laconia Citizen. It was generously supported by Catholics and non-Catholics alike.

It was on a very cold Sunday morning, when about a dozen trucks convened in the schoolyard after the high mass to travel their designated routes throughout the city to gather all the bundled papers left by the side of the street.

I climbed on a big furniture delivery truck with Fats Boudreau, Bobby Morin, and a couple of Boy Scouts to pick up papers. There was a sense of excitement, jumping off the truck before it even came to a complete stop and gathering the huge piles of newspapers and magazines. At times, there were so many piles of papers close together, we didn't even jump back on the truck. We just threw them on the truck and walked to the next pile, while the older boys stacked them neatly from the front to the rear of the storage box. In a couple of hours, we filled the truck and headed back to the schoolyard to deliver the bundled papers.

Somewhere in all this chaos, I began to bead in on comic books that were mingled in with the newspapers. It's as though I had radar connected from my brain to the buried comic books. I sensed when there was a comic book in a stack. I must have picked up twenty-five comic books that day. I was ecstatic. I hardly noticed the numbing cold weather. You see, I never had money to buy comic books. The only time I ever read about the adventures of Superman or Batman was when I went to Fats Boudreau's house. He had plenty of comic books. When we were through gathering papers, I tucked my comic books under my arm and walked down the street with Fats, heading for home.

Suddenly, Fats offered me a proposition. He also collected a bunch of comic books that day. From one ten year old boy to another, he offered to give me all his comic books if I backed off and let him have a chance to become Diane Bonneau's boyfriend. Such a deal!

True, I liked Diane Bonneau, but I wasn't crazy in love with her. I mean, I went to her house a couple of times, and we kissed on the front porch once, but I was more interested in that new little French girl, who moved to Laconia from Canada. That cute little Odell LeFleur.

A deal was made late that cold November afternoon. The door was open for Fats to enter Diane's heart and I, in turn, agreed to stop flirting with her in class and not walk her home after school, in exchange for a stack of comic books.

* * *

The year 1949 marked another baseball season that my beloved Red Sox lost the American League championship to those rotten New York Yankees again. This one was a heartbreaker. We clawed our way from thirteen games back at the All Star break to within one game of defeating the Yankees. Ted Williams had a great year. He batted .343 and was chosen the American League MVP. Mel Parnell amassed a fabulous 25 win—7 loss pitching record. Yet, we couldn't put the Yankees away.

In the crucial final series with the Yankees, Joe McCarthy's managing ability was seriously called into question again. Why would he pull our pitcher, who seemed to have the situation under control, for a pinch hitter when we had a lineup full of strong batters? We lost the game. McCarthy has to go. And the Yankees went on to beat their cross-town rivals, the Brooklyn Dodgers again, in five games to be crowned World Champions for the 1949 baseball season.

Not all was lost on the Red Sox. I was now rooting for my new favorite college football team, the Fighting Irish of Notre Dame. They would not disappoint. To the contrary, the Fighting Irish went undefeated that year and ended the season with a perfect 10—0 record. This was more than a football team. This was a dynasty.

This team, coached by Frank Leahy, won their third national championship in the past four years. Led by their Heisman trophy winner, Leon Hart, the Irish outscored their opponents 360-86! I loved the Irish! I was convinced that someday I would go to Notre Dame . . . . if that was at all possible.

Baseball season was over. Football season was over. It was now time to concentrate on winter sports. By Christmas, Claudie and I were whizzing around the French school skating rink practically every day after school. Finally, my skates fit me and my skating had markedly improved. I wasn't a fast skater, or even a fancy skater like my sisters, but I managed to cruise around the ice quite comfortably. Furthermore, I was not at all shy about taking one of my girl classmates by the hand to circle around the rink with.

As much as I enjoyed skating, I got more of an adrenaline rush from skiing. I just loved flying over a jump. Our neighbor, who lived in the next house up the street from us, had a nice hill in their backyard. Miss Huot lived with her brother and didn't have any children. They kindly allowed us to ski in their backyard.

One day, her brother came out with a hose and hooked it up to an outside faucet. We carved a narrow path down the hill and he proceeded to run water down our path. That night it froze over. I was then able to glide down the frozen path on my skates and fly over the jump I built at the bottom of the hill. Yes, I said skates. Sometimes, I even managed to land on my two feet!

I still continued my Saturday outings at Smith's hill. Claudie bought a pair of skis that year and allowed me to use her skis when she couldn't go skiing. Well, let me just be honest and say I took them sometimes. Her bindings were far superior to what I had been using. I could now actually make nice stem christie turns while going down the hill. I was skiing. It was exhilarating!

Quite often Claudie couldn't go skiing because she was too busy playing basketball. I was so proud of her. She was one heck of a basketball player. She started playing basketball in the 6th grade in the schoolgirl's intramural basketball program. O.K., I'll say it, she was the best player on the St. Joseph girl's team. She was such a good player; her talent didn't go unnoticed by Lenny Metcalf, who coached the Laconia Business College girl's basketball team. As an eighth grader, he recruited her to play for a college level team.

Girl's basketball rules were very different in those days. Each team had six players on the floor. Three guards and three forwards. The guards couldn't shoot or cross the centerline and vice versa. Claudie was a guard.

To me, her strength lied in her scrappiness and plain good basketball sense. She just had a knack of knowing what to do and when to do it. She was a fearless competitor and could often be seen chasing a loose ball or fighting with an opponent for a rebound. When she had the ball, she knew best where to pass it at the other end of the court. Hey, what can I say? She was good! It's a shame my mother and Ben never went to any of her games to watch her play. I went to her games as often as I could. I was her biggest fan.

I played for the junior boy's basketball team at St. Joseph's. We had the same coach that my sister did. In fact, Bert Morin coached all the St. Joe's basketball teams. Looking back on it, he was blessed with a great deal of patience, but a limited knowledge of basketball.

We did quite well in practice, learning to pass, dribble, and shoot lay-ups and foul shots, but when we played in the intramural league at the high school on Saturday mornings, you couldn't tell if we were playing soccer or basketball. It seemed like one boy would have the ball and nine other boys from both teams were trying to take it from him. Up and down, up and down, without scoring a point. We needed more than practice; we needed discipline. In time, we'd get better. We certainly couldn't get any worse. And I was just as big a ball hog as everyone else on our team.

*   *   *

I'll never forget January 17, 1950. I was at Fats Boudreau's house that afternoon. We were sitting in his living room watching television because it was too cold to play outdoors. The program was interrupted by a special news announcement. That historic event became known as the famous Boston Brinks robbery. It was the most daring and largest bank robbery in American history.

The Brinks building on the corner of Prince and Commercial Streets in the North end of Boston was robbed by eleven daring masked robbers in broad daylight that afternoon. The Brinks robbers managed to steal $1,218,211 in cash and $1,557,183 in checks and money orders. This epic event was covered by the media for days, weeks, and even months. The robbers had foiled the Boston police and even the FDI. According to the media, this was the perfect crime. No clues left behind. I had to wonder, since they pulled this off so masterfully, when and where would they strike again?

*   *   *

The 1950 Sacred Heart winter carnival broke all previous attendance records. This translated to more money for the parish. I honestly believed people were suffering from cabin fever and went to the parish carnival for a few hours just to get out of the house. Somehow, to me, it had lost its luster. Furthermore, I was getting tired of traipsing all over town in the snow and slush, in the dead of winter, to hustle people to buy raffle tickets.

I was earning a reputation as a little hustler. It was fine the first year, but I didn't want to be labeled a beggar. Now, I don't recall if I won it as a prize for selling the most raffle tickets or if my mother won it at the parish carnival, but somehow we ended up with an ugly three-foot tall plastic clown. I had no interest in it whatsoever.

My mother saw the clown as another opportunity to make money. The next thing I knew, I was again knocking on doors and dragging that stupid looking clown in the beer joints of Laconia on a Saturday afternoon, hustling my mother and Ben's drinking friends into buying chances to win a clown.

Yes, I was embarrassed. I was sick of hearing, *"That's Ora's boy."* Nevertheless, I did manage to bring in $42 that was supposed to be split between my mother and me.

As usual, she kept it all. "After all, it cost money to feed you and keep a roof over your head," she reminded me for only the eight hundredth time. I wish I had a dollar for every time I heard that.

I was always glad to see Lent come to an end. Not only because I had to go to church more often during that forty day period, but also because it generally signaled the end of another long, brutal winter.

As an altar boy, I sat in the altar pew whenever I went to mass. I also took my turn serving the priest during mass, which always made me nervous. I was scared I would goof up in front of the entire parish.

Sister Leo had a different system to coax us to attend mass during Lent. At St. Joseph's we received numerical grades, as opposed to letter grades, on our report card. She used that little tool as a bargaining chip to coerce us to attend mass. If you never missed mass, you received a grade of 100 for Catechism.

The only person I ever knew that achieved a perfect grade in Catechism was none other than my sister, Claudie. As much as Lorraine wanted to be a doctor, Claudie seriously wanted to become a nun. Perhaps because she was perceived as a tomboy and athlete, people failed to notice her deep religious convictions. She went to mass every day, not only during Lent. She even went to evening services at the church. She discussed her intentions with some of the other nuns at the convent and finally convinced our mother she was dead serious about serving Jesus and the Virgin Mary in a religious order.

Bear in mind, we never ever did anything in my lifetime as a family. We didn't even go to church together, let alone go to a restaurant or even take a car ride to the Weirs. Yet, on a Sunday afternoon that spring, my mother and Ben piled us all in the car and drove to Concord, New Hampshire, to the Carmelite sisters' new monastery.

This was definitely a very special occasion. This was the only day in history the Carmelite monastery would be open to the public.

The Carmelite sisters were known as the most devout, strict order in the Catholic Church. They essentially lived a hermitic life. While each convent may alter their rules slightly, generally, it is known they live a life of silence, solitude, and prayer, with devoted community service to the poor and less fortunate. The Carmelites abstain from talking from after evening prayers, usually around 7:00 p.m., until after the morning prayers, at approximately 9:00 a.m. the following day. Each nun lives in a very small cell, with only a cot and a pad to kneel on and constantly prays before a cross and statue or picture of the Blessed Virgin.

What really stood out with both my sisters during our visit that day was the youthfulness and beauty of the Carmelite nuns at that monastery. They were so much younger and prettier than the nuns we ever knew. This visit further inflamed Claudie's passion to join the order.

Soon it would be Memorial Day again. Oh, I looked forward to that day. In Laconia, we had a French Catholic cemetery and across the road was the city cemetery for Protestants. After services were held at both cemeteries, the organizations in town merged and marched from the cemeteries in a parade. The parade proceeded right down the middle of Main Street. There I was, proudly marching in cadence in my Cub Scout uniform, in front of all the people lined up on Main Street to watch the parade. That was always a proud moment in my life.

I hurried home immediately after the parade, put away my uniform, and changed into my "work clothes." The nearby lakes and streams were always crammed with fishermen that time of the year with hopes of catching a massive trout. For the most part, they brought their boats up from Massachusetts to take advantage of the beginning of boating season. By then, I had taken over the "family business" from my sisters.

Laugh if you want, but there was a good amount of money to be made selling worms to Oscar's Worm Ranch near the boat ramp on the edge of the Winnipesaukee River. I didn't sell the worms I gathered from our garden and the Clavette's garden directly to Oscar Mousette. No, instead I used a middle man.

I cut a deal with Marie Clavette's husband, Freddy Clavette. Freddy was my middle man and would drive to Oscar's bait shop and sell them for me. It was general knowledge that Oscar paid a better price for the worms he bought from adults. Mr. Clavette suffered from emphysema and couldn't work, so I picked as many worms as I could and put them into the cans he provided.

In the spring, the worms surfaced to the top of the plowed rows in the garden and were easily hand-picked. I relished a rainy day. That's when the worms would rise to the top and made for easy plucking. Plus, I would find a lot more night crawlers when it rained. Of course, my mother wasn't too pleased with me when I arrived home in my mud stained jeans and shirt. It was dirty work. The way I looked at it, dirt meant money.

My partner would pay me a penny for each worm and two cents for night crawlers. I was content with that arrangement and he kept anything above that amount he could negotiate with Oscar. That gave me spending money and provided Freddy with money to buy a few beers. It was a win-win for the both of us. With money in hand, I even contributed some of my earnings to Mr. Fournier's pinball machine, where I was beginning to hone my skills for bigger and better things in the future.

* * *

And what was Father #3 up to during this time? Quite naturally, I observed Ben closely to see what kind of role he would assume, if any, in our family. Would he endear himself to my sisters and me? Was he going to take me under his wing and teach me things like fathers do with their sons? Would he go ice skating with me? Would he teach me how to make repairs around the house? What would our relationship be?

The answer was simple. There would be no so-called relationship. It soon became obvious that Ben married my mother, not her three children. We weren't part of the deal. For one thing, he didn't know how to be a father; nor did he intend to learn. I had to remember he had been a bachelor for the past thirty-one years and spent his time gambling, drinking, and probably carousing around before he met my mother. That's all he knew. He was having enough problems adjusting to married life and trying to manipulate his new wife. As much as she may have loved him, Ora would always be in control. She realized she had to keep Benny Boy on a short leash, lest he go off and squander her money at the racetrack.

From my perspective, it appeared he was trying to gain her trust and was walking the straight line. They still went to her favorite nightspot on the weekend, but managed to make it to mass on Sunday morning. Shortly after they were married, he even quit his job driving the bread truck and took on another job delivering heating oil for Courtemanche Brothers Oil Company in the Franklin area. That was a physically more demanding job, but also paid more than delivering bread. Now, I could sarcastically tell my friends that Ben was in the oil business. When all was said and done, it appeared to me he was making an earnest commitment to settling down into married life.

If he was trying to test my mother, he learned his lesson soon after they were married. My sisters and I were still convinced he married our mother for her money. He wanted to use her money to give the appearance that he was a "big shot." Big spender Ben, using my mother's money. She may have been in love with him, but she wasn't about to let him squander away her hard earned money.

He made the foolish mistake of driving home one day with a brand new Buick he purportedly bought at Stafford Buick Company. Why, it even had the new dyna-flow transmission. My mother came unglued. How dare he go off and buy a car with her money without her permission. Did she ever tear into him. When the feathers quit flying, Ben had to take the Buick back to Stafford's and let them know he couldn't keep it. One thing for certain, that day he learned the Golden Rule: *"He who controls the gold, controls the rule."*

CHAPTER 10

PAPER BOY

Friday, June 16, 1950, was the final day of school at St. Joseph's for that school year. As soon as Sister Leo gave her little speech on how well we progressed in her class, and we countered back with how much we appreciated her, class was dismissed. I don't know who told the biggest lie, Sister Leo or her students? Either way, we were glad to be rid of her and I am sure she was equally glad to be rid of us.

As I walked home with my report card in hand, I was confronted with the dilemma of what was I going to do all summer. Not to worry, my mother already had a plan for me. I no sooner changed out of my school clothes to go play baseball with friends when my mother ordered me to hurry to the Railroad Station. The 30th annual "Gypsy Tour" motorcycle week was underway. The 100-mile national championship road races were again being held at the Belknap Recreation Area. The weather report forecast a beautiful weekend and the American Motorcycle Association (AMA) was already predicting a record attendance. They expected some 12,000 motorcyclists at the races that year.

The Chamber of Commerce set up a little white information booth near the Railroad Station. There, the cyclists could obtain a list of available lodging as well as information on local attractions in the area. This was a no-brainer. I stood in front of their booth and stopped the riders as they approached. By now, I had become a pretty good judge of people. If they had a sleeping bag rolled up on the back of their bike, they weren't there looking for a room. If they walked hastily toward the booth, it was a good bet they were looking for a place to sleep before everything was rented out.

As three older riders approached, I carefully checked them out. They didn't strike me as the type that camped out on the grass at Belknap.

I quickly tugged on the leather motorcycle jacket of the oldest one, and asked, "Are you guys looking for a room?"

The nice man smiled back and replied, "Do you know where we can find a nice room?" Before I could ask any more questions, I was riding on the back of Freddy Walsh's Indian motorcycle, guiding three riders to Ora Novak's boarding house at 46 Winter Street. I could tell my mother was pleased with the three nice "fish" I brought home that day.

Soon after the three riders dropped off their belongings, Mr. Walsh came down the stairs and asked my mother if she knew where the Indian motorcycle dealer was located.

I thought to myself, "If it's not near the Rod and Gun Club, she wouldn't know." Of course, I knew better than to say that. Instead, I blurted out, "It's at the top of Stark Street in Lakeport."

Before I could add anything to that tidbit of information, Mr. Walsh asked my mother for permission to take me along to show him where Carl's Motorcycle Shop was located. She was delighted to let me go. That's how my summer began.

As we rode to Lakeport, I was secretly hoping that some of my classmates would see me riding on the back of his motorcycle. Nobody I knew had ever been on a motorcycle. Nobody I knew rented out rooms to motorcyclists either. For a split second, I thought about the noise the motorcycles made running up and down Winter Street. I'll bet the neighbors didn't like that one bit. There goes that Ora Novak defying acceptable social behavior again. That just added more fodder to the pile of criminations they held against her. I hoped they weren't laboring under the misapprehension that she gave a shit!

While Mr. Walsh spoke with the owner of Carl's Motorcycle Shop, I wandered around the store looking at all the racks filled with fancy biker clothes. When it was time to leave, Freddy Walsh beamed as he handed me a new motorcycle hat. I couldn't believe it. I was thrilled beyond words. Nobody had ever done anything like that for me before. My new friend, Freddy Walsh, actually bought me a bright red fluorescent motorcycle hat.

He told me, "You've got to look like a motorcyclist if you're going to ride with me . . . partner." That was the beginning of our friendship.

That day, I rode on the back of Freddy Walsh's Indian motorcycle all over the area until dusk. As soon as I stepped in the house, I proudly showed my mother, Ben, and my sisters my new motorcycle hat. I don't recall ever being happier. Well, except for maybe the Christmas I got my Cub Scout uniform. Not only that, Fred was going to take me to the motorcycle races at the Belknap Recreation Area, both on Saturday and Sunday. Now, how was that for starting a summer vacation!

I went to the races with Fred and his friends both days. It seemed that everyone knew who he was. I learned that Freddy Walsh actually owned an Indian motorcycle dealership in Hartford, Connecticut. When he was younger, he was one of the top motorcycle racers on the East coast. He would only ride Indian bikes. That was unfortunate. By now, Harley-Davidson's were winning all the big races. And to think, he was my friend. I really felt sad when he left to return to Connecticut after the Sunday race. We promised to write to each other.

His parting words to me were, "I'll be back next year and we'll go to the races again."

I replied with the cute rhyme, "I'll be ready, Freddy!" I chocked up when I finally had to say goodbye.

It was shortly after Freddy Walsh left, when Father Chicoine lived up to an earlier promise. Father "Chic," as he was called by the kids at St. Joseph's, had promised to take our school baseball team to a Red Sox game. We gathered in the schoolyard and boarded the new maroon and gold Sacred Heart parish bus. Well, it wasn't really a new bus in that sense. It was an old bus someone donated to the parish for this kind of thing: To haul the school teams around. Off we went, on our way to Boston.

I sat in a seat along the first base line at the venerable Fenway Park, home of the Boston Red Sox. It didn't matter to me if they won or lost that day. It was just a thrill to be there to watch all the great players I followed. Mel Parnell pitched and the Red Sox beat Cleveland. I finally got to see Walt Dropo at first, Bobby Doere at second, Johnny Pesky at short. And #9 didn't let me down. The great

Ted Williams hit a home run that day. It didn't matter that I didn't have any money to buy sodas or peanuts like the other boys. I just savored the moment. Fenway Park. The Red Sox. Wow!

When the game was over, Father Chic even let us go to the parking lot behind the ballpark to try to get autographs. After the players showered, they left by the rear exit. A chain-linked fence separated the players from the public, but they often signed a few autographs before leaving Fenway. None of us were lucky enough to get an autograph that day. However, I'll never forget seeing Ted Williams walk out of the ballpark in his dress clothes. Now there was a man that exuded cool. He was God-like in appearance. Ted Williams stood 6' 3" tall, weighted in around 210 pounds. He was the proverbial tall, dark, and handsome man in every woman's dreams. That day, he wore a rust colored sport coat with matching slacks. Under his loose fitting sport coat, he wore a bright yellow sport shirt. He stood alone in a class by himself.

I thought to myself, "Someday that's exactly how I want to dress."

He was not only my hero on the field, but off the field as well. The man definitely had charisma. He was the greatest hitter of all time.

* * *

June was coming to an end. It was time for me to come down from the clouds. Everything was going too well in my little world. Time for a reality check. My first reality check came the following week when I was assigned to be the altar boy at the morning masses that week. Father Chicoine wouldn't be conducting the masses. As was the custom in the summer, we had a visiting priest in town. I suspected that's how they justified a little side vacation to another parish. Well, the visiting priest happened to be none other than our mean neighbor's brother.

Father Duquette came to visit his sister from his parish near Quebec, Canada. I spotted him walking from his car to their house even before I saw him in church. He was probably the most obnoxious looking man I had ever seen. He looked like a beached whale. He was so fat, he wallowed from side to side as he walked up the path to the wicked Mrs. Lafrabois' house. He even needed a cane to support himself. I wondered if he was as mean spirited as his sister.

Early the next morning, I learned the answer to that question. I waited in the back of the church for him to arrive. He didn't arrive until right before the mass. There was no greeting. No special instructions. He walked past me, as though I didn't exist, and proceeded to the altar.

The mass was going smoothly until it was time to deliver the water and wine to Father Duquette. I swear to God, he sneered at me and demanded that I bring him another cruet of wine. I never heard of a priest demand another cruet of wine. We didn't keep an extra cruet near the altar for some alcoholic priest to devour during mass. What a bizarre request. What could I do? I simply walked away from the altar and left him to continue the mass.

After the mass, as I was removing my altar boy vestments, Father Duquette motioned to me to come over to him. He didn't even ask. He just waved his fat hand at me to signal me come to him.

As I stared at his blood shot eyes, he proceeded to holler at me in French. "Demain Je veux deux vin, tu comprend?" he said. Translated: "Tomorrow you bring me two wines, do you understand?"

Except, he shouted those words at me and spit flew from his mouth when he said the, "TU COMPREND?" He was hollering at me so loudly, I was surprised someone didn't come to the back of the church to see what was causing all the commotion. He had his finger pointing at my face when he blurted out "DO YOU UNDERSTAND?" in French.

I was trembling when I nodded in the affirmative. I instantly hated this man who called himself a priest. I couldn't imagine anybody confessing their sins to this vile creature. I left the church in tears.

I thought about his tongue lashing for the rest of the day. And for the rest of the night. I pondered the questions, "Was he sent on earth by the devil? Was he a priest in disguise? How could he be so disgusting and still be a priest?"

I thought of telling Father Chicoine about the altar incident, but I changed my mind. I concluded that Father Chic would side with him in the end, so I let it ride. That is, until I saw that sorry excuse of a priest drinking wine in the closet in the back of the church after mass one morning. For the rest of the week, I did as I was told and brought him two cruets of wine — the blood of Christ — as he directed. I waited until after he returned to Canada before I finally told Father Chicoine about his drinking habit. As I suspected, Father Chicoine simply dismissed it and told me to disregard it. He was gone.

Just before the 4th of July, Roland "Fats" Boudreau came to my house to show off his new bike. It was one of those new fandangled 10 speed bikes with the skinny tires. In fact, it was the first one I had ever seen. Fats whizzed up and down Winter Street as though he was riding a rocket. He made pedaling look easy as he changed gears going up the street. He didn't let me try it out. He didn't have to. I was impressed. I wanted a bike. More importantly, I wanted a job so I could buy a bike.

Lorraine and Claudie had jobs that summer. They were earning money for school in the fall. Lorraine was promoted to the cashier position at the Colonial theater. Claudie landed several jobs babysitting. I was tired of doing without. I wanted to earn money too. I wanted a bike like Fats Boudreau.

My mother suggested I go to the Laconia Citizen office and see if there were any paper route openings, I did just that. Lucky for me, I was told Scotty Gallagher was trying to sell his route on North Main Street. I found Scotty delivering papers that afternoon and asked him about it. To hear him tell it, he had the best paper route in the city. That should have been my warning. I was only ten years old and prime for the taking. What did I know about delivering papers? All I saw was the dollar signs and big fat tips coming my way every week. Was I naïve.

I had to buy Scotty's paper route. He sold it to me for $21.00. That worked out to fifty cents a customer, for a total of 42 customers. That became the first loan I ever borrowed from my mother. She loaned me the money to buy the route. In return, I agreed to pay her one dollar a week until the loan was paid off.

Scotty handed me his little green book. It contained the names and addresses of my customers, with columns to be checked off each week to indicate their payment. At the time, the Citizen cost thirty-five cents a week. I delivered the papers Monday through Saturday. I collected from my customers on Saturday and went to the Citizen office the following Monday to pay them their share.

Of the thirty-five cents, the Citizen made twenty-five; I made ten. Whether I was able to collect from all my customers each week didn't concern the Citizen. That was my problem. I still had to pay the Citizen office $10.50 every Monday.

Every afternoon, I went to the rear of the Citizen office on Beacon Street around three o'clock to wait for the printing presses to finish printing the daily paper. The ink was still fresh off the press when the papers were counted by the supervisor, and then handed to the paperboys. There was a pecking order. The boys who worked there the longest got their papers first. Therefore, I got mine last. By the time I recounted my papers to be sure I had enough, it was approaching four o'clock. Time to get moving. I stuffed the newspapers in my canvas paper bag, with the name "Laconia Citizen" inscribed on the side and was on my way to North Main Street.

My first customer lived about a mile away from the Citizen office. My route began across the street from Bud's market, near the Opechee Park clubhouse. From the Citizen office to my last customer's house on North Main and back to my house, I covered a distance of five miles every day . . . for 42 customers. I soon learned I had the longest paper route in town, with the fewest customers. That didn't matter. What mattered to me was that I finally had a job. The summer weather was pleasant and I didn't mind the long daily walk. I reasoned I was strengthening my legs for the upcoming basketball season.

My paper route took me to another world. Until then, my life was filled with French speaking Catholics who belonged to the Sacred Heart parish. I was raised around names like, Doucette, St.Jacques, Paquette, Cote, Ouellette, Maheux, and so forth. I couldn't help but notice I didn't have one French name in my little green book. To the contrary, my customers had names like, Anderson, Bates, Brody, Graves, Prescott, Smith, and the like. So, I was transformed to a world of English speaking Protestants and Jews. Mostly affluent. Mostly well educated. Above all, they were not the condemning, self-righteous petty bigots I was accustomed to in my part of town.

What I liked most about my customers was that they didn't prejudge me. They didn't know my mother. They didn't care about her past. All they cared about was getting their daily paper on time, in their designated location. It was nice not being looked at with disdain. Why, my customers actually smiled and spoke to me.

* * *

One Saturday afternoon after I finished delivering my papers, my mother, Ben, and I went to Paquette's Sporting Goods on Canal Street to buy a bike. I had no idea what to look for in a bike. I would have been better off had I gone there with Fats. My mother didn't know anything about bicycles and Ben hadn't been on a bike in fifteen years, yet, he acted like he knew more about bikes than Mr. Paquette.

Ben was like a kid in a candy store. I stood on the side while he went over the different features of each bike with Mr. Paquette. He definitely favored this big, heavy glossy looking Schwinn bike. It was adorned with chrome fenders, a cross bar with a horn and key slot, and a basket. I liked the basket feature, but, to me, it was a clunker. It was pretty all right, but it was probably the heaviest bike in the shop. I just didn't think it was practical. It's not what I wanted. What I wanted didn't matter. That's what I got. "Listen to Ben," my mother said.

Mr. Paquette lived across the street from us and knew I had a paper route. The bike cost $50.00. I agreed to pay him a dollar a week until it was paid off. We left Paquette's Sporting Goods and headed back to Winter Street so I could practice riding my new chrome clunker, with the fancy gizmos on it. I should have been overjoyed. I wasn't. I never did like that bike.

As the summer wore on, I learned the little peculiarities of all of my customers. Some wanted their paper left in their mailbox. Others insisted I leave it between two doors. Still others wanted their paper placed in a specific location on their porch. I complied with all their requests, except for two customers. One of my customers had a long steep uphill driveway to their house. The woman wanted me to open the gate at the bottom of their driveway, walk up the long driveway, and place the paper in their breezeway.

I very diplomatically told her, "I just can't do that. You have an awfully long driveway and I can leave it in your mailbox if you want."

She could tell I wasn't going to back down. She didn't put up an argument. I suspected she was just feeling me out. I was glad I held my ground.

The other customer owned a beautiful house that set far back on their property. They didn't object to me leaving their paper in the mailbox. However, they wanted me to come to the front door on Saturdays to collect my money. Normally, I would do that, except they owned a vicious Chow dog. Their dog was eager to consume me for lunch if given the chance. I had some bad experiences with that canine beast. It was the only dog on my route that gave me a problem. Usually, he was kept inside. Unfortunately, every now and then he was outside when I delivered the paper. A couple of times, I had to kick him away when he tried to bite my ankle as I pedaled past their house. I actually walked or rode my bike on the other side of the street to avoid him.

Finally, I had enough. I bought a water pistol and filled it with ammonia. I carried the water pistol in my paper bag to protect myself. Sure enough, the next day killer dog came roaring out of his driveway. I placed my bike between him and me. When he came real close, I squirted him in the face with ammonia. That did it. Egor never bothered me again. Furthermore, I reached a compromise with Egor's owners. They agreed to leave my money in an envelope in the mailbox on Saturdays.

My paper route provided me a firsthand lesson in the study of human nature. Adults always intrigued me. I learned a whole lot by observing my customers. One of my customers lived in an old run down house across from Opechee Park. It was the only run down house on my route. I am sure his neighbors wished he'd move away or that the city would condemn his house. It was pathetic looking. More so, in view of the nicely kept homes in the area. You could hardly see his house. Vines hung from the house, obstructing any view. What could be seen was badly in need of paint. The grass was never mowed and the place was surrounded by wild blackberry bushes.

The kids in the neighborhood had all sorts of wild stories about the mean old hermit that lived alone in that rundown house. Everyone was scared of him. However, nobody could give me a reason why. I always threw the paper on his exposed front porch. Come Saturday, he left my money in a fruit jar near the front door. A month passed before I eventually saw the old man. The first time I saw him, he was sitting in an old kitchen chair eating blackberries on his front porch. He was surrounded by at least a half dozen cats. That explained all the dirty dishes I had seen laying out there. I watched him closely as I approached the porch. He was very unkempt. He looked like what I would expect a recluse to look like. He had a long overgrown white beard. He wore working boots. His khaki pants were filthy and he looked like he hadn't had a bath in weeks. For a moment, I didn't know whether to throw the paper on the porch or get off my bike and hand it to him. Something inside me told me to get off my bike and meet this old man. I'll never regret that I did.

I don't recall his name. It was one of those long Russian names that are hard to pronounce. I could tell he was quite surprised that I wasn't afraid to walk up to him. He didn't growl. He didn't bite. To the contrary, in his broken English he thanked me for the paper. As I was turning to walk away, he asked me if I wanted some blackberries. That began our friendship. For the rest of the summer, he met me at his porch and offered me a small bowl of blackberries. We didn't talk much. I think he was embarrassed that he couldn't speak English very well. Anyway, I sat on the front steps and pet the cats while I ate my blackberries. He sat in his chair by the door and smiled at me in a comforting sort of way. When I was done, I thanked him and jumped on my bike to continue my deliveries. What a kind, gentle man. How easy it is to misjudge people.

My new bike was both a help and a hindrance. Where the land was flat it really came in handy. At least until it turned cold. I pedaled my bike from our house to pick up my papers on Beacon Street, a little over half a mile away. From there, I pretty much pedaled it until I reached the incline on North Main Street. It was just too heavy and not worth the hassle. If I kept it with me, I had to push it up two hills, so I locked it and left it in one of my customer's driveways when they weren't home. I knew when they were gone. They always cancelled their paper before they went away.

There was a lot more going on beside my paper route that summer. The union was trying to become firmly established at Scott & Williams, the largest employer in Laconia. In late July, when the company refused to give in to the union's demands, the worker's went on strike. A strike was a new phenomenon in Laconia. Of course, the company thought the workers couldn't hold out and would return to work in a few days. Were they ever wrong. However they did it, the union mobilized the workers to hold out for more. As time passed, some of the less fortunate, or less determined, couldn't afford to stay out of work. They had families to feed and bills to pay. I am sure they held out as long as they could. Others were more determined and refused to give in until the union's demands were met.

That caused some of the saddest, most terrifying times in the annals of Laconia's history. When the so-called "scabs" crossed the picket line in front of the factory they were beaten with bats and clubs by the strikers. The strike pitted brothers against brothers. Neighbors against neighbors. Friends against friends.

People stood across the street from the plant on Union Avenue to watch the daily activity. I knew it was inhumane to dote on another man's suffering. Yet, I was as bad as everyone else. In the afternoon, I joined the rest of the crowd in Normandin Square in eager anticipation of an outbreak across the street.

The strike lasted five weeks; the scars from the strike lasted a lifetime. When it was all said and done, many family relationships were shattered. The bitter feelings among neighbors would never go away. It took a few generations to forgive and forget the strike of 1950.

*　*　*

The biggest surprise of all happened later that summer. If I were older, I probably wouldn't have believed it. However, I was too young to realize the impact of what was happening. My 39-year-old mother was pregnant! I didn't realize how unusual it was for a woman her age to have a baby. Nor did I understand the ramifications it would have on her life. I didn't know if this was something she and Ben planned. I didn't know if they were just being good Catholics and abstained from birth control. I didn't know anything. All I knew is that my 39 year old mother was pregnant.

Because of her age, my mother had to quit her job at the shoe factory a few months before she was due to deliver. I was told the baby was due in late October. I also surmised that Ben couldn't afford to support her and a baby on his salary. I am sure they discussed such matters between themselves. I was never privy to anything they discussed.

I'll admit Ben surprised me. He quit his job delivering oil in Franklin and went to work at Laconia Malleable Iron. He may not have been a father to me, but I would always respect him for his work ethic. Laconia Malleable Iron or "the foundry" as it was called, had a reputation in town. It was considered to be the most demanding place to work. If you couldn't find a job and were desperate for money, you worked at the foundry as a last resort. Reportedly, it paid well, but you worked your ass off for every penny you made. Slackers need not apply.

It was particularly tough for Ben to work at the foundry. He only weighed about 150 pounds. He wasn't French, and he wasn't from Laconia. He was from Franklin. Besides that, he was new. He had to earn the other workers' respect. He was severely tested that summer. They gave him the worst jobs to do in the foundry, while his coworkers watched in hopes he would crack and quit. Ben was not a quitter.

One day, he forgot to bring his lunch pail to work. My mother had me deliver it to him at his workplace. I couldn't believe the atrocious working conditions in the black, soot filled foundry. Even before I opened the door, the smell of burning iron filled my nostrils. As I opened the door, I saw the hot smoldering iron flowing from the huge vats into the waiting molds. It was dark, dank, and terribly hot in there. I barely detected men moving about through the haze of gray dust. The only light came from the smoldering fire in the vats. There weren't any windows. There was no air conditioning. The only ventilation came through the open doors at the end of the building.

A big dark man with a gruff voice approached me and asked, "What do you want in here?" He said it as though I was in a forbidden place.

I told him, "I'm bringing Ben Novak his lunch."

He shouted loudly, "Novak, Novak."

I spotted Ben. He was crouched over a wheelbarrow full of iron forms he was hauling to another station. He looked exhausted. He appeared to be embarrassed that I had to see him that way. I couldn't help but think, "I'll bet this wasn't what he thought he'd be doing a year ago when he married my mother." Notwithstanding, he earned my respect that afternoon. That place had to be the equivalent of hell on earth.

Poor Ben. He arrived home from work around five o'clock every afternoon. He was exhausted. I don't know how that feisty Pollock managed to stick it out. He did though. He was covered with soot from head to toe as he slowly made his way up Winter Street. As soon as he walked in the house, he headed for the shower. After he showered and changed out of his work clothes, he and my mother sat in their rocking chairs on the front porch and drank a couple quarts of beer.

They would comment on the people returning home from work. Perhaps it was more like gossip. After all, that was the favorite pastime of the people that worked in the sweat shops of Laconia. Sometimes they would say, "Hello" to the people passing by. Sometimes not. They knew who was friendly toward them and who would snub them before they even reached our house. It didn't matter. They didn't hide from anybody. They always sat out front and drank their beers in broad daylight for the rest of the world to observe. Good for them. They deserved that much. Besides, they weren't fighting like in the old days with Harold. My mother appeared to be happy. I am sure she was concerned about their finances, but never mentioned anything to my sisters or me.

What other earth-shattering event could possibly happen that summer? While we had our own homegrown strike at Scott & Williams, there was a much bigger strike happening on the international front.

According to Sister Leo, if we ever went to war again it would be against Russia. She was wrong. Who would have ever thought that the good old USA would stick their nose into some internal conflict between North and South Korea? I certainly didn't. They didn't attack us. Yet, there we were, smack dab in the middle of another war.

As I followed the war, by reading about it in the Laconia Citizen, I realized this wasn't just about unifying Korea. We had a more vital reason to get involved. This was really a war pitting Communist vs. Non-Communist countries. I learned that Communist China was supporting North Korea in their battle to reign over Korea. If they defeated South Korea, China could expand communism by going after Japan. Therefore, it was in our best interest to come to the aid of South Korea.

Once the North Korean forces invaded South Korea on June 25, 1950, President Truman appointed General Douglas MacArthur, Supreme Commander of the allied forces. We expected this little skirmish to be resolved quickly. Were we ever wrong.

Who would have thought that the Korean War would last three long years? When it was all said and done, 1.8 million American soldiers served our country during the Korean War. Fifty-four thousand American soldiers were killed and another 103,000 were wounded. It was estimated that the toll on Chinese and Korean casualties was at least ten times as much.

Even though we claimed victory because an armistice agreement was signed on July 23, 1953, nothing had changed in the eyes of the Koreans. The center of the conflict, the 38th parallel, remained the dividing line between North and South Korea. If anything, the Korean War probably played an important role in the presidential victory of Dwight D. Eisenhower. The Armistice was agreed upon only after he threatened to deploy a nuclear attack on North Korea. It just goes to prove, he who has the biggest bomb wins.

When my sister, Claudie, wasn't working, she could usually be found playing basketball. The St. Jacques owned a small convenience store directly across the street from Scott & Williams. Both my sisters, as well as other teenagers, hung out at the store. They had two boys, Ernie and Kenny, who excelled in sports. The boys attached a backboard to the back of their garage and converted their yard into a small basketball court.

Often, I went there to watch Claudie play. She really held her own with the boys. They treated her just like one of the guys. I must admit, at thirteen, she was well developed. Such matters didn't even occur to her. All she thought about when she was on the court was winning.

One day, while playing at St. Jacques court, she was driving to the basket for a lay-up when one of the boys reached for the ball. Instead, he accidentally found his hand on her breast. If I hadn't said anything, it wouldn't have been an issue. Instead, I made some stupid remark about my sister's boobs. She was infuriated.

I knew I was in trouble. She chased me all the way home. When we got there, she held me down, opened a jar, and grabbed a handful of marshmallow. She then proceeded to rub it all over my head. When she finally let me up, I immediately ran back to St. Jacques to show the big boys what my mean sister had done. I thought they would sympathize with me. Not! They just broke out in total laughter. I was quite a sight with my white marshmallow-covered head. I instantly was dubbed, "the marshmallow kid." It took a while for me to live that one down. Claudie still teases me about that. I keep telling her "paybacks are hell." It will always be a family joke between us.

*   *   *

School wasn't a joke though. Not when you have the dreaded Sister Rudolph for a teacher. It's drudgery. She couldn't have been more appropriately named. She was the strictest teacher in the entire school. Maybe, in the entire world. She was a short, strapping, fiery nun, who blew up like Mount Vesuvius with the slightest provocation. She was a legend among demonic teachers.

This was one teacher you didn't want to irritate. When she blew up, she flung erasers, chalk, or whatever she could get her hands on right at you. I swear she had eyes behind her head. She purposely went to the blackboard with her back to the class. If you so much as whispered to a classmate in the next aisle, she saw it.

When she caught you, she literally ran over to you, made you stand beside your desk, placed her face three inches from yours, and ripped into you like a drill sergeant. You stood there and cringed while she broke you down and humiliated you in front of the class. I couldn't help but notice the saliva flying from her mouth as she berated my classmates. Being chewed out for some minor infraction was much more favored than being told to lay your hand, palm down on your desk. That really hurt when she took the ruler and smacked your exposed hand. That was sure to bring a tear to your eye.

I'll never forget the time Rudolph completely lost it. Eddie Martel was one of the better students in our class. He made the unfortunate mistake of talking back to her once. She went to the corner of the room, grabbed her umbrella, and hastily walked to his desk. Her eyes were bulging out by the time she reached him. Suddenly, she whacked Eddie right across his face with her umbrella. His nose began to bleed. He was sent to the office. The office sent Eddie home. Rudolph had broken his nose.

How could she get away with such behavior? I didn't know the answer to that question. What mattered was that she could. Fortunately, no other teacher was as mean and crazy as Sister Rudolph. I would have thought there would have been some sort of investigation by a parish committee or something like that. Nothing. Such was life at the French Catholic School in Laconia.

Claudie began her high school freshman year at St. Joseph's. Three weeks later she transferred to Laconia High. She enrolled in St. Joseph's because she was a devout Catholic and intended to become a nun. Poooof!! That all changed during that brief period at the new St. Joseph High.

It happened on a cool September morning. Claudie wore a sweater, with a blouse underneath that unforgettable day. As she entered the classroom, her teacher proceeded to embarrass her in front of the entire class. She blatantly accused my sister of exposing herself. Claudie was simply chastised for being better developed than the other girls in class. She was confused and humiliated. She cried. That nun's behavior was totally uncalled for. Consequently, right then and there, she decided she wasn't going to endure any more abuse. The next day, she walked over to Laconia High and enrolled herself in the city public high school.

*   *   *

There I was, ten years old. With my paper route and tips, I was making about $5.00 a week. Of that, I had to pay Mr. Paquette $1.00 toward my bicycle and $1.00 went to my mother for the money she loaned me. That left me with $3.00 to spend on myself. I wasn't about to squander my money or spend it foolishly. I knew I wanted to be in Boy Scouts. I was saving a little each week to buy my Boy Scout shirt and kerchief. I reasoned I could buy my belt and pants later, after I collected my Christmas tips. I also needed a pair of sneakers. The ones I wore had holes on each side. And they smelled foul. I had to wear them for everything. That's all I had.

I was embarrassed to wear them. My mother wasn't working. I didn't think it was Ben's responsibility to provide for me. Neither did he. He never offered to buy me anything. I was Ora's boy; not his.

I saved every penny I could to buy my Scout shirt and a pair of sneakers for school. They were for school. They were for my paper route. They were for playing basketball. They were all I had. So, it came as a surprise to me, when I asked my mother for toothpaste so I could brush my teeth before going to school.

She looked at me matter-of-factly and said, "Now that you're working, you can buy your own toothpaste and soap and the other things you need."

I was stunned. If I didn't know her, I would have thought she was kidding. But, I knew better. She had carefully calculated this moment. This was the critical moment in my life that she plotted to free herself from ever having to provide anything more than food and shelter for me from that day on.

From that day forward, I was responsible for buying everything I needed. From the time I was ten years old, I supported myself. What goes through your mind at that critical moment? Answer: A lot. First, in my mind, I made a mental list of what I needed. Next, my mind shifted to how much money I would need and how I would earn it? As fate would have it, that became my lifetime model for living. I just didn't expect it to be forced upon me so soon. Without any fancy Management course to guide me, I taught myself to set goals and initiate plans to achieve my goals.

That day I made a list of my needs. Such things as clothes, shoes, coats, soap, shampoo, toothpaste, toothbrushes, socks, underwear, hair tonic, school supplies, pencils, bike payment, loan payment, winter boots, mittens, a basketball, sneakers, movie money, and so on. That's how my "Needs" list began. I excluded any notion of a "Wants" list, which would have included such frivolous items as a doughnut from time to time, or candy, chocolate milk, a sweater, a movie, or even Christmas presents. I knew I just couldn't afford such "luxuries." I certainly knew I had to augment my meager $5.00 weekly earnings to fulfill my basic "Needs" list, but, my paper route was all I had at the time. From that day on, I lived with the constant frustration of never having enough money to even purchase my basic needs. However, I managed. Oh, did I ever manage!

Nothing would stop me from joining Boy Scout Troop 62 that fall, even if I couldn't afford to buy myself a lousy Boy Scout kerchief. I needed scouting. It had a profound influence on my life. It filled a void. I wanted a value system. That wasn't available to me at home. It was up to me to develop a value system to live by. I needed to develop character; to live by a creed of honor. I took the ideals spelled out in the Scout Oath, Scout Law, Scout Motto, and Scout Slogan seriously. At times, even too seriously!

Troop 62 was an active troop. Every fall and spring we camped in the woods at the Belknap Recreation Area. I never camped out overnight until I became a Boy Scout. I had so much to learn. Bobby Morin and I shared his tent. Bobby had it all. He had an official Boy Scout tent. He had a knapsack, sleeping bag, hatchet, canteen, scout knife. You name it, Bobby Morin had it. I didn't have anything. I was just fortunate to have him for a camping partner.

When it was time to go on the three day outing in the woods, I had to beg my mother to let me borrow a blanket. I stuffed my blanket in a pillowcase. That was my knapsack. I didn't even know enough to bring eating utensils. I didn't even bring a pot to cook my can of soup. Heck, I didn't even know to bring matches to light a fire. Thank goodness, my friend was there to bail me out. Actually, all the other boys were quite gracious. Nobody made fun of me, at least not to my face. They loaned me an axe and shovel and whatever else I needed. Some boys brought extra food they willingly shared with me. Bobby had camped with his Dad before so he knew a lot already. He was a big help. He taught me not to touch the outside of the tent in the early morning. If I did, the dew would seep right through. He taught me lots of little things like that.

The proof lies in the pudding. My fellow Scouts achieved the goals of scouting by sharing and experiencing the principles they were taught. Although I was often embarrassed, my first camping trip was a positive experience. I wouldn't be such a goon the next time out. I definitely learned what I needed for the Spring Jamboree. As soon as I finished paying my mother the money I owed her, I would start saving to buy a canteen, an axe, and a sleeping bag. Now, I had a new goal.

*　　*　　*

A few days before my brother was born, my mother sent to stay with Grammy and Grampy Garneau. My mother had to go to the hospital early in case there were any complications. My grandmother, Laura Garneau, was a fastidious homemaker. She prided herself on the cleanliness of her home. I didn't know my grandparents very well. Up until now, I had very little contact with them. Oh, she knew about me, but I didn't know anything about her, except that she was involved with the women's auxiliary of the *St. Jean de Baptiste Society*. They wore fancy gold capes and maroon dresses, the colors of Sacred Heart School, when they marched in the Memorial Day parade.

My grandfather, Joe Garneau, was well respected in the French Catholic community. If you owned your own business, you were held in higher esteem than the poor Frenchmen that worked in the factories. He owned a barbershop on Main Street. My mother sent me there for free haircuts. That was all right by me when I was younger. However, Joe was really beginning to slip in his craft. I looked forward to the day when I could make enough money to have Mr. Lyman cut my hair.

My stay with my grandparents was pleasant enough. I had no great expectations. They never took me out to eat or go anywhere that might cost money. They pinched every penny they earned, just like my mother. To my surprise, my grandparents had a nice guest bedroom in their basement. They paneled in a 12' by 12' section and converted it into a spare bedroom. It was so clean; you could eat off the floor. Other than the fact I was a bit scared sleeping in the cellar, I rather enjoyed the privacy of having my own room away from them.

My routine didn't change when I stayed with my grandparents. I went to school in the morning, and delivered my papers in the afternoon. It was dark by the time I arrived at their house. We ate supper and watched a little television. I said goodnight to them around eight o'clock and went to my room. I didn't dare tell them what I wanted to watch on the television. I really wanted to watch the news to find out the latest on the Korean War or the Kefauver hearings. Unfortunately, they weren't interested in world affairs. If it didn't happen in Laconia, then it didn't happen. Like most French people, they thrived on gossip and they didn't classify the Kefauver hearings as gossip. As my grandfather asked me once, "Who in the hell is Kefauver?" He didn't matter.

It was October 31, 1950, —Halloween. I hurried home from school to finish my paper route early to go Trick or Treating. For months I anxiously looked forward to Halloween; the day I gathered my annual supply of candy. It wasn't to be. Grammy Garneau was waiting for me at the door to tell me the news. My mother delivered a 7 pound, 2 ounce bouncing baby boy earlier that day. They named him Bennie Jr., after his father. I didn't quite know how to react to the news. I was just glad my mother was O.K. and that there weren't any complications. Now they had their own complete family: My mother, Ben, and little Bennie Jr. I had a family too: Lorraine, Claudie, and me.

I wanted to visit my mother at the hospital, but wasn't allowed in the maternity ward. I finally saw her again when she came home with the baby in her arms. He was so cute. He was a little blond, blue-eyed baby. He had this cute little pug nose, much like a Chinese Pug dog. My first reaction was to nickname him "Pudgie." It stuck. From that day on, Bennie Novak Jr., would always be known as "Pudg" or "Pudgie."

Ora didn't return to work for a few years after Pudgie was born. She stayed home to take care of her infant son. Ben became the sole provider. Of course, she still had income from the two apartments and the garages she rented. To supplement that, she took on more curtains to clean. She now had more time to devote to that business. That meant Claudie was stuck spending more of her time helping her mother wash and dry curtains. Lorraine wasn't available. By the fall of 1950, she was working at the Laconia Western Union office after school and on weekends. That was quite a prestigious job for a girl still in high school. My big sister was now an official telegraph operator.

Claudie wasn't a complainer. She always was a team player and willingly did whatever my mother asked her to do. However, now that she was in high school, she was hoping to at least be able to go to the high school football games on Friday night. That's all she asked. That wasn't to be. My mother denied her that simple privilege.

From our house, you could hear the noise of the crowd and see the lights at the high school football field on Friday nights. I saw the disappointment on Claudie's face when she heard the roar of the crowd when a touchdown was scored. Instead of being in the stands cheering with her friends, she was in the cellar stretching curtains on wooden curtain racks. Like Lorraine and I, she was biding her time until the day she could move away from home forever.

*   *   *

By Thanksgiving, I no longer rode my bike on my paper route. I put it in the storage shed for the winter. There were two temperatures between November and April . . . cold and colder. It was a brutally cold winter. It became colder and colder as each day passed. It was a constant battle between me and the elements. To survive, I strategically planned the stops on my route. It was beginning to turn dark by the time I reached Bud's market to begin my deliveries. The mercury dropped rapidly as the afternoon sun vanished by mid-afternoon. I stopped in Bud's just long enough to warm my face and hands, then moved on to my next stopover point, Prescott's flower shop. Prescott's was always nice and warm. No time to linger. I had to keep moving.

By the time I reached Edgewater Avenue, I was numb again. The wind was howling across Lake Opechee. I stopped at Mrs. Roubo's house to inquire how her son, Joe, was doing in the Navy. Any excuse I could think of to warm up momentarily. There weren't any other predetermined stops until I reached the end of my route at the veterinarian, Dr. Smith's, house. Looking back, I don't know how I made it. It was so cold; I would lift my paper bag to my face to block it from the howling wind and bitter cold. My feet were frozen and my hands were numb by the time I reached Doc Smith's. I didn't ask. I needed to thaw out. I took it upon myself to enter the mudroom and rest on his storage box until my fingers stopped tingling.

Doc Smith's house was the end of my route. However, I still had to make the two and a half-mile trip back home every day. And, I still had eight papers to deliver to the houses on North Main between the north and south end of Edgewater Avenue. By then, it was totally dark out. Often, it snowed and the roads were immersed in freezing slush. My feet were soaking wet and frozen, as ice clung to the side of my canvas sneakers. This was not the winter wonderland you saw on postcards. For me, this was all about survival.

By December, I swallowed my pride. If I timed it to arrive at Doctor Smith's before five o'clock I could stick out my thumb and hitch a ride from one of the workers leaving the Laconia State School. That helped. I hitched rides to the north end of Edgewater Avenue, got out, and finished my route for the day. My daily delivery routine became more difficult as the winter wore on. I was determined to stick it out. At least until I could collect my Christmas tips.

The Citizen sold us Christmas cards that said, "From Your Paperboy." I bought some and placed them in my papers about ten days before Christmas. Christmas fell on a Monday that year. That was a blessing. That meant I could make my collection on Saturday, December 23, just at the peak of everyone's Christmas spirit. I purposely started my route late that afternoon to catch my customers at home. I didn't finish my route until after seven o'clock. My face was beaming when I counted up all my Christmas bonuses. I suspect that many of my customers figured I wouldn't last until then. Because I did, I was amply rewarded. When I finished adding it all up, I made over $48.00 in tips that day. Was I ever happy.

My mother asked, but I didn't tell her how much I made. I didn't want to have to give her "her share." I learned my lessons well from observing my older sisters. However, I paid her the balance of what I owed her for the loan. I also made a payment of $10.00 to Mr. Paquette the next week. That still left me enough money to buy a nice pair of lined rubber boots to wear on my paper route and a few Christmas presents for my family.

I was inspired by clichés like, *"When the going gets tough, the tough get going."* and *"Winners never quit, Quitters never win."* Hey, that's me! I mentally thought of those clichés as I braved through storm after winter storm. By January, I changed my tactic. After I finished my deliveries on Edgewater Avenue, I wisely doubled back and delivered the papers to the usual final customers on North Main Street. By making that change, when I finished my route at Doctor Smith's, I could hitch a ride all the way to Main Street. Often, people gave me a ride all the way home. It took me a while to realize that some of my customers were coming to my rescue.

Looking back, Doc Smith would tell me, "I need to go to town. Do you want a lift?"

At first, it didn't occur to me that he waited to run his errands, if any, until I made it to his house late in the afternoon.

Likewise, Doctor Brody often doubled back to town in the evening under the pretense that he had to go to the hospital for something. I think my customers really respected me. They were genuinely concerned and looked out after me. They went out of their way to help me out. I became quite attached to them. Despite the misery, I wasn't about to let them down.

*   *   *

I didn't have to deliver papers on Sunday. I looked forward to a leisurely afternoon of skating at the ice rink. After mass, I put on my skates and headed to the rink.

One Sunday morning, as soon as I hit the ice, I heard the chant: "Three Pop Virgin! Three Pop Virgin! Three Pop Virgin!" The repetitive chant was being bellowed loudly across the skating rink by the class bully, Fats Boudreau.

I tried to ignore him by skating in another direction and acting as though I didn't hear his spiteful verbal assault. That only encouraged him, and his band of followers, to pursue me until they cornered me on the edge of the rink near a snow bank.

The chant continued even louder, "Three Pop Virgin! Three Pop Virgin!"

I was confused and didn't know how to respond to that. I didn't get it? Let's see, I had one father, named Charlie Virgin, so what did he mean by the "Three Pop" reference? Did he mean Pop, Pop, like Bang, Bang? My last name was Virgin, but I didn't understand what he was driving at.

At first, I stood there looking stupid trying to muster a half smile, as though I acknowledged his humor. However, under the veil of my façade, I sensed he knew something about me that I didn't even know. He was a bully and languished in the knowledge that I was helpless to defend myself against him. I tried to defend myself before, only to be held in a chokehold, and then thrown to the ground.

As I stood there helplessly, with my skates still on, I waited to find out how the bully was going to punish me this time. When I refused to raise my fist to throw a punch, Fats, who outweighed me by at least fifty pounds, secured my head in a headlock and squeezed hard to inflict his brand of pain. I wouldn't fight, but I also wouldn't cry. After a while, he tossed me face first into the snow bank.

About that time, a grownup came to my rescue. He commanded Fats and his followers to, "Leave him alone and get away from there."

Of course, they told him, "We're just playing."

The man helped me up and asked if I was all right. My pride was hurt. I was still confused by Fatso's chant. All in all, I wasn't bleeding and I was able to walk away. The man offered me a ride home. Fortunately, I lived next to the skating rink. I was done for the day. I returned to the comfort and safety of my home in less than two minutes.

*   *   *

On Saturday mornings, I played basketball for St. Joseph's in the city intramural league. Our team played much better than we did the previous year. I missed several practices because of my paper route, but still made the first team. I was a starting guard. I learned a good deal about the game watching Claudie play. With my Christmas tip money, I bought a basketball. After supper, I went to the cellar and dribbled the ball on the concrete floor for hours on end. I mentally visualized myself playing in a game. I practiced as often as I could. Like Claudie, I was earning a reputation for my ball control and hustle. I excelled at stealing the ball from an opponent and dribbling all the way down the court for a lay up. I realized there was always room for improvement and I thrived to be the best I could be. I loved the game. It was an escape from the realities of my existence. I probably had that Type A thing Lorraine told me about.

As winter passed, so did the customary rituals at Sacred Heart. There was the annual winter carnival at the parish hall. I sold raffle tickets again to raise money for whatever causes the Sacred Heart parish felt they needed to raise money. I didn't understand why they were always conducting one fund raising event after another. To me, they had a gold mine. After all, they passed the collection plate every Sunday at mass. They made money whenever someone lit a candle in church. They also charged people for weddings and funerals. The parish hall was full at Friday night Bingo. And, they sold "*torquay*,"those French meat pies, and religious Christmas gifts at the church Christmas bazaar. In class, they were always after the students to buy something.

To secure my position in Sister Rudolph's good graces, I bought my mother a nice 8" tall ceramic statue of the Virgin Mary and a smaller statue of Saint Jude for Mother's Day. I was quite pleased with my selections. My mother told me that Saint Jude was her favorite saint. She said she prayed to him all the time for "special favors." Sister Rudolph told me Saint Jude was the saint you prayed to for "impossible causes." I interpreted that to mean if you needed a miracle you prayed to Saint Jude. Maybe she prayed to him to have Pudgie?

Maybe she prayed to Saint Jude to have me bring in a lot of money from the raffle tickets she coerced me into peddling again that winter? I wondered why she couldn't conduct her annual Ora Novak fund raising event in the summer when the weather was nicer. This time I had to make some rules with her. Rule #1: This would be the last time I do this. Rule #2: I would not sell her "chances" to any of my paper route customers.

That year, the winning prize was the magnificent pressure cooker she pulled out of her closet. Just what everybody wanted! Need I say how embarrassed I was, knocking on people's doors with a pressure cooker under my arm? Where they would have bought three chances in the past, they were being gracious to even buy one. Mostly, they acted very disappointed they couldn't buy a ticket because they already had a pressure cooker.

I felt a bit awkward when I asked, "Are you sure you don't need another one?"

The usual Saturday afternoon patrons at Paul's Lounge and Freddie's Cafe didn't let me down. They bought the most chances. A few of them asked, "How's your mother doing these days?" or add on to that with, "We ain't seen her around." Then, someone at their table would invariably ask, "Who's that kid?" "You don't know him?" "*That's Ora's boy!*"

I had fun joking with the drinkers. When one of them would say something like, "What to hell am I gonna to do with a damn pressure cooker?"

I always had a quick answer, like, "You can put your beer in it" or "It makes great home brew." Whether it was funny or not, they all laughed.

When I got home, it was already dark outside. I worked longer because I had to spend a few hours delivering my newspapers. I didn't sell many chances. Not that many people were interested in her pressure cooker. When the lady who won it came by the house to pick it up, she was ecstatic.

She told us, "I have never won anything in my life."

You would have thought she won a brand new car. In fact, my mother handed her the cooker as though she were handing her keys to a new car!

That Mother's Day, my mother and Ben were sitting in their rocking chairs on the front porch when I approached her. I held her surprise Mother's Day gift behind my back. First, I gave her a Mother's Day card. It seemed like it took her forever to read it. I couldn't wait to give her the nice statues I bought her.

After she removed them from the special wrapping, she stared at them for a moment. It was as if she was trying to figure out what they cost. Then she looked at me with a sort of disappointed look. I didn't know what to think. I waited patiently for over a month to give her these special gifts. She put them down beside her rocking chair without saying a word. I was crushed. My feelings were hurt. I excused myself. I just wanted to get away from them and go in the house and cry. I would never forget that Mother's Day.

While my friends were watching shows, such as, "Howdy Doody," "The Mickey Mouse Club," and "Queen for a Day," I was far more interested in watching the latest update in what was commonly referred to as, "the Kefauver Hearings." From May 1950 until April 1951, the Kefauver Committee held hearings in fourteen major cities. The purpose of the committee was to investigate crime in interstate commerce. Many of the committee hearings were televised nationally. To many Americans, this was their first glimpse of organized crime in the U.S.

It made for great television when mobster's like, "Joe Batters" Accardo, Louis "Little New York" Campagna, Mickey Cohen, Frank Costello, Meyer Lansky, and Paul "The Waiter" Ricca, appeared before the committee. Many of the hearings were aimed at proving that an Italian-Sicilian organization controlled a vast crime conspiracy in the United States. Despite calling more than 600 witnesses, the Kefauver Committee never came close to justifying their claim. However, one notable outcome was that the Director of the FBI, J. Edgar Hoover, admitted that a national crime syndicate existed and the FBI had done little about it.

What the committee didn't do, that I expected them to do, was catch the crooks that pulled off the famous Boston Brinks robbery. Nevertheless, I was fascinated by the hearings and watched them as often as I could.

When the Spring Boy Scout Jamboree came around, I couldn't attend. My backup for my newspaper route was also in Boy Scouts. That left me without anybody to cover my route. I handled it like a grownup. I had a business. That came first. There would be other Jamborees, and other boys to train as a backup.

I was still determined to go camping. Bobby Morin and I were working on earning our Camping merit badge. One of the requirements was to camp out overnight in a self-made lean to. We set out on our camping outing one Saturday afternoon after I finished my paper route. We hiked seven miles to our destination out near the airport. Back then, there was nothing but sand bunkers and brush along the side of the runway.

The rain was pouring down when we arrived. We were soaking wet, but determined. First, we cut some brush and built a fire to keep us warm. Next, we dug a small cave in the side of a sand bunker. We then stripped branches and laid them across each other to build a cover over our cave. We tied the branches together with ropes. Then, we placed whatever else we could gather on top of the branches. Voila! We had a comfortable hut for the night. We changed out of our wet clothes and proceeded to cook beans and hot dogs. Finally, the rain stopped. Bobby and I talked until we fell asleep to the sound of crickets and frogs in the nearby pond. The next afternoon, we cleaned up our campsite and hiked back to town. It was a wonderful experience and to top it off, we earned our Camping merit badge.

CHAPTER 11

DO A GOOD TURN DAILY

The Saturday after Bobby Morin and I returned home from our camping trip, my mother, Ben, and Pudgie went shopping. They were gone all day. Late that afternoon, they pulled into the driveway in a brand new 1951 Buick Special. Ben got his new Buick after all. It was a beauty, and even had the new Dyno-Flo automatic transmission. I don't know who paid for it, but I suspect my mother did. She was a different person with Ben than she was with Harold.

She never demonstrated any affection toward Harold. She never showed him any respect. They fought all the time. Conversely, she apparently loved Ben. With her new baby and new husband, she acted as if it was her first marriage. It was as though she was trying to erase her past and start a new life. She certainly was less critical of him. Even though she wasn't working and Ben brought in less money than Harold, I never heard her complain about a lack of money. They must have been doing well. After all, they just bought a new Buick.

Ora openly showed her affection toward Ben. He seemed to dote on it, like some sort of prized bull. From my perspective, I saw Ben as a narcissist. He saw himself as God's gift to women. I couldn't understand how he could be so vain. I thought he was very superficial. When he showed affection toward Ora, it was only to draw attention toward him. My mother didn't see it. Then again, maybe she did. Regardless, she was determined to make this marriage work — even if she had to spend all her money on him to do it.

Pudg didn't lack for my mother's love. She loved that boy. Possibly to the point where Ben was jealous of his own son. Ben was as indifferent to Pudg as he was to me. He rarely held him. He never checked on him when he came home from work. He didn't show any fatherly affection. I suspected that was a reflection of his childhood relationship with his father. Aren't we all a product of our environment?

After observing Ben for some eighteen months, he definitely had established a discernible pattern. He preferred being alone in the cellar rather than socialize with my mother or anyone else. After he cleaned up, he always seemed to have a project to work on in the workshop he built on the tenant's side of the cellar. He was constantly bringing home tools and hardware to build something. He subscribed to Popular Mechanics. He even had a collection of Popular Mechanics near his workbench. After supper, he went to his workshop, turned on his radio, smoked cigarette after cigarette, until it was time to go to bed. That was pretty much his routine.

He never finished anything. I have no idea what he worked on down there. Neither did anyone else. He simply preferred to be alone in his hideaway, immersed in completing nothing.

Occasionally, he joined my mother in the parlor to watch television. We always had to watch what Ben wanted to watch.

My mother would say, "He works so hard and needs to relax watching his shows."

I didn't watch much television with Ben and my Mom. It wasn't that I didn't care to watch his shows. What really got me was this: He would sit in his favorite green naugahide recliner, devour an entire box of chocolate covered Pom-Poms, and never offer anyone else even one stinking Pom-Pom. He had the manners of an ape. Ben only took care of Ben. I never saw him pick up his young son and sit him in his lap. Pudg was definitely becoming a Mama's boy.

Another school year ended, Friday, June 15th. I was anxiously awaiting the arrival of Freddy Walsh. He called my mother earlier in June to reserve a room. When he arrived, late that afternoon, he greeted me with a big hug and as soon as he unpacked, we were off to Carl's motorcycle shop in Lakeport. Once we got there, he had a surprise waiting for me. Fred had enrolled me as an official member in the American Motorcycle Association (AMA). Then he gave me my membership card and a nice AMA pin to wear on my fluorescent motorcycle hat. Freddy Marsh certainly was nice to me, yet, instinctively something about him made me suspicious.

The next day, I couldn't go to the races with Freddy. I had to deliver my newspapers and, besides, it was collection day. He understood.

He told me he had another surprise for me. "What is it? What is it?" I begged to find out.

He told me he was not only taking me to the big race on Sunday; he was actually racing in it. That was a big surprise all right. You see, Freddy was at least 40 years old. Nearly all the racers were in their early 20s. Besides, BSAs and Harley-Davidsons had dominated the races for the past 10 years. Indians had fallen out of favor in the motorcycle racing world. I couldn't reconcile why he was taking such a big risk. Was it for me? Or, was it for himself? I didn't know him well enough to answer that question.

We left the house early the next morning. Fred wore his leather racing pants and boots and his pullover shirt with the "Indian" logo imprinted on it. When we arrived at the Belknap Recreation Area, his two mechanics were waiting for him. They unloaded his race bike from the trailer, located their pit assignment, and began fine-tuning the deep red racing machine. I wasn't allowed in the pits, so I stood behind the picket fence and watched the race.

His practice runs didn't go well. I heard him tell his mechanics, "I'm having carburetor problems. Try turning it two clicks to the right."

They kept tweaking the engine, but they couldn't get the speed the Harley's were getting. Maybe it was the rider?

I overheard bikers making comments like, "Hang it up, Freddy" and "You don't have a chance." He ignored their remarks.

Because of his qualifying times, Fred Walsh began the race near the rear of the pack. He was losing ground on every lap. By the thirtieth lap, the leader lapped him. It was soon over for Freddy Marsh. He pulled into the pits with a discouraged look and took his helmet and leather-racing jacket off. I accurately surmised before the race that he didn't have a chance. It was time to retire from racing. That day he did.

I could tell he was sad. There was nothing I could say or do. He watched the rest of the race in the pits. I watched from behind the fence. Early the next morning, Freddy and his two mechanics left Laconia and headed back to Hartford.

*   *   *

That summer marked the second year on my paper route. I actually enjoyed my paper route in the summer. There was no rush to complete my deliveries. I could ride my bike most of the way. By then, I knew my customers well enough to stop and chat with them when they were outside. The Chow dog stayed away from me. He must have known I still carried my water pistol with ammonia in it. I became friends with Doctor Brody's sons. Often, I stopped and played with them after I finished my deliveries. They dispelled much of what the nuns told us about Jews. They didn't act like snotty, rich kids. They treated me like an equal and didn't look down at me because I worked. If anything, I think they respected me.

One day, early that summer, the Citizen asked me to come by the office. The woman behind the desk asked, "Would you be interested in delivering newspapers to the Laconia State School?"

She indicated I could probably pick up three or four more customers. It didn't take me two seconds to decline her request. For one thing, it would add nearly another quarter of a mile to my route. There was no way I was going to add any more distance to this route. It took every ounce of energy and determination I could muster just to make it to Doc Smith's house in the winter. Besides, they couldn't pay me enough to deliver papers to that place.

The people in Laconia likened the State School to a house of horrors. It was supposedly where society cast off the "feebleminded." I was told that's where they placed all the "wreckage of humanity: the diseased, the insane, the imbecile, the epileptic and the criminal." It was said that during the Great Depression, families sought to place their children there when they couldn't provide for them.

Photographs taken in the early 1950s showed the deplorable living conditions those poor downtrodden people had to live in. The "residents" lived in large, drafty rooms, walled in brick and tile, with drains on the floor. They didn't have any privacy. There were no stalls in the bathrooms or seats on the toilets. One building that housed 80 residents had one toilet and one shower. The stench of urine and feces was overwhelming. The Portsmouth Herald likened conditions at the Laconia State School to the concentration camps in Nazi Germany. That was not an exaggeration. At one time, it housed over 1,000 of these poor deformed or deranged social rejects.

Often, on cold, still winter nights, I heard screams of terror coming from the confines of the State School as I hitchhiked on the road by Doc Smith's house. It was frightening. There was no way I would go near that place, let alone deliver the newspaper.

Always quick with an answer, I suggested, "Maybe they should pick up the Citizen at Bud's market. That way, they would have it sooner than I could deliver it."

I loved animals. Doc Smith always kept five or six horses in the stalls below his barn. He raced the horses at County fairs and Sulky racetracks all over New England. The big horses fascinated me, and I often stopped by the stables after I finished my route. When they were training on the track behind the barn, I watched them run.

Doc Smith employed a retarded man to clean the stables and take care of the horses. He probably came from the State School and Doc Smith took him in. Somehow, I didn't feel comfortable around him. Call it intuition. He always approached me when I went to the stables. He gave me the creeps.

One day, I was behind the barn watching one of the horses they were training for a race. The stable hand came up behind me. I didn't hear him. Before I knew it, he had his left arm over my shoulder and reached down to touch my crotch with his right hand. I pulled away. For a split second, I looked at his face. He had this strange unfamiliar look. Oddly enough, I wasn't scared of him even though he must have weighed over 250 pounds. I even thought of punching him or kicking him in the groin. For a split second I thought of how best to handle this.

Instead, I told him, "Don't you ever come near me again or I'll tell Doc Smith." He got the message loud and clear.

I didn't tell Doc Smith what happened that day. I never told anyone. As badly as he acted, he didn't harm me and I didn't want him to have to go back to the State School. I wouldn't wish that on anyone. I let him off the hook. He never bothered me again. However, from that day on, I made sure there were other people around whenever I went down to the stables.

My biggest complaint about being a paperboy was having to chase deadbeat customers to collect my money. The majority paid me on time. But, there were always a few I had to chase down. Funny, it was always the same customers. Eventually, I collected from them. Sometimes, I surprised them and showed up at their doorstep late in the evening.

There was one customer who stiffed me big time. He was the head pro at the Laconia Country Club. He lived in a modest Cape Cod style house on Edgewater Avenue. I could understand that he spent long hours at the Country Club in the summer. However, I didn't understand why he couldn't leave the money he owed me somewhere. I should have stopped delivering the paper after he fell five weeks behind. I guess I was enamored by the fact he was a professional athlete. In fact, I know I was.

I went by his house at seven, and even as late as eight o'clock at night. He still was not at home. Yet, sometime in the night, he must have come home because the paper was gone the next day when I returned. One time, I caught his wife at home. She was rather haughty and indignant to me. How dare a lowly paperboy question their integrity. She let me know she left such matters to her husband. I didn't believe her. I let her know I really needed my money. She assured me I would be paid the next week. This dance went on for twelve weeks. I finally stopped delivering the paper to them. The big shot pro won the city golf championship that summer. He never did pay me. I was screwed by another adult again. Incidents like that made me distrust them even more.

One of my customers was a single woman that lived near the top of the hill on North Main Street. I reckoned she was in her early 50s. I rarely saw her. She usually left my money in a cup between her two front doors. If she forgot to leave the money, she would answer the door and pay me. This one Saturday, she must have forgotten to leave the money.

I knocked on the door. When she opened it, I was stunned. Maybe, more than stunned. It was late in the afternoon. There she stood, in all her glory, in a see-through negligee with nothing on underneath. Now that was a surprise!

In the sexiest voice she could muster, she said, "Come on in. I'll be right with you." She slowly sauntered back toward the kitchen, with an exaggerated hip movement to draw attention to her derriere.

I found her show to be curiously entertaining, as long as nothing was expected of me. While I waited for her to return with my money, I began to sweat. I had never encountered anything like that before. Frankly, I didn't know what to do, except I knew I wanted to get out of there.

She finally returned from the kitchen with my money in her hand. This time, she appeared with the front of her negligee completely open, exposing her old floppy breasts and genital area for my eyes to gaze upon.

I thought to myself, "Oh my God, is this where Saint Jude comes to my rescue?" If I ever needed a "special favor" it was now! I had no idea what this woman's next move would be, but I knew mine was to get out of her house as quickly as possible.

She looked at me with a wry smile and said, "I think you're blushing?"

I was so flustered, I think I replied, "Maybe I am, but I got to get going. Got a lot of customers to collect from." Hell, I don't know what I said, but I am sure it had something to do with getting out of there fast, before I passed out. Whew!

She realized that this little paper boy wasn't ready for a sexual encounter and let me leave. I was sweating bullets when I stepped out into the fresh air. As I pedaled my bike away from her house, I wondered, "Did she realize how much trouble she could be in for exposing herself to a minor? How desperate could she be?" In some odd way, I was actually concerned about her feelings. I hoped I hadn't offended her by my rejection. Anyway, that was another incident I never told anyone. I didn't want to see her go to jail. No harm done. I just felt sorry she had to stoop to hustling an eleven-year-old paperboy. An altar boy at that.

Fortunately, these instances were rare. Most of my customers were pillars in the community. Why, I had the school superintendent, the high school principal, and at least a half dozen schoolteachers on my route. I also delivered to doctors, lawyers, and business owners. They were educated people. If I had my way, that's where I wanted to live. These people had style. They had grace. They were refined. I learned a great deal just by observing them.

For instance, Mrs. White lived with her husband on the corner of Edgewater Avenue, directly across the street from Lake Opechee.

Never did I see that woman when she wasn't well dressed, with her hair perfectly coiffured. She was extremely tidy. Her house looked like something out of Better Homes & Gardens. Moreover, she always spoke softly and kindly. Typically, she wore a nice gray wool skirt with a dark cashmere sweater. Alternatively, she might wear that skirt with a beautiful white silk blouse. I noticed things like that. Appearances were important to me. After all, people often judge others by the way they look. The woman exuded class.

On the other side of the spectrum was the nice old hermit who shared his blackberries with me. I thought as much of him as I did Mrs. White. One day, I figured it out. It wasn't how well you looked that counted. It was how well you treated people that really mattered. Now I understood why they called it the Golden Rule: *"Do unto others, as you would have others do unto you."* Not a bad rule to live by.

*　　*　　*

I went alone to the Fourth of July celebration at Opechee Park. The grandstand was packed. There must have been over 2,000 people there to watch the fireworks. The city went all out to put on an excellent fireworks display every year. My guess was that half of the people there were visiting the area on vacation. Cars were parked on both sides of North Main Street for at least a half a mile. The fireworks were awesome. On my way home after the fireworks, I wondered if anyone might have lost a wallet or some other valuable item around the grandstand while watching the fireworks. Perhaps there would even be a reward if I found something? Bright and early the next morning, I went back to Opechee Park to look for lost items.

I scoured under the bleachers for a lost wallet or watch or anything of value. I didn't find anything there. However, as I walked near the tennis courts, I found a checkbook that belonged to the owner of a local insurance company. It was easy to identify the owner. His name, address, and phone number was inscribed on his checks. I was sure he was frantically looking around his house for his checkbook. I was pleased my search was not in vain. Now I could return it and fulfill the Boy Scout Slogan, *"Do a Good Turn Daily."*

I handed the checkbook over to my mother. She notified the insurance agent that we had his lost checkbook. When he arrived at our house, my mother met him at the door and handed it to him. I was a bit disappointed. No reward. I didn't even get a "thank you." I don't know if she told him I actually found it. She probably took the credit. We were never thanked for doing anything at our house. It was always just expected of us. A nice "thank you" would have certainly made me feel better.

*   *   *

That July, I was working toward earning a merit badge for Bicycling. One of the requirements was to make a long trip on a bicycle. The Boy Scout manual never mentioned it, but I assumed they thought anyone going on a long trek would carry a canteen of water and a backpack with sandwiches and snacks. Forget what a good Scout might do. To me, that was just extra weight to carry. I never carried snacks and water on my paper route and that was five miles. The ride on my bike to Grammy Bourgeois would be a twenty-eight mile round trip, from Laconia to Franklin and back. I was certain she'd prepare a sandwich for me at her house.

I hadn't seen Frank and Lena Bourgeois since the wedding. That was nearly two years ago. I was sure they'd be glad to see me again. I certainly was looking forward to seeing them. That was my motivation for this trip. Not only would I earn a merit badge, I would also be visiting my grandparents . . . . well, they were kind of like grandparents.

I chose to ride Lorraine's old English bike for my journey. I don't think I would have made it pedaling up and down all the hills with the "clunker." My sister's bike was vintage World War II, and then some. However, it was easy to pedal and didn't have a cross bar to climb over. I should have bought it from her instead of buying the fancy Schwinn bike that Ben favored.

When you're eleven, you don't think about the dangers of riding a bicycle on one of the busiest and narrowest stretches of highway in the entire state. For most of the ride on U.S. Route 3, there wasn't a shoulder on the side of the highway. I pedaled my bike right down the driving lane with all the cars whizzing by. This was summer. Most of the tourists drove on this highway to get to the Lakes Region. Was I crazy? No, just young. Well, maybe a little crazy.

With all the hills I had to navigate, it took me four hours to make it to Franklin. I pushed my bike up some of the steeper hills. That also allowed the large line of frustrated drivers to go around me. Gee, I didn't realize I was bringing forty or fifty cars to a crawl. Those Massachusetts people weren't too friendly.

Finally, I pushed my bike all the way up Chestnut Street to Frank and Lena Bourgeois place. Were they ever surprised to see me! Perhaps "stunned" would be more accurate. Grammy Bourgeois could have laid an egg, just like one of her hens, when she saw me pushing my bike up her driveway.

"Ach you grow up my Sonny. How you get here?" she asked.

I told her, "Grammy, I just came to see you and Frank. I'm a Boy Scout now. I'm working on a merit badge." I don't think she heard a thing. She was so excited. Frank sat back in his rocking chair in the tiny enclosed porch, sucking on his empty pipe. He just nodded and kind of gave me a half smile. Nothing rattled old Frank.

She fixed me a ham and cheese sandwich with fresh tomatoes from her garden. I gobbled it down. She fixed me another one. I gobbled it down. I didn't realize I was so hungry. After I finished my second glass of lemonade, Grammy Bourgeois was rushing me to return home. I don't know if she didn't want to be blamed for my trip or was afraid I'd get killed on my way back. I could tell she was more than a bit concerned.

"Well, Grammy, I need to head down the road. I got a long way to go." I am sure she was worried for me, but was also relieved that I was leaving. I smiled and waved goodbye. This was the last time I ever saw them.

There was more traffic returning to Laconia then there was going to Franklin. By now, I learned I had to pull over more often to let all the cars go by. I made my way through Tilton, then over the Winnisquam Bridge, past the St.Francis home, and down the hill heading into Laconia. When I arrived home, it was after six o'clock.

My mother scolded me because I wasn't home at five o'clock for supper. I told her what I had accomplished. That didn't interest her one bit. She couldn't care less. Her only concern was that I wasn't home at the appointed hour. There would be no "nice going" for this kid. She was always so indifferent to what I did. She didn't even ask how Frank and Grammy Bourgeois were doing. Sometimes she could be so callous.

Years later, I asked Lorraine if she knew what happened to Frank and Lena Bourgeois? She said, "Oh, you didn't know?"

"No, I didn't. That's why I asked."

She told me Frank died shortly after my visit. Grammy Bourgeois remarried and moved away. One day, my mother called Lorraine and asked her, "Have you heard the news today? It's all over the papers."

Lena Bourgeois' next husband beat her to death with a hammer. Then, he finished the job by bludgeoning her with an axe. The most heinous, brutal way a person could die. What a tragic ending. When I heard that, I sat silently in total disbelief. What a way to die. And to think, she made the best flapjacks in the world.

* * *

One day in early August, the mailman left his mailbag and a pile of mail, strapped to a belt, on our front porch. I noticed the mail on our porch around 11:30 that morning. By one o'clock, the mail was still on our front porch. I became concerned. Did he get sick? By one-thirty that afternoon, the mail was still there. I reasoned, "It's about time I help the poor mailman out." I had to leave by three o'clock to pick up my papers at the Citizen. I could help him until then.

Before I began, I noticed the mail was neatly sorted by addresses. I hoisted his leather mailbag over my shoulder and proceeded to deliver the mail for him. I crisscrossed up and down Winter Street, then down Summer Street, dropping off mail at the designated addresses. I was sure I would get a nice "thank you" for helping him.

Along the way, people greeted me at the door. Many of them thanked me for bringing their mail. Others asked, "Where's the mailman today?"

I answered, "I don't know. I'm just helping him out."

What a breeze. In slightly over an hour, I delivered all the mail in the neighborhood. When I was done, I left to begin my paper route. I felt good about that. I was able to, *"Do a Good Turn Daily."* I was sure the mailman would appreciate it.

I arrived home from my paper route, shortly after 5:00 p.m. My mother was frantic. Questions were flying at me before I could even get off my bike.

"What did you do? Did you deliver the mail on Winter Street? Do you know the neighbors have been calling me all day? Did you know the cops were here? You've got some explaining to do."

When I told my mother what I had done, she actually had a grin on her face. I told her I thought the poor mailman might have become ill so I delivered his mail for him.

She told me I missed the highlight of the day. She relayed to Ben and me, the look on the mailman's face when he came to pick up his mail and it was gone. He rang the doorbell. When my mother answered the door, he asked if she had seen anyone take the mail. She didn't know anything. And she really didn't. His leather pouch and strap were on the porch but the mail was gone.

From there, he frantically knocked on neighborhood doors to try to reconstruct what happened. Eventually, someone let him know that *"Ora's boy"* said he was helping the mailman out and he delivered their mail. "Such a nice kid." He returned to our house and began questioning my mother again.

Again, she told him, "I don't know anything about my son delivering your mail." He knew he was in hot water.

Within an hour, two men in dark suits were knocking at our front door. They showed my mother and Ben their badges and identification. They asked to speak to me.

We all went into the living room and the two men asked me to recount the events of that afternoon. I noticed one of them couldn't hold back a grin as I told him how I just was trying to help the mailman. They proceeded to tell me I had committed a Federal offense, punishable by a big fine and possible time in prison.

"What, for helping the mailman?" I asked.

For some reason, they didn't scare me. I pretended I was worried to make them feel better. Down deep, I knew I wasn't going to jail.

Before they left, they softened up a bit and just told me to, "Never help the mailman again."

I assured them I wouldn't. I also told them, "He should tell people when he's going to be gone for a couple of hours." Later, I overheard that he may have been visiting a lady in the neighborhood. That was a matter for the U.S. Post Office.

CHAPTER 12

LAKEPORT

It was early August, a month before school began. Lorraine and the varsity cheerleaders were in our backyard practicing cheers for the upcoming football season. Lorraine would be a senior this year. This was her final year at LHS. Claudie was out there taking it all in. She was going into her sophomore year. She didn't try out for the junior varsity cheerleading squad last spring, but thought perhaps she just might try out for the varsity squad next spring. That's when they selected the cheerleaders.

"*Rah, rah, for old Laconia, banners wave on high. We are marching onward, on to do or die, rah, rah, rah . . .*" I heard the cheerleaders sing the high school fight song so many times, I knew it by heart. And, I was only going into the seventh grade at St. Joseph's in the fall of 1951.

It was quite an honor to be selected for the high school varsity cheerleading squad. Many girls tried out, very few were selected. Generally, the varsity cheerleaders came up the ranks from the junior varsity squad. It was unusual to be selected your senior year. I was surprised my big sister even tried out. Somehow, she managed to work in all the practices and games around her busy work schedule at the Western Union. And, she still had her heart set on attending college after she graduated.

Claudie had a job packing blueberries at Harrington Farms that summer. It's no small wonder the boys who worked there couldn't wait to go down to the barn and flirt with her. Everybody liked Claudie. Not only was she attractive, she also had a great personality. Claudie had a lot of friends. She didn't try to be popular, she just was.

My seventh grade teacher's name was Sister Albert. If I were to describe Sister Albert in one word, it would be "nice." Any teacher after Sister Rudolph would be "nice." Like most of the teachers, she was firm, but fair. She set the boundaries and told us her limits from the first day of school.

I was a good student. I enjoyed school and thrived to make good grades. Although, I certainly could have studied more. There was always room for improvement. However, to my way of thinking, if I made good grades without studying, then why study? Besides, there wasn't any emphasis on academics at our house. Our mother only went to school through the eighth grade. She didn't understand the value of an education. To her, a paycheck was more important than a good education. Fortunately, we didn't share that belief.

My Boston Red Sox folded again. They finished third in the American League that year. I was beginning to accept disappointment gracefully. Like all Sox fans, I thought things would be different now that we got rid of Joe McCarthy. The new manager, Steve O'Neill, wasn't any better. Just another damn Boston Irishman. They were out of the race by mid-August. I was beginning to take losing in stride. No point being upset. I had to get use to the fact they weren't as good as the Yankees. Those damn Yankees won the American League pennant for the third year in a row.

Their opponent in the 51' World Series was the New York Giants. What an unbelievable year they had. The Giants were 11 games behind the Brooklyn Dodgers at the beginning of September. They came back from being down 11 games to tie the Dodgers on the last day of the season. They beat them in a three game playoff to win the National League championship. In the final game, Bobby Thompson hit a home run to win the game. It became known as, "the shot heard round' the world." I think every TV set in the country was on for that game. Anybody who watched it will never forget it. It was one of those great moments in baseball history.

I was so pumped up after watching the final Dodgers vs. Giants game; I just had to watch the first game of the World Series. I knew the Giants were going to kill those Yankees. The problem I had was that the game was being played on a school day. I solved the problem by writing a note to Sister Albert, signed by Ora Novak, telling her that Lucien had to stay home sick that day. That might have worked had I watched the game at home. There was a problem with that. My mother was at home.

I heard the game was being shown on a large screen TV at Tardiff Park. Sometimes, I just didn't think. I went to Tardiff Park to watch the game. When I got there, all the seats were taken. There must have been 50 or 60 men there. Well, I just plopped down on the floor in front of everyone and watched the game. The damn Yankees won it 5 to 1.

You just can't trust those Frenchmen. Wouldn't you know it. One of them just felt he had to do his duty and let the school know I skipped school and watched the game at the Tardiff Park clubhouse. The next day, before school even began, I was summoned to the principal's office. Sister Superior and Sister Albert were waiting for me. I figured out what happened before they even opened their mouths. I wisely chose not to give them the fabricated note with my mother's forged signature. There was no point in lying. I was caught dead on. They called my mother at our house, right in front of me. She told Sister Superior she'd deal with me when I got home from school. Also, I had to stay after school for over an hour that day to write, "I will never skip school again" 500 times on a pad of yellow lined paper.

When I got home, my mother laced into me. "The next time you skip school, I'll tell Ben. Do you hear me?"

"Yes, Mom. I'm sorry. It won't happen again," I replied.

"You better get going on your paper route. It's getting dark outside," she snarled back.

It was already dark when I left the house to go to the Citizen office to pick up my papers. I genuinely felt repentant. I don't know if I felt sorrier for skipping school or for being so stupid for going to Tardiff Park to watch the game.

The week after the World Series, Troop 62 was off to the Belknap Recreation Area for the Fall Boy Scout Jamboree. When we arrived, Bobby and I put up his tent in a torrential downpour. While some of the Boy Scouts were building a large fire in the middle of our campsite, I was busily digging a trench around our tent for the rain to flow through when our Scoutmaster came by to check on us. We had everything under control. After he left, we changed out of our wet clothes and stuffed our faces with potato chips and cookies. It

The present from Freddy was an Indian motorcycle sweatshirt. I liked it because it had the word "Indian" printed across the front. Unfortunately, it was too small. It fit too tightly and the sleeves weren't long enough. It would be O.K. to wear around the house. Mom and Ben gave me a couple of shirts for school and a warm pair of mittens. Those mittens would come in handy on those cold winter days on my paper route.

The paper route was a real grind. I was weary from it and knew I didn't want to do it another winter. I planned to sell it in the summer when the weather was nicer. Maybe the boy I hired to substitute for me would buy it? I made sure he only filled in for me when the weather was nice. As much as I liked my customers, when I did the math it just wasn't worth it. It took me roughly 2 1/2 hours a day, 6 days a week to deliver my papers. That's 15 hours a week. I earned an average of $5.00 a week. The bottom line was that I was freezing my ass off out there for thirty-three cents an hour! I should be able to make $5.00 a week doing something else.

My real dilemma was that I needed to work. I needed to support myself. I was always thinking of how I could make money if I sold my paper route. I always came up blank. There was just no demand for a five-foot tall, twelve year old kid. I had the heart and the spunk. I was willing to do anything. There just were no jobs available.

To make matters worse, one night I was at the skating rink playing "snap the whip" with Claudie and her friends. Since I was the smallest, they put me at the end of the line. The end of the whip. That meant I would be traveling the fastest when they snapped the whip around. The person holding my hand suddenly let go. I went flying across the ice, hit a bump, and fell down face first. Thump. At first, I thought I was knocked out. When I put my hand to my face, blood came out of my mouth. Everyone stooped over me as I sat there on the ice. My mouth hurt. Claudie told me to open it so she could check me out. When I did, she noticed my upper front tooth was gone. I knocked it out on the ice. Worse yet, it wasn't completely gone. It was split off right at the gum line. The roots and a small sliver of tooth were still intact in my mouth. To a casual observer, I was missing my front tooth. There was no way of hiding the gap when I opened my mouth.

Barely five foot tall, big ears, and now a missing front tooth. Naturally, I was self-conscious. Very self-conscious. I didn't smile very often as it was. Now I had to smile with my mouth closed. I certainly didn't have money to have a dentist take the rest of the tooth out and make a bridge or something. I figured that would cost hundreds of dollars. I didn't like it, but was helpless to do anything about it. I had to accept the fact I would have a missing front tooth for years, until I earned enough money to have it replaced. Meanwhile, it was impossible to brush the small piece that remained near my gum line. I thought that perhaps eventually it would rot and the rest of the tooth would fall out.

I must have been a sight to see on the basketball court. As it was, I was the smallest player on our team. There goes the toothless midget, dribbling the ball down the court on his way to another basket! I didn't think about it when I played basketball. Wasn't it the great Vince Lombardi who said, "*Winning isn't everything, it's the only thing?*" His quotes were part of his legend. Actually, that was taken out of context. What Lombardi really said was, "*Winning is not everything, but making the effort to win is.*" Either way, I was in another world when I was on the court. Winning was everything to me.

*   *   *

That winter, there were posters in the front windows of the stores on Main Street, with a picture of the all-Negro basketball team that was coming to town. They were playing an exhibition game against a team called the New Hampshire All Stars. The game was to be played on a Saturday night at the Laconia High gym. This was quite a novelty. I knew Negroes were great basketball players from watching the Harlem Globetrotters on TV. However, there was only one Negro family in the entire Lakes Region. All I knew was that Negroes lived in the South somewhere and didn't like cold weather. They weren't Abe Saperstein's famous Harlem Globetrotters, but, hey, there was no way I would miss that game. Why, I was even prepared to ask them if I could be their ball boy.

The morning of the big game, I was sitting in the bleachers at the high school waiting for our turn to play. Suddenly, to my surprise, five or six of the Negro basketball players came into the gym. As I reflect on it, we weren't prejudiced in Laconia. If anything, we welcomed Negroes to our town. We were clueless about the way white people treated them in the South. I am sure they were concerned and curious as to how they would be received up there in the boondocks of New Hampshire.

I immediately went to where they were sitting and started a conversation. I thought they were very nice. They were just hanging out, waiting for their game that night. I let them know I was playing in the next game. They told me they would stick around and watch my game. I was thrilled. Mr. Toothless just had to play his best game. I did play well that day. Of course, I didn't pass the ball very often. I wanted to be the high scorer. I wanted their approval.

I don't know what possessed me. After my game, I asked them if they'd like to come to my house. Who knows? Maybe they had never been in a white kid's house? I didn't even give it a second thought. I just wanted them to feel welcomed. I wasn't surprised when they accepted my offer. I thought nothing of it. Off we went; me and five black giants, walking down Dewey Street, through the French schoolyard, across the ice rink, to my front door. Then it hit me. What would I tell my mother, walking in the house with a Negro basketball team?!

Sometimes, my mother surprised the heck out of me. This was one of those times. When I walked into the kitchen with my new found friends, my mother graciously greeted them with a smile. She was amazing. I was so proud of her. She asked all the right questions. She even joked with them. It was one of the happiest moments of my life. She offered to make them a sandwich, but they declined her offer. She asked them if they had seen our Main Street. She told them of the stores and restaurants on Main Street. Whew, I was glad she didn't mention the Rod and Gun Club or Mom's Tavern in her tour of attractions.

Before they left, they gave us four tickets to the big game. My mother didn't accept them. That's alright, I did! After they left, I said, "Mom, you were great. Thanks." I went over and gave her a hug. She didn't say anything. We both looked at each other and smiled.

*   *   *

At the end of January, Father Chicoine came to one of our Boy Scout meetings. He was there to tell us about the Ad Altare Dei medal. Until then, I didn't know what it was. I found out that Ad Altare Dei meant, "To the Altar of God." It's the highest Catholic honor you can receive in scouting. To receive it, you have to at least be a First Class Scout and served with "loyalty and fidelity" as an altar boy during your tenure in Scouts. He informed us that we also had to pass an interview with him to be recommended for the medal.

I was up to the challenge. Father 'Chic" told us to be prepared to answer numerous questions about the Catholic faith during our interview. He told me to call the rectory to make an appointment for my interview when I felt I was ready. As the big day approached, I became very concerned I might not pass Father Chicoine's test. So concerned, in fact, I skipped school the day before my interview to prepare for any questions I might be asked. I stayed in the bathroom and poured over my Catechism books for eight straight hours. I never studied that hard for anything before. This time I had my mother's permission to stay home. She knew this medal meant a lot to me.

The next day, Father Chicoine's secretary guided me down the hall of the rectory and instructed me to wait outside his office. When I entered his office, he stood up near his desk and shook my hand. I always felt comfortable around Father "Chic." He was in line to replace old Father Robichaux as the parish Monsignor. We rarely saw Father Robichaux. It was always Father "Chic" who attended our sporting events and popped in from time to time at our Scout meetings. He was much younger and more active in the day-to-day activities of the parish.

I served mass with him many times and he knew me on a first name basis. He actually called me "Sonny," just like my family and friends.

His first question was, "Did you prepare well for this interview?"

"Yes Father, I feel I am ready," I replied.

"Good, I believe you are ready to receive the Ad Altare Dei medal."

He smiled at me and extended his hand. That was it. I couldn't believe it. He didn't ask me one single question. And I spent all those hours preparing for the interview. I reached out, clasped his hand, and smiled back . . . with my mouth closed. What a relief!

The following Sunday afternoon, the four boys from our parish who were to receive the medal drove to Manchester with Father Chicoine. The medals were presented by Bishop Brady in Saint Joseph's Cathedral. What an irony. That's where I attended mass on Sunday mornings when I was at St. Vincent de Paul's orphanage. This is the same bishop I was accused of hitting with a snowball.

I couldn't help but think about my days there as we drove right past the orphanage to the parking lot across from St. Joseph's Cathedral. I never forgot St. Vincent's. I wish I could have. That place would haunt me forever. At least I didn't have to go inside the building again. I wondered if Bishop Brady remembered the snowball incident.

The scouts receiving the Ad Altare Dei medal sat in the front pews of the massive church. Sounds in the cathedral resonated off the walls, as the highest priest in the state spoke. When my name was called, I walked up to the bishop and knelt before him. He pinned the medal to my Boy Scout shirt. After he shook my hand, I returned to my seat. At the end of the ceremony, Bishop Brady announced there would be a lunch and reception for all in attendance at the parish hall. The scouts proceeded out of the church first. We marched to the huge open ballroom across the street from St. Vincent's.

To my surprise, my mother and Ben attended the ceremony. I didn't know they would be there. My mother told me she was proud of me. I must say, I was quite proud of myself also. We never spoke a word about the horrible school across the street.

*   *   *

In the winter, I skied whenever I could. I loved skiing as much as I loved basketball. I had to overcome a few problems before I hit the slopes. First, there was a little matter of getting there. The Belknap Recreation Area was six miles away. Usually, I stood on the corner of Union and Gilford Avenue and hitchhiked to Mount Belknap. There were always skiers going to the mountain that were glad to give a kid a ride to the Area. It didn't bother my mother at all that I hitchhiked all over the place. The lifts didn't operate until 9:00 a.m. I stood on the corner with my thumb out, long before then. I often hitched a ride with one of the ski instructors going to the mountain early in the morning.

Proudly displaying my Ad Altare Dei medal - February 1953

My other big problem was money. Lift tickets cost money. If I couldn't afford to buy a lift ticket, I simply couldn't go skiing. Whenever there was a winter snowstorm, I hit the streets early, with shovel in hand, to try to make a few dollars before all the snow was shoveled from the walkways. I saved that money for my ski fund. I didn't have money to buy lunch at the Area, but that didn't matter to me. I wanted to be the first one on the mountain in the morning and the last one off at night. That's how much I loved the sport.

During the week, the Belknap Area had night skiing under the lights. That's the only time most of the local working folks could go. I bummed rides from my friends whenever I heard they were going skiing with their parents.

Back in the early 50's, the ski equipment was crap. The sport hadn't gained widespread popularity yet. It was only popular in a few places like, Colorado, Utah, Vermont, and New Hampshire. Skis were still made of wood and step-in bindings hadn't been invented yet. Binding cables were known to "freeze up" and wouldn't snap open and release when they needed to. However, there was something magical about whizzing down the mountain, wind slapping you in the face, as you tried to maneuver those two boards into carving beautiful parallel turns. I lived for that thrill.

In the first few years I skied, I saw accidents at Mt. Belknap that would make most people shy away from the sport. One Sunday afternoon, I was skiing down Phelps slope, oblivious to anything around me. It was late in the afternoon. There were very few people on the mountain. Suddenly, I heard this terrible, frightening scream. It sounded like a cat being devoured by a fox or something. From the distance, I saw a body lying in the snow, some fifty yards or so in front of me. As I approached, I noticed it was a woman. When I reached her, I almost vomited on the spot. She was lying on the snow with the tip of a ski pole lodged in her left eye, as if someone chucked a spear at her. I didn't dare touch her.

I quickly gathered my senses and told her, "Please don't move. I'll get the ski patrol as fast as I can."

I didn't even think. I needed to get to the first place that could help her. With the image of that ski pole stuck in her eye, I skied through an unauthorized area to the lift attendant at the bottom of Phelps slope.

I shouted at him, "Get the ski patrol. Get the ski patrol on Phelps," while I was still in motion. There wasn't time to talk about it. Time was critical.

He stopped the lift and called the ski patrol as I was telling him what I saw. The ski patrol brought the woman down the mountain in a toboggan. I don't know if she lost her eye. I suspect she may have. It made me more aware of the possible dangers of skiing. I will always remember that day. After seeing that pole stuck in her eye, I was nauseated for hours.

Another time, I was skiing on a Wednesday night. The lifts shut down at 9:00 p.m. I was taught to be careful using the rope tow that pulled the skiers to the top of Phelps slope. Phelps was the only run open that night. You grabbed onto the spinning rope with both hands as it lurched you forward up the tow lane. When you reached the top, you pushed off, away from the rope. It would then continue its path to the giant wheel some thirty yards away and spin back down the towline. It was like a revolving rope line constantly moving between two giant wheels. One at the bottom. One at the top. Power was generated by a huge motor at the bottom.

You had to wear leather mittens or gloves. Otherwise, in no time at all, the spinning rope would tear wool mittens to shreds. Also, you had to be careful not to let your ski jacket or sweater get twisted into the spinning rope. All these warnings were posted on a big sign at the bottom of the mountain.

It was almost quitting time. There weren't many skiers left on the mountain. There was a big lag between skiers going up the tow. It took all my strength just to lift the heavy rope above the snow. Even grownups had trouble keeping the turning rope up. There were two men going up the tow ahead of me.

Near the top, the man in front of me pushed off. He immediately began screaming, "Help, Help, Help, someone Help."

When I got to the top, I saw what was happening. The man in front of him couldn't remove himself from the rope tow. He was wearing a wool sweater. His sweater was all wrapped up in the towrope. He couldn't release. There wasn't an attendant at the top. The lift operator at the bottom couldn't hear us yelling. Soon, the man was lifted off the ground. His right arm was sucked into the giant wheel at the top. The wheel severed his arm completely off.

143

Oh, my God. That was sickening. That's how he was freed from the rope tow. He fell to the ground and passed out from the shock. Eventually, the rope tow stopped. The ski patrol arrived. They briefly turned their heads when they saw the poor man laying there.

I wasn't immune from being injured either. About the time I fancied myself as a pretty good skier, I met my Waterloo. I was flying down Phelps in a race tuck that Sunday afternoon. I'll never know what I hit. A chunk of ice? Maybe an exposed rock? Could have been a stump? I don't know. I remember flying in the air, out of control. When I landed, I felt a sharp pain attack my left knee. The pain got worse before it got better. I couldn't move my left leg. I didn't want to move it either. It was my turn to take a toboggan ride to the bottom of Mount Belknap. An ambulance took me to the hospital. I had a broken kneecap.

They operated on my knee that day. I was more concerned about my paper route than my knee. The doctor put a pin in my kneecap to keep it together. He told me I would be on crutches for at least a month. Crazy thoughts were going through my mind as I laid there on a hospital gurney. Now, I had a good excuse to avoid selling raffle tickets for my mother. I was praying that my backup would be willing to do my paper route.

My mother and Ben came to the hospital to get me. She seemed rather angry. It's as though I interrupted whatever they were doing. She never asked how the accident happened. She wasn't concerned. I felt like I was imposing on them because I interrupted their Sunday afternoon. I should have known better than to expect a little sympathy.

I didn't bother to tell them the gory details of my big ski accident. I knew they didn't care. I told myself everything would be O.K. I was silent all the way home. So were they. I would figure a way to take care of myself. I promised myself I'd be back on the mountain next year. A broken kneecap wasn't going to stop me from skiing again.

The pain in my knee kept me awake most of the night. The next morning, I called the Citizen to find a replacement to deliver my papers. I called there early to let them know about my accident. The woman I spoke with suggested I contact the boy that knew my route first. It was before 7:00 a.m. when I called his house. I spoke with his mother. Mrs. Bradley was very sympathetic.

She told me, "Don't you worry, Billy will gladly deliver your papers. You just get better O.K."

That afternoon, Billy Bradley came by my house to pick up my green book. I was relieved. I didn't know when I would be able to do my route again. After a week, Billy told me he was ready to take over my route if I wanted to sell it. We made a deal. I simply gave it to him. I didn't want to sell my customers. I just wanted them to have a good paperboy. He already had told most of them about my ski accident. I don't think they expected me to come back. It was time to move on. I was glad to be rid of it. Maybe the ski accident was a blessing in disguise. God had strange ways of looking out for me.

I missed a week of school. I carefully hobbled over to St. Joseph's when I returned. The snow melted into puddles on the sidewalk in the daytime, but froze over at night, as it manifested into frozen footsteps by morning. If I accidentally fell on the ice, I would severely damage my knee. As time passed, my knee healed. I still had to stay on crutches the entire month. I couldn't hobble very far, so I spent my afternoons at Fournier's candy store. The high school boys often bet money at the pinball machine. Aha, I was on to something. By then, I just happened to be a pretty good pinball player. Besides, I hated to lose. I had to be careful. I didn't want them to know I could beat them.

One afternoon, I asked a couple of older boys if I could get into their game. They responded with, "Your money's as good as ours." I am sure they expected to win. We swapped wins back and forth for the first six or seven games. Once I felt they were comfortable allowing me to play with them, I carefully orchestrated the game to end up barely ahead at the end. I walked away from there $1.25 richer. That launched my new career.

There was a small variety store next to Scott & Williams. I mean right next door to Scott & Williams. It was named after the proprietor, Francis Truchon. It was simply called Truchon's. It might have been even smaller than the Fournier's candy store. The place was filthy inside. We suspected Mr. Truchon was a bookie. I couldn't prove it. I didn't care. Men walked in and out of there all day long. I didn't see them buy anything. Mr. Truchon was very unkempt. He had big bags under his droopy eyes, looked like he rarely shaved, wore the same filthy sweater every day, and actually scared people away that didn't know him. What I liked about Truchon's was the pinball machine in the back room. The men who worked at Scott's played the machine for money.

At first, I hobbled in there on my crutches to watch the grown men play. I was probably the only kid that dared go in there. The place smelled like stale urine. Never mind, I was more interested in the quarters on the top of the pinball machine. I watched and cheered them on for a couple of weeks so they would become comfortable with me on their turf. Then I made my move. I asked if I could get in the game with them. At first, they told me to get lost.

"Why, I shouldn't even be in there," one man said.

I made my move. I replied, "Are you afraid that I'll beat you?"

That did it. I was in the game. I was careful not to pour it on. All I wanted was a couple of dollars.

"Hey, the kid's good," one of the men remarked.

I walked away two dollars richer. I was a good pinball player. I knew it. I also knew my limitations. There were men that could beat me. I wasn't cocky. This was my bread and butter. I carefully selected my opponents. After all, I couldn't afford to lose.

It was well over a month after my ski accident before I was able to walk without crutches. I had to be careful when I put weight on my left foot. At times, my knee would buckle and I fell forward, flat on my face. I never went back to be checked out by a doctor. My mother assured me that wasn't necessary. It wasn't her knee that wasn't healing.

She kept telling me, "It just takes time to heal."

I hobbled to school on my crutches until late March. I didn't feel safe putting weight on my knee. I was right about that. One Sunday, Lorraine and I went to mass together. We took our time walking to church. We were very careful. All was going well until I went to genuflect before entering the pew. As I began to kneel, a sharp pain shot straight to my injured knee. I yelled out, "Ahhhh," from the pain as I fell to the floor. I didn't care how I looked laying down there. I was more concerned about how I was going to get up. Fortunately, we arrived at the church early. We were one of a handful of people there. Lorraine and a man helped me to sit in the pew. I felt like I was going to pass out. I was dizzy. The church was filling up fast. I just wanted to go back home. I was discouraged. I should have been walking without any pain by then.

Lorraine and I proceeded slowly back to the entrance of the church. Maybe I should have asked for an ambulance? I wanted one. Then I remembered. That cost money. I would rather limp home in pain than listen to my mother preach about how I was costing her money again. My sister held my arm, and I slowly limped all the way home. I wasn't ready to walk without crutches. At least not until April.

Mom was right. It just takes time to heal. By early April, I could walk without crutches. I couldn't run with my classmates yet, but it didn't hurt when I genuflected in church. That was a big relief. In a couple of weeks, I would receive the sacrament of Confirmation.

Confirmation is one of the seven sacraments through which Catholics pass in the process of their religious upbringing. Call it a right of passage. According to what Sister Albert taught us, when we're confirmed, we receive the Holy Spirit and are accepted as adult members of the Catholic Church. She told us that it marks the time when we become morally responsible for our actions. I interpreted that to mean we were old enough to know right from wrong. Perhaps so, however, I didn't always agree with Sister Albert's beliefs of what was right and what was wrong.

For instance, according to her, it was a sin to read such popular magazines as Life, Reader's Digest, Look, and even the Saturday Evening Post. I failed to see what was wrong with reading those magazines. She was quite resolved in her stance that Catholics shouldn't look at filthy pictures of semi naked aborigines running in the barren lands in Australia. Or, look at pictures of Negro tribesmen in their African villages. True, I did go out of my way to find pictures of women with exposed breasts. If necessary, I would tell that to the priest in confession. However, I didn't think all those magazines were going to hell because of their pictures. Particularly, National Geographic. What was the point of studying Geography, if we couldn't accept the different customs of the different cultures?

Sometimes, you just have to do what you have to do. I didn't argue with Sister Albert. Other kids in class did. It wasn't worth it. Besides, I didn't want to jeopardize my Confirmation. It was to be. One Sunday during mass, the brilliant students of the seventh grade at St. Joseph's school received their Confirmation. I was now a mature adult in the eyes of the Catholic Church.

*   *   *

That was in mid-April. When I arrived home from church after my Confirmation ceremony, my mother and Ben were busy putting our kitchen dishes in boxes. I had no idea what was happening. This was just another instance of my mother not telling me what was going on. It's as though I didn't have a right to know. I was upset. Ora was keeping everything to herself again.

All she said was, "I'm busy. I'll tell you what we're doing later."

I waited outside for later. I was confused. I didn't like what was happening. Worse yet, I didn't know what was happening.

Later that day, she told me, "We sold the house. We're moving to Lakeport."

Just like that; we were moving to Lakeport. That was the only information she'd pass on. No explanation given. My mind danced with all the unanswered questions. Would I have to change schools? When were we moving? What about my friends? How would I explain that my mother sold our nice house on Winter Street to move to Lakeport? It's a good thing I didn't keep my paper route. I grew up on Winter Street. The skating rink was practically in our back yard. Lakeport was at least a mile from school. So many unanswered questions.

I didn't see our new house until the day we moved in. I hardly believed my eyes when I saw it. 642 Union Avenue was an old crumbling building compared to our house on Winter Street. We didn't even own it; we just rented there. It was a dilapidated duplex with a barn in the back. It didn't even have wood siding. It had dark gray asphalt shingle siding. The Johnson family lived on the right side, we moved in on the left. All the rooms were very small in comparison to our last house. It was disappointing. I couldn't understand why she had to sell our house. Were we broke? At least she had rent coming in at our old house. Were they paying off some of Ben's gambling debts? If we're broke, why did they buy a new

Buick? Of all the places to rent, why did they pick this dump? Nothing made sense to me.

We entered the house from the rear door right into the kitchen. The linoleum floor was grimy and faded. There was a small window above the kitchen sink that faced the barn in the rear. Next to the kitchen was a small utility room. It was too small to be of any practical use. My mother put a couch and night stand in there. Perhaps Pudg could play there in the winter? Toward the front of the house was the living room. All that remained downstairs was an enclosed front porch. Why, it was hardly five feet from the sidewalk and the traffic on Union Avenue. That was my bedroom in the summer. I had to learn to sleep with all the noise from the passing traffic.

The bathroom was at the top of the stairs. To the left were two bedrooms. Two very small bedrooms. The first one would serve as the master bedroom. My mother, Ben, and Pudg slept there. They barely had room for his crib and a dresser. Next to their bedroom was another small room. I don't know what it was originally intended to be. There wasn't even a door separating that room from theirs. Lorraine was graduating from high school in a month. This was probably their way of forcing her to leave.

That wouldn't be necessary. Lorraine was counting the days until she would move away. Until then, she and Claudie, who was going into her junior year, had to sleep together on a twin bed in the room next to theirs. To get to their room, the girls had to walk right through my mother and Ben's room. It was a lousy situation. Claudie would have to pass through their room every night until she too could move away. We felt like they were forcing us to move out as soon as we could. They definitely didn't make us feel welcomed. Until she graduated, Claudie didn't have a choice. She and I were stuck there.

From the back door in the kitchen, there was a long covered walkway to the barn. The Johnson's had an entrance to their side of the barn from Moulton Street. We had access to the barn from the driveway we shared with the house on our left. Ben parked his Buick on the grass between the barn and the kitchen. It was a huge old-fashioned barn with two wide swinging doors. That was a good thing. My mother had more furniture stored in the barn than she had in the house. Was this going to be a permanent move? She wouldn't tell me.

Luckily, Lorraine didn't have to live there very long. My big sister finally made it. She was the first one in the family to earn a high school diploma. To Lorraine, graduation from high school wasn't an ending, it was just a beginning. She had her heart set on going to medical school. She desperately wanted to be a doctor. One of my mother's "friends" from the Rod & Gun Club actually had some influence at Colby Junior College in Massachusetts. He offered to help her get accepted at Colby. Lorraine really wanted to go to a medical college, but Colby would be a beginning.

When she spoke with her high school guidance counselor about it, the counselor told her, "Well, Lorraine, I don't think you would be "comfortable" there."

Lorraine got it. She didn't belong there. She wouldn't fit in with all the rich preppy girls from Massachusetts that went to Colby. She had to accept reality. Ora wasn't going to contribute a cent toward her education and she just didn't have the money to go to college.

My mother and Ben didn't even attend her graduation. They didn't even give her a graduation present. Of course that hurt. First one in the family to graduate and her mother didn't even bother to watch her daughter walk across the stage to receive her diploma. Lorraine recalls that Aunt Evie, bless her soul, sent her a graduation card and a little gift. Lorraine was grateful. That meant a lot to her.

She didn't have the money to go to college, but she certainly had enough money to get her own apartment in Laconia. She rented a small efficiency apartment on Union Avenue the week after she graduated from LHS. Free at last! It wasn't much, but it was hers. By then, she passed the Western Union's test and was a qualified commercial telegrapher. That summer, she worked at the Laconia Western Union office on a full time basis. She was making more money than Ben.

CHAPTER 13

SOAPBOX RACING

I was happy for Lorraine. She made it out of the house. Good for her. Yet, I was worried for Claudie and me. Lorraine and my mother had bitter arguments the last few years. Lorraine never yielded from her principles. She was my rock; my foundation. She kept our mother at bay. Until the day she left, I felt she was our protector, our guardian. She was also my source of inspiration. My mother actually had a love-hate relationship with her oldest daughter. She confided in Lorraine. She respected her. Yet, I could tell she was jealous of her. Lorraine was goal oriented, and it wasn't about money. Ora didn't understand that. With my protector gone, she could lash into me for no reason and nobody was there to protect me.

Claudie had her own issues. One of which was that she had to go through their bedroom every night to get to her room. She couldn't even put a light on in her room at night. It would shine directly into their room. She was stuck in a very undesirable situation. She dealt with it the only way she knew how. She stayed away from the house as often as she could. Claudie wasn't a complainer. She kept things bottled up within her. She never showed anger or disappointment, but quietly erupted like a volcano within herself. Who was I to complain when my sister wouldn't? Grin and bear it. Someday, we'll be out of there. That was the day we were both living for.

The day after we moved in, there was a knock at the rear door. It was the boys next door, Bobby and Richard Johnson. We were about the same age. The boys welcomed me to the neighborhood. They told me about all the other boys that lived around us. There was Allie Drake, who lived on the street directly behind ours. Dick Wells lived across the street. My cousins, Lou Cormier and his brothers and sisters, lived only a block away on Mechanic Street.

My cot was set up on the front porch. There was a six-foot plywood partition separating our porch from the Johnson's. Bobby and Richard also slept on their porch in the summer. That made for some fun nights. We talked across the partition at night until we fell asleep. If we happened to talk too loudly, Mrs. Johnson would scold the boys and that would end our nightly conversation.

Within a week, I met Allie Drake. Although we were the same age, Allie was nearly a foot taller than I was. Allie was an only child and lived in a big white house on the nice quiet street behind Union Avenue. His house was right next to the parking lot of the Scott & Williams's plant in Lakeport. The Drake's had at least an acre of land that sloped down to Lake Opechee. As their yard sloped down toward the lake, the concrete wall separating their yard from the Scott & Williams's parking lot became higher and higher. That summer, I spent many nights camping outside with my new friends down by the lake in Allie's backyard. I certainly had my fill of marshmallows.

The second week of June I fell asleep to the roar of motorcycles parading up and down Union Avenue all night long. The roar of the motorcycles was so loud, we couldn't hear each other talk over the partition. The 32nd Annual New England Gypsy Tour and 100 mile National Motorcycle Championship was underway. I was so occupied playing with my new friends, I almost forgot about motorcycle week. I never heard from Freddy Walsh that year. We certainly didn't have room for him to stay with us. My mother never said anything about him. Honestly, I didn't care. I liked to watch the 100-mile race, but the novelty of riding on the back of a motorcycle had worn off. I wasn't upset that Freddy hadn't called or showed up at the house. I didn't even tell the Johnson brothers about my escapades on the back of a motorcycle. My fluorescent motorcycle hat was buried in some moving box never to be seen again. It probably didn't fit anymore anyway.

I kept very busy in the summer of 1952. Just before school let out in June, the nun that played the organ in the church approached me and asked me if I would like to sing solo at funeral masses in the church. I was thrilled. Actually, I was honored. She told me that funeral masses were being held for the dead soldiers returning from the Korean War. In some small way, I felt I could do my part to honor our dead heroes by singing my heart out at their final ceremony. Besides doing my patriotic duty, I was being paid seventy-five cents a mass. I thought, "Not bad for an hour's work."

I practiced after school for a week with the organist. I sang the Latin prayer "Tantum Ergo" and, at the end of the mass, when the casket was being carried out of the church, I poured my heart out singing, "Ave Maria." Often, I became emotionally caught up in the moment. I would step down to the end of the choir balcony, extend my arms like an eagle, and bellow the "Ave Maria," with tears coming from my eyes. I was touched. I couldn't help myself. People leaving the mass looked up at me singing my heart out and often cried along with me as they left the church. I must admit, I loved working the crowd! I received several compliments for my heart-pouring rendition of "Ave Maria." I thrived on the recognition. I was getting the admiration from singing at funerals that I never got at home.

That summer, I sang at one or two funeral masses a week. The organist didn't pay me. The priest, usually Father Chicoine, paid me. One time, he told me he didn't have my seventy-five cents with him and would pay me later. A week went by and he forgot to pay me, Seventy-five cents might not seem like much, but when you have nothing it's a lot. I counted on every cent I could make. That sent up a warning flag to me. I had been stuck without being paid too often on my paper route. Certainly, the church charged the family of the deceased for my singing. Probably ten dollars or more. All I wanted was to be paid for my work. The next time the church called me to sing, I told them I needed to be paid before the mass. They got the message. It was a win-win situation all around. I probably would have sung for nothing, but I certainly wasn't about to tell them that. I was becoming quite street savvy.

One night, while camping in Allie's back yard, I told Allie about my neat summer gig at the church. I was bragging a bit and told him how I made people cry when I sang. He said something interesting. Allie heard that someplace a family opened the draped casket of their dead son to retrieve some memory of him, but, when they opened the box, there wasn't a body in there. What they saw was a pair of boots and some weights. I couldn't believe what I was hearing. We talked for hours about that.

"You mean I'm singing my heart out to a pair of shoes?" I asked.

"Maybe. Not always," he responded. He went on to tell me, "You know, some of these bodies were found buried in the snow, months after they were killed."

I felt flush. A thousand thoughts raced through my mind. I recalled all those poor people weeping in their handkerchiefs as they walked out of the church. What if there was only a pair of boots in the casket? I didn't want to know. I had to believe the Sacred Heart Church wouldn't allow that to happen.

My mother didn't acknowledge that I was receiving compliments for singing, but Grammy Garneau sure did. One day, she called me directly and asked if I would sing a song for the Saint Jean de Baptiste women's auxiliary meeting. She must have heard about me singing in the church. Here was my chance to show my grandmother I was good at something.

Their meeting was held at the new Tardiff Park clubhouse. When I walked in the door, my grandmother greeted me with a big smile and even came over and hugged me. She proceeded to let the other old ladies know I was her grandson. When the women were all seated, I took the mike and began singing, "I'm Looking over a Four Leaf Clover." I was such a ham. I concluded my little program with a step-shuffle-step-step tap dance that Lorraine had taught me.

I heard one of the women say, "Oh, how cute."

Another one asked my grandmother, "Who is that cute boy?"

She proudly said, "That's my grandson. *That's Ora's boy!*"

Even though we moved to Lakeport, I still went to Laconia to play with my old friends. One of them, Paul Lemay, lived on Winter Street. I enjoyed going to Paul's house. His father was a building contractor and the Councilman for Ward 2. One time, Mrs. Lemay showed us how to make maple syrup from scratch. They tapped a spigot right into the maple tree in their back yard. In early spring, sap oozed from the tree into a bucket attached to the spigot. We drank the sweet water-like sap right from the bucket. Mrs. Lemay boiled the sap and converted it to maple syrup. Then, she rolled apples in it and put them in the refrigerator to harden. When we were through playing, she treated us to those delicious apples, coated with maple syrup and confectionery sugar sprinkled on top.

I was always comparing other families to ours. I couldn't help it. The Lemay's genuinely loved their children and openly showed their affection to them. Paul was disciplined, but he was disciplined for the right reasons. He was raised to respect other people. They cared about his education. They encouraged him to get good grades in school. They even helped him with his homework.

Fortunately, for him, Paul was raised in a caring, nurturing environment. That's what I observed when I went to his house. Oh, how badly I wanted to be in a family like his. Sadly, I knew I would never have a good home life. It wasn't in God's plan for me. I didn't live in a family like Paul's, so I made it a point to expose myself to people who raised their children the way I wanted to be raised. That's the best I could do.

One day, Paul told me that "we" needed to get "me" a new front tooth. He must have been hallucinating. I listened to what he had to say. He told me about a new dentist in town and suggested we approach him and offer to mow his lawn and do any other chores he might have us do in exchange for a new front tooth. I was touched. Here was this friend, willing to help me without any compensation so I could have a front tooth and wouldn't be embarrassed to open my mouth any longer.

That day, we visited the new dentist, Doctor Joseph W. Gage, at his new office across the street from Laconia High. He was just starting out in his first practice. The contractor was still hanging drywall and there was debris scattered everywhere. I let Paul do the talking. I was surprised when Paul told Dr. Gage he wanted to be a dentist someday. I could tell Dr. Gage was impressed by Paul. Before I knew it, I was sitting in Dr. Gage's new dental chair, as he examined my severed front tooth.

We made an agreement. He agreed to make a partial mouthpiece for me that would look like I had a front tooth. In exchange, Paul and I would put the debris in the dumpster and mow his yard every week until the grass stopped growing. I was so happy. I was going to look normal again.

True to his word, Paul met me at Dr. Gage's office every week to mow the lawn and do any other chores that needed to be done. I'll always remember Paul for that. I am sure he turned out to be the fine young man his parents raised him to be.

*   *   *

If you lived in Lakeport in the summer of 52,' there's a good chance you were involved with Soapbox Derby racing. It was a very popular sport back then. Lakeport was considered the mecca of Soapbox racing in the Lakes Region. Races were held on Wednesday nights and Sunday afternoons on the Belvidere street hill. Officer Dan Clare was the kingpin that made it happen. He was solely responsible for the success of the racing program in Lakeport. He was an iconic figure. Dan, as everyone called him, was nearing the end of his career on the Laconia Police force when I met him.

Everyone admired Dan Clare. They could have easily put in a traffic light to control traffic turning to and from Elm Street and Union Avenue. That wasn't about to happen, as long as Dan Clare was willing to stand in the street and direct the oncoming traffic through one of the busiest intersections in the city. I don't know how many lives Dan touched in his long police career, but I know he was admired by everyone who knew him. He was a good man. He unselfishly gave of himself until the day he retired.

When I first met Dan, he was walking up Belvidere street hill with his police hat in hand, collecting donations from the crowd to be shared by the winning racers. There were probably 200 people lining the hill that night. I am guessing there were probably 14 or so racers at the top of the hill. The first time I looked up Belvidere Street, I couldn't believe anyone was crazy enough to race down that hill. Other than Pine Street, we had nothing that steep in Laconia. Not only was it steep, the street was sort of rounded from side to side, so you wanted to stay in the middle to improve your chances of winning your race. With two racecars s in each race, there was only room for one in the middle of the street. That often resulted in racers banging into one another to gain the advantage of being in the apex of the street. The crowds loved it, that's what they came to see.

Looking up the hill, on the right hand side there was a fence with a drop off of at least thirteen feet into someone's garden down below. I could easily visualize a racer careening out of control, crashing through the wooden fence, and ending upside down in the garden. As if that wasn't dangerous enough, there were all those people standing on the sidewalk on the left side. It wouldn't take much to lose control and crash into one of the onlookers, or worse yet, crash into someone's rock wall, built to hold their front yard in place on the steep slope.

That evening, I watched the racers in their sleek home-built racecars, zooming down Belvidere Street until there were two racers left who hadn't been beaten in their heats. There was an energy, an excitement in the crowd, which was contagious. I didn't even know those kids. Yet, I found myself screaming for the blue car to win. And he did. I found out the winner's name was Donald Douglas. Everyone in Lakeport knew him as "Ducky" Douglas. I was hooked.

As luck would have it, the Laconia Police department was impressed by the popularity of the races in Lakeport. They decided to conduct Soapbox Derby races in Laconia. By word of mouth, I learned they were going to hold their races on Thursday nights on Fairview Street. Compared to Belvidere Street, it wasn't much of a hill. However, they couldn't race on Pine Street. There was too much traffic on Pine and no place to slow down and turn your racecar around at the bottom of the hill. Fairview dead-ended at the top of the hill, so there was far less traffic. The bottom was fairly flat and you could slow down enough to make a U-turn. A police officer was stationed at the bottom to control traffic.

I learned through the grapevine that Ralph Carignan's father built a Soapbox racecar for his son, but wouldn't allow him to race. He thought it was far too dangerous. It didn't take me long before I was knocking on his door to see his racecar. By no means was it a good-looking racecar. It was more like a tanker. It had a metal barrel attached above the floorboard the racer sat on. Mr. Carignan cut out a section of floorboard and hooked a spring from the inside of the barrel to a hinged piece of wood with a rubber underlay to be used as a brake. A rope was tied to the front axletree by eyebolts and that's how you steered. There was one thing about Ralph's green Soapbox racecar that was different from everyone else's. It had fat inflated tires. Everyone else used tires that came off carts.

I got right to the point. "Ralph I hear your Dad won't let you race your car. Can I race it for you?" I asked.

As expected, he had to get his father's permission. My deal was that we would split all our winnings 50-50. Ralph wanted to see his car race down Fairview Street. His Dad gave us permission to race it, as long as I was the driver. We were off to the races! I had no idea how we would do. Compared to the other sleek racecars, nobody thought we had a chance. Since this was my first time racing, I didn't really expect to win anything. That's a lie. I always expected to win!

"How could we possibly win in that tub?" someone asked, as we pushed our racecar up the hill to the starting line.

Well, it just so happened that the ugly fat car with the funny blown up tires came in third place the first night of racing in Laconia.

Ralph and I split our winnings, as we agreed we would. It wasn't much. The word hadn't spread around Laconia yet. As the weeks passed, more people showed up at the Thursday night races. Meanwhile, I was learning the little secrets to winning. One of the secrets was to use a very fine oil to lubricate the wheel bearings. They actually made official Soapbox Derby oil. That was a well-guarded secret. Another one was to put carbon tetrachloride into the ball bearings. That took away any paint or contamination that might get in there and cut down on friction in the wheels. These were just some of the tricks I learned from my friends in Lakeport.

Before long, Ralph's ugly fat racecar was winning the Thursday night races in Laconia. Yes, that Sonny Virgin was a hell of a driver. I even had a cheering section rooting for me. Kids rushed to me when they saw Ralph and I turn onto Fairview Street.

They would ask, "Sonny, Sonny, can I push it?"

Of course, I let them. If it were up to me, they could push it from Ralph's house to Fairview every week. Pulling it to the races was the part I didn't like.

There was only one thing missing. This wasn't Lakeport. Winning in Laconia wasn't the same. Ralph's car wouldn't stand a chance in Lakeport. It was built far too high off the ground. It would easily tip over on Belvidere Street. The other racers would push me into a ditch in no time.

I'll never forget the final week of the racing season in Laconia. To my surprise, four of the racers from Lakeport showed up for the final race. Their racecars were offloaded from a large flatbed truck. Everyone knew they came to show us up. I recognized the racers. I don't think they knew I lived in Lakeport. They had a swagger about them. I am sure they thought they were going to show us how the big boys did it. I wasn't intimidated one bit. If they won, good for them. That's the way it should be.

A funny thing happened that night. Their cars might have been right for the steep hill in Lakeport, but the heavier racecars we raced in Laconia were faster on the less steep incline. At the end of the day, Ralph Carignan's ugly, fat green tank, driven by Sonny Virgin, won the final race of the season. We sent the big shots from Lakeport back to their hill with their tails tucked between their legs. What a great way to end the season. Now the Lakeport boys knew who I was.

*   *   *

The first thing I noticed my first day back in school was that the boys all looked three inches taller and the girls now had boobs. Me, I had a new front tooth. Immediately, Sister Bebianne launched into her annual rhetorical of how she would punish us if we didn't abide by her rules. I thought to myself, "This is the last year I have to listen to this crap." While she was speaking, I had already deciphered that her nickname would be, "Sister B-B-Gun."

Actually, Sister B-B-Gun was a very good teacher. I fully expected her to side with the Catholic viewpoint on issues we discussed in class. Nevertheless, she promoted open discussion on current events. She encouraged me to use my brain and formulate my own opinion. We had some good constructive arguments. I didn't take her criticisms personally. At times, my opinions differed from hers.

New Hampshire's claim to fame is its First in the Nation presidential primary election status. Its real importance comes from the massive media coverage it receives. Since 1952, the New Hampshire primary has been a major testing ground for the presidential candidates of both parties. Candidates who do poorly there, frequently drop out. While those who do well, suddenly become serious contenders. Lesser known candidates know that if they do well in New Hampshire, they can garner large amounts of media attention and campaign funding.

In 1952, the primaries were held in March. Senator Estes Kefauver, who chaired the televised investigations of organized crime in 1951, defeated the incumbent, President Harry S. Truman, in the New Hampshire primaries. Kefauver's victory stung Truman. It was enough for him to announce he wouldn't seek reelection.

The battle for the Republican nomination was between General Dwight D. Eisenhower and "Mr. Republican," Senator Robert Taft of Ohio. New Hampshire's Governor, Sherman Adams, managed the "draft Eisenhower" campaign in the state. Ironically, Eisenhower never even campaigned in New Hampshire. The Democrats had held the Presidential office for 20 years. The Republicans saw "Ike" as their only chance of defeating the Democrats in the national election.

Adams literally campaigned for the General. Eisenhower didn't commit to a presidential run until he saw the results of the New Hampshire primary. Governor Adams went on the road to every nook and cranny in the state. While General Eisenhower was serving as the Commander of the NATO Allied Forces in Paris, Sherman Adams campaigned relentlessly for Ike. In the end, Eisenhower scored a major victory in the New Hampshire primary, as a write-in candidate, giving him a huge upset victory over Senator Taft.

That year, General Eisenhower ran against Adlai Stevenson in the presidential elections. The bloody and indecisive Korean War was dragging into its third year. In a major campaign speech, Eisenhower announced that he would go to Korea and put an end to the war. His great military prestige, combined with the public's weariness with the conflict, gave him the boost he needed to win. On Election Day, he soundly defeated Stevenson 55% to 44% in the popular vote and by a larger margin in the Electoral College. For his efforts, Sherman Adams was well rewarded. He became President Eisenhower's Chief of Staff in the White House, a position he held for six years.

It was no secret that 99.9% of French Catholics in New Hampshire were Democrats. Thus, it wasn't a surprise to me that Sister Bebianne assured the class that the intellectual Adlai Stevenson would win the election. Not only was she a Democrat, she believed that Eisenhower didn't deserve to win because he didn't even have the "decency" to visit New Hampshire during the primaries. While the class stayed silent, I spoke out in defense of Ike. "For crying out loud, Sister, don't you think he has a very important job to do in the military?" I asked.

She knew I had a good point. I really twisted the knife in her back when I reminded her of General Eisenhower's promise to end the war in Korea if he were elected.

To finish it off, I asked, "What did Stevenson promise?"

She gave me that soft smile of hers, but failed to come back with a reply. I liked politics. I though, "Maybe I could run for a political office someday?"

At the house, I teased my mother and asked her who she was voting for? I always got the same answer.

"It's none of your business," she would say.

I made her feel uneasy when I talked politics. She knew I followed the elections. I watched the state primaries unfold on television. She and Ben hardly ever watched the news. She wasn't interested in national politics.

How well I remember the local level elections when we lived on Winter Street. It never failed. The snotty people in Ward 2, who talked about my mother behind her back, were very sweet to her at election time.

They'd call and ask, "Ora, do you need a ride to the polls tomorrow?"

And the Ward Captain would call and ask, "Ora, how's it going? Is there anything you need at your place?"

I was fascinated by that. That's how the big political machine churned its wheels at election time. Just like the big boys in Boston. There was no doubt that Ora was a Democrat. Born and bred. True and true. Same as Sister Bebianne.

Perhaps, my mother should have asked the Ward Captain for some food after we moved to Lakeport. We didn't have a garden, and the cupboards were practically empty all the time. There were cans of soup and tuna fish, and usually some crackers to eat with the soup. Often, not much else. I couldn't help but notice that my mother was becoming thin and frail. She wore the same pair of checkered slacks and her favorite old frayed green sweater around the house every day. Ben and my mother quit going to the Rod & Gun Club on Saturday night. If they went out at all, it was to play cards at Grammy Garneau's house. Grampy Garneau always had a bottle of

Canadian Club whiskey available for their visits. They took Pudgie with them so my grandparents could see their favorite grandson. I was glad when they left. I could watch the Gillette Saturday night fights on TV.

A bottle of beer every now and then became a treat for them. Obviously, money was tight. They were barely getting by on Ben's salary from the foundry. My mother was restless. I sensed she wanted to go back to work, but she couldn't. She had to stay home to take care of Pudgie. He was only three.

I didn't know their financial situation. However, I felt an uneasy tension. For my part, I didn't ask for anything. I spent the money I earned that summer to buy my school clothes for the coming year. By the time school started, I was broke again. I needed to earn money somewhere. There weren't any paper routes available in Lakeport. Everyone shoveled their own snow in the winter. We lived too far away for me to shovel snow in Laconia. By the time I got there, all the walks would have been shoveled.

Finally, I came up with an idea to make some money. I hadn't used my bicycle all summer. I walked everywhere. I didn't need it anymore. So, I decided to try to sell it back to Paquette's Sporting Goods or Bean's Used Furniture store. I looked all over the barn for it. It wasn't there. Then, I looked for Lorraine's bike. I couldn't find her bike either. Had someone stolen our bikes? I was upset, but I didn't panic.

I went inside the house and asked my mother and Ben if they knew where my bike was? "Nope," they said.

What about Lorraine's?" I asked.

"Haven't seen it," she said.

Was it possible that they just left them on Winter Street when we moved? I had to be careful not to accuse them of anything. I didn't want them to get angry. Yet, their calm demeanor concerned me. I couldn't help but suspect they might have sold both bikes and kept the money. The following Saturday, I went to Paquette's Sporting Goods and Bean's Furniture Store to see if I could spot my bike. It wasn't there. I didn't dare ask if my parents had sold it to them.

Fortunately, one day early in the school year, Sister B-B-Gun asked the class if anyone would be interested in a job after school. She went on to explain that Sister Superior was looking for someone to sweep the hallway floors in the afternoon. Nobody raised their hand. I wanted to, but I didn't want anyone to know that I was desperate. I asked Sister Bebianne about the job at recess. She told me to talk to the head nun at the end of the day.

That afternoon, I went to Sister Superior's office. She explained the job to me. The school had classrooms on two floors, with stairs on both ends of the long corridors. They kept a barrel of fine cedar shavings in the basement.

In broken English, Sister Superior told me, "You need to scatter this here dust (shavings) on the stairs and den do da floors with your dustpan. Do you understand?" "Then, you need to sweep da halls with this push broom and den do da stairs with this brush. Do you understand?" She told me it should take me about an hour a day to sweep the floors. She wanted me to sweep the floors five days a week. I told her I couldn't do it on Wednesday's. I had another commitment. She reluctantly agreed.

After school that day, I began my new job. It was after 6:30 p.m. by the time I finished. It took me nearly three hours to do both floors and the stairs. I missed supper. My mother scolded me for coming home late. She let me know if I wasn't home at five o'clock when they ate supper, I would have to do without. I hadn't eaten all day. I was starving when I went to bed.

I was sure Sister Superior would compliment me on the fine job I did when I saw her the next day. Instead, she said, "You missed dat spot over dere. Do you see it?"

What I saw was a few shavings in a tight corner on one of the stairs. She proceeded to let me know I needed to do a better job. I swear she walked the stairs and both floors with a magnifying glass in her hand, looking for a sliver of red cedar shavings.

"What did I get myself into this time?" I wondered.

No matter how hard and how fast I worked, it still took me at least two hours every day to sweep both floors. Consequently, I missed supper every night. In addition, every morning, Sister Superior found some tiny fault to bring to my attention. I hated to quit. I just wasn't a quitter, but I couldn't go without eating supper any longer and her daily nagging was wearing thin. If I could have found another job, I would have quit that job in a heart beat.

At the end of the week, I went to her office to be paid. When I took the job, I never thought to ask how much I would be making. Sister Superior reached in her desk, as though she was guarding some Top Secret classified document. She cupped her hand so I wouldn't see what she was doing. Then, she handed me a dollar bill. A dollar bill!

I couldn't help myself. I asked, "Sister is this a mistake? Is that all I am being paid?" Perhaps she didn't realize I had worked over ten hours sweeping the floors? I could tell she was a little put out that I was questioning someone in a position of authority. I suppose good Catholic boys didn't do that. On the other hand, I had to remind myself that the nuns took a vow of poverty and she probably considered one dollar to be sufficient.

I don't know what she thought, but I wasn't going to work ten hours a week and miss supper every night for one lousy dollar a week.

I told her, "I'm sorry Sister, but you're going to have to find someone else. I have to be home by five for supper."

I was so disappointed. I wanted to tell her what she could do with her dollar bill. Of course, I didn't. Damn, I hated being screwed by adults. I just told her that I couldn't do it anymore.

As I was walking away, she called me back. Her whole disposition changed. She was desperate too. She needed me to sweep those floors. After talking it over, we reached an agreement. I would do one floor and one set of stairs a night. That cut the workload in half. She also agreed to raise my pay to $1.50 a week. I agreed to try it out, but left the door open to quit if it took much longer than an hour a night. $1.50 wasn't much, but I needed every cent I could make. How was I going to buy socks and toothpaste, or go out with my friends every now and then if I didn't have any money? Working also meant I missed basketball practice after school.

I didn't have to practice football to play in the annual football game against our archenemy, Saint John's school. That was the other Catholic school in town. They were the Irish Catholics. We were rivals at everything. The big game was held on a Sunday afternoon at the Laconia High School football field. Coach Morin was really desperate for players. He begged me to come out and play in the big game.

I told him, "Coach, I don't even know the plays. I haven't even been to a practice." "What to heck, it doesn't matter," he said, "I'll put you in the line at Tackle. All you have to do is block the other guy. Try to keep him from tackling our guy in the backfield."

I thought, "Oh well, I might as well do one for Coach Morin!"

That Sunday, we put our football uniforms on in the school basement. I was more concerned about the mess I would have to clean up the next day than I was about the stupid football game. It was raining when the game started. In no time, the field was a mud bowl. I played in the line opposite Bobby LaFrance. He was a linesman all right. He was all muscle and outweighed me by at least 30 pounds. Play after play, he knocked me on my butt and was in our backfield tackling one of our players. Obviously, I was the weak link. I couldn't stop him. By the end of the first quarter, Coach Morin realized he had to run plays away from me.

The final score was 6 to 6. We had a better backfield. They had a better line. I wasn't a football player. I was way too small. I knew my limitations. So did everyone else. From then on, I would stick to basketball. At least we didn't have to forfeit the game that day. I was the 11th player they needed to have a team.

I must confess, I wasn't much better at baseball than I was at football. I had this depth perception problem. I misjudged the ball. I always seemed a little out of sync. Either I swung the bat a little early or closed my glove too soon when I fielded a ball. I wasn't a bad player, I just wasn't good.

Allie thought that I should get my eyes checked out. He surmised that was my problem. He might have been on to something. In class, I sat in the front row so I could see the blackboard. If I sat further back, everything seemed blurred. Again, my problem was money. I couldn't afford to have my eyes tested. I definitely couldn't afford a pair of glasses. It wasn't a problem when I played basketball. There, I was dealing with a big round ball that wasn't coming at me at 60 miles an hour. I had time to adjust to a pass. Besides, I was a better ball handler than I was a shooter.

I couldn't have played much worse than the 1952 Boston Red Sox. I would never give up on the Sox, but that didn't mean I couldn't cuss them out. I had good reason to. They were getting worse every year. What an embarrassing season. They ended up in

6th place in the American League. It hurts to say it. The Yankees won the American League pennant for the 19th time. They went on to win their fourth consecutive World Series in seven games against the Brooklyn Dodgers. We were certainly no match for those damn Yankees. I quit saying, "wait til' next year." I saved that cry for my favorite basketball team, the rejuvenated Boston Celtics.

Last season the Celtics made it to the NBA playoffs. They barely lost to the New York Knics. I was a diehard Celtics fan too. I knew it was just a matter of time before we'd become a basketball dynasty. That season, the great 6'1" point guard, Bob Cousy, led the Celtics. They called him the "Houdini of Basketball." The Celtic fans adored "the Cooz." I did too. He averaged 21 points a game and led the team in assists. He was also an NBA first team nomination. I couldn't get enough Cousy. I wanted to play just like him. I couldn't wait for the upcoming basketball season

*   *   *

The reason I couldn't sweep the floors at the school on Wednesday night was because I made a commitment to be a Cub Scout Den Mother's assistant. When I was in Cub Scouts, the Den Mothers had volunteer Boy Scouts help them at their weekly den meetings. I looked up to Mrs. Morin's assistant when I was in Cub Scouts. He knew what to do. He was a valuable asset to her and to us as well.

I was assigned to assist a Mrs. Ledoux. She lived in a nice Cape Cod style house on Gilford Avenue. She volunteered to become a Den Mother because her son was in Cub Scouts. That was usually why they became involved. When I first met her, I sensed she was a bit skeptical of me. I felt she wanted someone else to be her assistant. I couldn't put my finger on it, but this wasn't new to me. I knew rejection. Perhaps someone told her some bad rumor about me. The French people were good at that. She had no reason to dislike me. Unfortunately, my mother's bad reputation loomed over me like a dark gray cloud everywhere I went. People victimized my mother, without giving her the benefit of the doubt. I had been exposed to the Mrs. Ledoux of Laconia before. All I could do is be myself. I was there to help her.

Our first den meeting went well. She took the job seriously. I did too. She had read the training manual and had prepared an agenda. The Cubs stayed occupied. I helped the boys do arts and crafts. Every week, Mrs. Ledoux prepared a snack for the scouts. Since her husband owned a grocery store, she always had plenty of food on hand. In no time at all, she and I blended well. The boys looked up to me. I valued that. Whatever she was told about me didn't matter. In time, Mrs. Ledoux became my staunchest supporter.

We would talk after the meetings. At first, it was about scouting things, but after awhile it became more personal. She wanted to know my plans for the future. She encouraged me to do well. Eventually, I confided in her about my home life. She genuinely felt sorry for me. We became good friends. I finally met an adult I could confide in. We never discussed her problems, but I sensed she was hiding something. I never pushed the issue. If she wanted to tell me, she would.

It was obvious to Mrs. Ledoux that I was scrawny and undernourished. She didn't want to embarrass me, but she was concerned. Without saying anything, she prepared twice as many snacks as we needed for the meeting. At the end of the meeting, she'd ask me to do her a favor and take them with me.

She would say something like, "I don't like to keep sweet things around the house. Here, do me a favor and take these with you."

One time, she prepared a dozen cupcakes. It was snowing hard that day. Only four kids showed up for the weekly meeting. We ended it early because of the weather. She knew I had to go all the way to Lakeport. She offered me a ride home. I thanked her, but declined her offer. I didn't want her to see the dump we lived in.

Finally, she said, "Here, take these for me, please."

She placed seven cup cakes in a paper bag. One by one, I ate all of them on my way home. After I walked into the house, I placed the empty bag in the garbage can.

I didn't see much of Lorraine after she moved to her own apartment. She was busy. I was busy. That's the way it goes. I should have at least dropped by the Western Union office to say, "Hello." She would have liked that. Before I could do that, she called the house and told Mom she was moving away. It was time for her to see a little of this country. By October, she was on her way to a new job with Western Union in Presque Isle, Maine.

I couldn't wait to go to school and find Presque Isle, Maine on the map. I finally found it. What had my sister done? Heck, Presque Isle wasn't even on the principal map. It was so far off into the boonies, they showed it on an extended page. It was above half of eastern Canada. I envisioned people walking around in snowshoes, wearing buckskin clothing, and driving around in dog sleds. You couldn't be much further north and still be in the United States. If it were anybody but Lorraine, I would have been worried, but she was so wise and mature for her age, I knew she'd be fine. I only hoped she would call and let us know how she was doing from time to time.

By mid-October, it was becoming too cold to sleep on the front porch. I had to move inside. The Johnson boys moved inside their house a month before I did. My mother left my cot out on the porch. For the winter months, I had to sleep on the couch in the small room next to the kitchen. At least I would be warm.

The first night in my new bedroom, I woke up to a noise in the kitchen. I though it came from around the sink. It sounded like something hitting a pan. When I put on the light, I saw a rat dash across the kitchen counter. Oh, no, that's all I needed. I was scared to death of rats . . . . even mice. What a miserable experience. For the rest of the winter, I slept with my head covered underneath the blankets. My body trembled. I heard the rats running around in the kitchen every night. I cringed at the thought of them running over my covers. I had also seen rats running in the barn. The house was probably infested with them. I never went down to the basement. I just wanted to move away from there. I prayed to Jesus to protect me.

CHAPTER 14

MERRY CHRISTMAS, MAMA

My cousin, Lou Cormier, lived next to the cemetery on Mechanic Street. On Christmas Eve of 1952, he and I were sledding down the long slope in the cemetery. That wasn't the smartest thing I've ever done. There were rows of roads in the cemetery for cars to drive through. You had to maneuver carefully down the slope to avoid hitting one of the rows directly. If you didn't angle your sled just right, you might find yourself flying in the air into a tombstone. On the other hand, that was part of the fun. We played in the cemetery until the afternoon sun went down.

When I arrived home, the Christmas tree was lit, my little brother was sitting on the floor in my bedroom, and my mother was standing over the sink looking out the kitchen window. I took off my boots and jacket before entering the house. We weren't allowed to wear shoes in the house. When I walked in the kitchen, I noticed my mother's red eyes. She must have been crying. Ben wasn't in the room.

When I tried to talk to her she turned away. Suddenly, Ben came up the cellar stairs. He looked angry. That was nothing new. He always looked angry. You could cut the tension in the house with a knife. Even Pudgie looked scared. I assumed they had been arguing again.

Soon, their argument escalated out of control. They were standing in the living room hollering at each other. I was worried for my mother. Ben wasn't Harold. You could see the anger in his eyes. My mother was scared of him. I overheard him threaten to leave with Pudgie. Ora pleaded with him not to do that. I stayed in the kitchen away from the fray. In the heat of their argument, Ben pushed my mother backwards right into the Christmas tree. She fell on her back and knocked over the tree. Ben raced through the kitchen. I stepped aside, clearing the way of his path to the rear door.

Immediately, after he stormed out of the house, I ran into the living room to help my mother up. Tears were streaming down her face. I began to cry with her. As well, my little brother sat on the floor bawling without understanding why. We heard Ben rev the engine to the car. Before long, he drove off into the night. I helped my mother sit in her favorite chair. She was crying uncontrollably. The sonofabitch ruined her Christmas.

I sat on the floor, holding her hand while she wept. She sat there, physically, mentally, and emotionally drained. She had tried her very best to make this marriage work and it was now disintegrating before her on this Christmas Eve. Even though Mom wasn't hurt physically, the emotional scars she acquired that day would last a lifetime. The luster had worn off the knight's shining armor. Above all, she felt the despair of a failed third marriage.

After awhile, she stood up and wiped her tears away. She asked if I was hungry. I was, but I told her that I wasn't. She looked so sad. I just wanted to be there to comfort her; to let her know I was there for her. We didn't know where Ben went on that sorrowful Christmas Eve. We didn't even know if he would return. My mother wandered about in a daze. I am sure a million things were racing through her mind. In a way, I was glad he was gone. I didn't have to tip-toe around the house and carefully avoid him when he wasn't there. Secretly, I was hoping he would never come back. Somehow, we could manage without him. And I felt we would be better off.

I didn't worry much about the rats that night. I was more concerned about my mother's mental state. She was helpless. For the moment, her future was out of her control. She spent the night in the living room waiting for a phone call that never came.

The next day, we spent the most somber Christmas of my life. She wanted me near her, yet, she didn't want to talk about it. By then, I figured that Pudg was the ace in the hole. If it weren't for Pudg she might proceed with a divorce. Ben, on the other hand, knew how much that boy meant to my mother. He would threaten to take him away as his bargaining chip whenever he wanted his way. My sisters and I were right all along. He married her for her money.

Now they were stuck with a young child. That kept them bound together in an unhappy marriage.

She didn't call Marie or any of her other friends. She certainly wasn't going to tell my grandmother what happened. The last thing she wanted to hear was, "I told you so." She didn't call the police either. There wasn't much I could do to comfort her. She didn't want to share her thoughts or even her emotions. As always, she kept everything bottled up within her. We were supposed to go to Grammy Garneau's for Christmas dinner. It took all Mom had to hold back from crying over the phone.

I heard her tell Grammy, "Pudgie is very sick. We're gonna have to stay home. Might even have to take him to the hospital."

By the day after Christmas, she seemed to be doing better. She stopped sobbing. I don't know whom she spoke with on the phone, but when she was through talking to the other party, her old business face had returned.

I thought to myself, "He may not love her, but he's not going to get her money."

With Mom, money was her security blanket. She may look poor and act poor, but she wasn't poor. She had money saved somewhere that Ben didn't know about. That much I knew about my mother.

Three days after he shoved her into the Christmas tree, we heard the Buick pull into the driveway. I waited and watched with my mother. He came into the house sobbing. It was an Academy Award performance. I watched this grown man groveling for forgiveness. I watched to see what my mother would say and do. Ben's story was that he didn't remember anything. He snapped out of his spell driving down a freeway in Massachusetts. He swore he didn't remember anything.

"You wouldn't understand," he explained. "I have these blackouts from getting malaria in the war." He went on to say, "When I was a POW, I caught malaria. I get these attacks and don't know what I'm doing."

It was a convincing story. I think my mother wanted to believe it. She was clinging to a ray of hope. Anything that would let her think he didn't betray her would do. I wasn't completely sold on his malaria story. I knew the big Veterans Administration (VA) hospital in Manchester took care of the war veterans. If he had malaria, then why didn't he go there for treatment? I had friends in school whose fathers went to the VA hospital. He lived with us for four years and suddenly he has a malaria attack? Why hadn't he told my mother before that he had malaria? I just wasn't buying it.

My mother sent me outside to play. I went to the gym at Our Lady of the Lakes parish in Lakeport. Since we were on Christmas break, the gym was crowded with kids playing basketball. I released all my pent up frustrations of the last three days on the court. That day, I played with more determination than ever. When Norm Douglas guarded me too closely, I plowed right into him and knocked him down. He could tell I was angry and backed away.

When he asked how my Christmas went, I said, "Fine, now let's get on with the game."

I got home in time for supper. The table was set with Mom's finest silverware. Ben reheated the ham while I was at the gym. We finally sat down and ate a belated Christmas dinner. Everything was hunky dory. My mother and Ben had made peace. All would be well until he would have another one of his malaria attacks. I couldn't help but wonder how much money he lost at the track this time.

*   *   *

Without realizing it, Claudie and I took our frustrations out on the basketball court. We played the game with more intensity than anyone else. She was now playing for the Peoples National Bank girl's team. They traveled all over New England to play. Playing away didn't bother Claudie. She did everything she could to stay away from the house. What bothered her most was that she was supporting herself with what little money she could earn babysitting on weekends. If she had a weekend game, she had to play and couldn't babysit. It was difficult to pretend you lived like everyone else, when you didn't.

She did her best to mask her family life from her friends. Sometimes, that didn't work. If you're around someone all the time, they see through your façade. Such was the case with her teammates. One time they went to Massachusetts to play in a tournament. They planned to eat at a restaurant on the way back. Claudie didn't have money to eat in a restaurant. She was prepared to say she wasn't hungry again, although she was every bit as hungry as the other girls on the team. You can't get by on the oranges you suck in the locker room at half time.

As the team walked into the restaurant, her coach, Freddy Weeks, took Claudie aside. He took fifteen dollars out of his wallet and handed it to her. One of the girls on the team caught the flu and couldn't make the trip. Mary Jane Gamache gave coach Weeks the fifteen dollars for Claudie to have a meal at the restaurant. Claudie will never forget Mary Jane's act of kindness.

I was playing CYO basketball for the Our Lady of the Lakes team in Lakeport and for Saint Joseph's in the Saturday morning intramural league. Allie Drake and Bobby Johnson were playing on the Junior High team. We were best of friends, but not on the basketball court.

My most memorable moment ever on a basketball court happened on a Saturday morning at the High School gym. We were playing the Junior High team. They were supposed to be a better team than we were. After all, their team was made up of the best players from all the elementary schools in the area. We just came from one school. Nevertheless, we had played together for four years and could pretty well hold our own.

There were more people than usual watching the game that day. At the half, the Junior High team was up by six points. In the second half, we hung in there with good defense. I had a couple of steals and Jack Garneau held Allie Drake in check. He was usually their high scorer. With less than a minute to go, the score was tied.

The people watching were shouting with excitement. The other team threw a long pass down the court. I saw it coming and darted over to intercept it. I had possession of the ball. With time running out, I drove to the basket to make a lay-up. As I got near the hoop, there were four outstretched arms waiting to stop me. My reflexes took over. I dribbled under the basket and toward the out of bounds line to look for a teammate running down the lane. Nobody made a move toward the basket.

I thought, "If I take a turn-around jump shot, maybe someone will foul me."

I just heaved the ball in the direction of the basket without even looking. Swishhhhhhh. Basket! The horn sounded; game over. We won, 36-34. The place went wild. My teammates grabbed me and lifted me off the floor.

Then someone in the stands chanted, "Cousy . . . Cousy . . . Cousy."

Everyone picked up on that cry and joined in a chorus of "Cousy . . . Cousy . . . Cousy." From that day on, my new nickname became "Cousy." I loved it. I couldn't have been more honored. I became known as "Cousy" Virgin.

That season the Boston Celtics beat the Syracuse Nationals in the NBA playoffs. In the final playoff game they played in a quadruple overtime thriller. My idol, Bob Cousy, ended the game with 50 points. He made 30 out of 32 free throws that night. The game is regarded by the NBA as one of the finest scoring feats ever. "The Cooz" averaged 7.7 assists a game that season and won the NBA assist title. However, for the third time in a row, the Knics defeated the Celtics in the next round. I felt the Celtics desperately needed a scoring center.

On Tuesday, January 20, 1953, Dwight D. Eisenhower was sworn in as the 34th President of the United States. There was no school on Inauguration Day. Allie Drake invited me to an Inauguration party at Patty Blane's house in Lakeport. Allie was popular because he was a big shot athlete in Junior High. I went with Allie to the party to meet the so-called "in crowd" from Lakeport who were in his class.

They were friendly enough. I don't know if it was because I was with Allie or if I was "accepted" because both my sisters were varsity cheerleaders. That seemed to be the goal of every girl in high school. One thing made me skeptical about them though. I noticed that none of the Douglas boys or any of the other kids who raced on Belvidere Street was at the party. On second thought, maybe I didn't fit in with Allie's friends. Time would tell. I would be joining them at Laconia High in the fall.

Since we moved to Lakeport, I didn't have many opportunities to play with my friends from St. Joseph's. After school, I was stuck sweeping the school floors. That left little time for play. I did manage to see them at our Boy Scout meetings. One day that winter, Bobby Morin didn't show up for school. That was unlike him. I assumed he was sick. It was a lot worse than I would have ever imagined. I was shocked when I heard that Bobby's mother died. I simply couldn't believe it. She must have only been in her mid-40s. Why, she was my den mother in Cub Scouts. This couldn't happen to her. I didn't even know she was ill. That was the first time in my life that someone near and dear to me died. To think, she was my friend's mother. I felt so sad for Bobby. I felt his despair for the loss of a mother he would never see again. She was such a sweet lady.

The entire class went to Simoneau's Funeral Home to pay our respects to Mrs. Morin. I was without words. I simply hugged Bobby and we cried together.

I asked myself the question, "Why did God always have to take the good ones?"

In the early spring, Sister Bebianne asked me to be in the school play. That was quite an honor. Every year the school put on a play at the parish hall. It was a big event. Practically everyone in the parish went to the play. That year, we did "Les Miserables." It was all spoken in French. I played the role of the young son. A boy and girl who were students in the new Saint Joseph High School played the father and mother. We practiced and practiced for the play until I could recite my lines in my sleep. Finally, the first night of the annual school play arrived.

The parish hall was packed. It was exciting. I noticed Grammy and Grampy Garneau were in the audience. I didn't expect my mother and Ben to be there. As the saying goes, *"Blessed are those who expect nothing, for they shall not be disappointed."* So, I wasn't. However, I was thrilled when I looked down at the audience. Mrs. Ledoux was sitting in the very first row. That made all the practice worthwhile. I really hammed it up that night. When the gendarmes were carting my father away for stealing a loaf of bread, I went down on my knees and reached for him.

With my outstretched hands, I cried out, *"Papa, oh, mon Papa."*
I heard people in the audience gasping, "Ohhh."

That was the saddest moment in the play. I pulled it off! When it was over, Mrs. Ledoux came backstage and gave me a hug. She said I was marvelous. And, for a brief moment, I thought I was.

* * *

I never knew quite how well I was doing in school. We were all treated equally. Oh, we received report cards and kind of knew who the smart kids were. I put Maureen Wright at the top of that list. She was always studying. And Andy Belisle wasn't any slouch either. Although I rarely studied, learning came easy for me. My mother never had to go to the school to explain why I was falling behind in my studies. Actually, she never went to school for anything. I must have been doing O.K. I was always the last one standing in class when we had spelling contests. I'll admit, I was having a little trouble with Algebra. I didn't understand why I needed to do math that way.

One day, Father Chicoine showed up in our classroom and announced that he was taking the top five boys in the class to Assumption College in Worcester, Massachusetts, for academic tests. I was surprised to learn I was one of the boys selected.

The snow had completely melted when we arrived at the campus of Assumption College. We were staying there for two nights. The first day, we were given a tour of the campus and told the history of what was then known as Assumption High School and Assumption College. Later, we had dinner in the school cafeteria with the other students who came from all over New England to take the tests. I estimated there were about one hundred of us there.

I learned that Assumption High was a secondary boarding school operated by the Catholic order of Augustinians of the Assumption. It was closely associated with Assumption College. In fact, the school was located on the campus of Assumption College. We were told the instruction was French oriented and often given in the French language.

The priest giving the lecture also informed us that, "philosophically, the priests at the school emphasized using rational analysis in the pursuit of truth" . . . whatever that meant.

More importantly, he told us that basketball was the most popular sport in the school. Now, that had my attention. Perhaps that was influenced by the fact that Bob Cousy played his college ball at Holy Cross, on the other side of Worcester. Regardless, I really liked the campus and felt I would fit in well at Assumption.

After the dinner meal, the boys gathered in the school gym. When I made my way to the gym it was too crowded to play basketball.

Boys were just standing around in the middle of the court. It was a first class gym. I imagined myself playing there. There was an indoor track on the floor above the gym. That's the first one I had ever seen. Since the gym was crowded, I took off my shoes and ran around the track in my stocking feet.

We slept in the high school student dormitory. The students must have been home on spring break. Even though it was an open dorm, it didn't feel at all like Saint Vincent's. The beds were twin sized. Each student had an ample locker with his name on it behind his bed. The rooms had huge windows with plenty of light shining in. They also had a study room in the building and a "break" room with a television and a Ping-Pong table.

I thought to myself, "If they just had a pinball machine, I could make some nice spending money here."

The next day, we were up bright and early to take the tests. After a hearty breakfast, it was time to get down to business. Testing lasted all day. I didn't think the tests were particularly difficult, except I knew I missed some of the math questions. That evening, we were allowed to roam the campus again or spend time talking with the priests. I wanted to ask when we would know the test results, but I didn't. There was nothing to be gained by setting myself up for another disappointment. Even if I did well on the tests, I knew my mother wouldn't pay for me to go to this fancy prep school.

Father Chicoine arrived around noon the next day to take us back to Laconia. It was only a three hour drive, at most. However, when we arrived in Manchester he let us off on Elm Street. He told us he had business to attend to and would be back soon to pick us up. That was the longest "soon" I ever experienced. It was practically dark outside when he finally returned. We were anxious to get home. We were also hungry.

Father "Chic" took us to a real nice restaurant on the outskirts of Manchester. Here I was, thirteen years old, and had never been to a nice restaurant in my life. I made up for it that night. I must have eaten a half dozen of their delicious popover rolls. I didn't care what Father Chic or the other boys thought. I was going to cherish every moment of my fine dining experience. I finally arrived home around 9:30 p.m. Everyone was in bed, soundly asleep. I hung up my clothes, laid down, and dreamt about how wonderful it would be to go to school at Assumption High.

*   *   *

Even though it was late April, we still ran the furnace on cold days and nights. It wasn't uncommon to have temperatures in the low 20s that time of the year. Since we were renting the house in Lakeport, Ben probably never thought to ask the owners when the chimney was last cleaned. When you burned coal or wood in a furnace, I knew you should have your chimney checked and cleaned every year. We always had ours checked when we lived on Winter Street. Not just for our sake, but also for our tenants. My mother learned the hard way that the chimney in Lakeport hadn't been cleaned in a long time.

When I arrived home from school late that afternoon, the house was filled with smoke. The fire department had just left. My mother and Pudgie were safe. Windows were opened everywhere to let the smoke dissipate from the rooms. Ben was still at work. Claudie was helping my mother move furniture around. The smoke was so thick, I could barely make out their silhouetted figures on the other side of the room. I began coughing as soon as I entered the house. I was just thankful that nobody was hurt. Thank God, the chimney fire didn't happen at night when we were sleeping.

My mother declined the offer to stay with the Johnson's that night. She told Mrs. Johnson we would be fine. My eyes burned for several hours until the smoke found its way out the open windows. The odor from the smoke damage clung to our furniture for months and latched on to all the clothes we owned. Claudie and I had to wear our smoke-filled clothes to school the rest of the year. However, what some people saw as a misfortune, my mother saw as an opportunity.

For the next week, she feverishly documented everything that needed to be replaced because of the fire. She didn't miss a thing. She may have even added a few items that were stored in the barn. She recorded everything, down to the last handkerchief, and then some. This was an opportunity for her to "make well again" whatever was damaged by the smoke.

To me, this looked like some zealous form of entertainment for my mother. She was determined to squeeze every cent she could from her insurance claim. Unfortunately, she failed to recognize the damage done to Claudie's and my clothes. She didn't overlook Pudgie's though. Perhaps she forgot to add ours to her claim since she didn't buy them. I have no idea how much she collected from the insurance company, but it was obviously enough to purchase new furniture and clothes for her, Ben, and Pudgie.

*   *   *

The graduating class of 53'at Saint Joseph's had been together a long time. Most of the kids had been classmates since kindergarten. Soon, we would separate and go off in different directions. Some would remain at Saint Joseph's; others chose to break from the pack and go to Laconia High. I was in the latter group. Before we parted company, we decided to have a class graduation party. One last get-together.

Mrs. Ouellette offered to let us have the party in the basement of Mike's Diner:— on the condition we remove all the trash and clean the place first. We should have examined it before we agreed to hold it there. The place was a mess. That was a wise bargain on Mrs. Ouellette's part. No matter, we had fun working together cleaning the room and decorating it for the party. We never had a class party before. Now, we were a pack of frisky teenagers, ready to release all those pent up hormones.

It was one thing flirting with the girls at recess, but an entirely different matter when we were together in a dim lit room with soft music playing in the background. Most of the boys were shy and hung together on one side of the room. The girls stood on the other side, just waiting for the boys to ask them to dance. This party was going nowhere. Fortunately, my sisters taught me how to dance. I was their guinea pig when they were learning. Besides, I wasn't shy around girls. Someone had to break the ice and get this party off the ground.

Joyce Houle was fourteen, but could have passed for eighteen. Joyce was knockout good looking, stacked for her age, and very mature. She always had a smile for everyone and although I didn't know her that well, I always regarded her as a friend.

So, I went over to her and said, "Joyce, let's get this party going."

I grabbed her hand and we made our way to the middle of the room to dance. We danced to a slow song, then a fast one. Nobody joined in. It didn't take us long to realize that maybe the boys in our class didn't know how to dance. It's no wonder, we didn't have dance classes at the French Catholic School.

We turned the record player off for a moment, called everyone to the center of the room, and offered to teach them some basic dance steps. Mike's mother turned the record player back on and we proceeded to teach our classmates some basic moves. Soon everyone was ready to try dancing. I asked them to form a circle. Boys walked to the left. Girls walked to the right. Mrs. "O" operated the record player. As we walked in our circle, when the music stopped, we changed dance partners. When the music started again, we danced with a new partner. It worked. Before long, the boys were asking the girls to dance and everyone was mingling.

The party even got better when someone suggested we play spin-the-bottle. Mrs. Ouellette was our chaperone. She kept the game under control. Naturally, the boys were shy to kiss the girls in public. Likewise, some of the girls didn't want any part of that.

Nobody was forced to play and some of the kids chose not to. It was all just in fun. The party broke up by ten o'clock. Some kids had to be home by then; while others had their parents come by to pick them up. Mrs. "O" figured we partied enough. I sure enjoyed our one and only class party.

The final week of school, Sister Superior called me to her office. She sincerely thanked me for sweeping the school floors for the entire year. Then we had a somber conversation about my future. She was genuinely concerned for me.

She told me, "I want you to seriously tink about going to da Laconia High School."

She really meant well. It was her opinion that I would be lost in the big public school. She correctly declared, "Dere you going to be a small fish in a big pond."

She went on to let me know I would have a much more personalized education at Saint Joseph's. I heard what she was saying. I didn't doubt her at all. I knew she had my best interest at heart. Frankly, I was confused. At the time, I just wanted a change. I wanted to meet other people from different religions and different backgrounds. It was time for me to spread my wings.

The next day we had our class picture taken in our caps and gowns in front of the Sacred Heart church. Then we went to the parish hall to receive our diplomas. My mother didn't attend my graduation. *"Blessed are those who expect nothing, for they shall not be disappointed."* Little did I realize, this was an ending to an important chapter in my life. Looking back, I probably should have taken Sister Superior's advice.

CHAPTER 15

SOME YOU WIN, SOME YOU LOSE

How many times have you heard someone ask, "Do you want the bad news first or the good news first?"

More often than not, you take the bad news first. It's like saving the good news for dessert. In early June 1953, the bad news happened first. It came in the final week of school. The previous weekend had been unusually hot and muggy all over New England. Temperatures reached 90 degrees in the southern part of New Hampshire. That was very unusual. Back then, air-conditioning was unheard of in New Hampshire. No self-respecting right-minded Yankee would have an air conditioner in their home, even if they had been available.

It was Tuesday, June 9. Across the schoolyard, kids were talking about the killer tornado that touched down in Flint, Michigan, the night before. In class that day, Sister Bebianne told us that it was more than likely caused by some Atom bomb testing the Government had conducted just prior to the tornado. I was a bit skeptical about that. I hurried home to watch the news on TV to find out what really happened in Flint.

By the time I arrived home, the temperature had dropped at least 15 degrees from the previous day. It was now in the lower 70s. The heat spell was over. I watched the four o'clock news from Boston. What I learned was that at 8:30 p.m., the night before, a category F5 tornado struck the northern Flint community of Beecher, killing 116 people and injuring 844 more. Most people were at home, with their children in bed, when it hit. By the time people heard the storm's roar, their houses were being torn apart. It was the deadliest tornado in Michigan's history.

As I watched the news, the newscaster announced that the New England Weather Bureau has just issued a "severe thunderstorm watch" for western Massachusetts. No sooner had he uttered those words, when, at approximately 4:25 p.m., a tornado touched down in a forest near the town of Petersham, Massachusetts, and proceeded to move east through the towns of Rutland and Holden, where 11 people were killed. At around 5:00 p.m., it moved into the city of Worcester. By then, the tornado had grown to a mile wide path as it ripped right through the campus of Assumption College and a nearby large residential development. The funnel maintained its 48-mile path as it passed through Shrewsbury, Westborough, and finally killing three more people when the Post Office collapsed in Southborough. Around the time it ended, at 5:45 p.m., 84 minutes later, a tornado warning was issued. Far too little; far too late.

When it was all said and done, the tornado that touched down in western Massachusetts that day accounted for 94 deaths and over 1,300 injuries as it traveled on its 48-mile journey. Some 10,000 people were left homeless. Later, it was learned that the Weather Bureau didn't use the word "tornado" in their broadcast for fear of "unnecessarily exciting the public."

I didn't understand things like a high-pressure mass in the north, colliding with a low-pressure mass from the south to cause the conditions for a tornado. This was New England. We weren't supposed to have tornadoes. That only happened in places like Texas, Oklahoma, and Kansas. Like many others, I just couldn't believe what happened. I couldn't help but recall my time on the Assumption College campus, just two months before. My dream was gone. There would be no Assumption High School in my future. It was like losing one of my own when I heard that a priest and two nuns from Assumption were killed in the tornado.

I couldn't help but wonder, "Why did God choose them?" I didn't sleep that night.

The next day, our Boy Scout leader called an emergency meeting after school. He asked for volunteers to go to Massachusetts on Saturday to help with clean-up operations in one of the towns that had been devastated by the tornado. Every single scout volunteered. I looked forward to it. That's what scouting was all about.

We arrived in the town of Shrewsbury by 8:00 a.m. that Saturday. I had never seen mass devastation like that before. Even at that early hour, the town was packed with volunteers from all over

New England who came, like us, to help out in any way they could. There was plenty of work for everyone. I gazed around in awe, like a farm boy in the middle of New York City, at the destruction that surrounded me. Roofs were torn off houses, windows were blown out, people were living in tents, and trees were down everywhere. I was assigned to a group of Scouts whose job was to pick up fallen tree limbs and branches and put them in piles at designated locations.

Everybody worked very hard that day. In some small way, I felt proud to be doing my part to help bring this town back on its feet. One thing really struck me that I'll never forget. Conspicuously noticeable, in the middle of town, was a white catering truck with a big red cross painted on the side. I had been told the Red Cross was always there when a disaster struck to help the poor victims. Perhaps they did.

Nevertheless, I was appalled when I heard they were selling coffee to the volunteers for fifty cents a cup. Fifty cents a cup for a small cup of coffee, served in a paper cup. And, this was in 1953. I was informed they did this to raise more funds to help with their ongoing emergency assistance. I couldn't believe it. Neither could other volunteers who gave their time and energy to help the poor tornado victims. Many of the volunteers were infuriated about that. A minister from one of the local churches was so irate, he had members of his congregation hand out free coffee and water to anyone who wanted some.

I was hungry when I got home late that night. A few free cups of water and a doughnut was all I had to eat that day. I rummaged through the refrigerator and ate whatever wasn't tied down. It had been a long day, but a very satisfying one. I felt grateful I was able to help those people. As I lay on my bed on the front porch, all the scenes of devastation I had seen earlier that day flashed before me. Soon I was sound asleep.

*   *   *

That was the bad news for the summer of 53.' The good news came a week later.

I was sitting in my mother's rocking chair on the front porch, bored out of my mind. Motorcycles were roaring down Union Avenue when Claudie burst into the room.

"Sonny, I've got some good news for you," she announced.

Semi-concerned, I inquired, "What's that, Sis?"

She told me that Jimmy Smith was selling his Soapbox racer. Jimmy had one of the fastest racecars in Lakeport. He didn't win the championship the previous year, but still managed to win several races on Belvidere Street. That got my attention. I stood up and began discussing the prospect of buying his racecar with my sister. He was in her class in high school. In fact, they were good friends. That's how she found out he was planning to sell it. Jimmy was sixteen now and was working at his father's Goodyear station.

Technically, you couldn't race in the Soapbox Derby after you reached sixteen. Besides, he didn't need the money since he was working full-time for his father. I didn't have to think about it. I knew this was a gift from God. I took off like a rocket and ran down the street to the Goodyear station. When I got there, Jimmy was changing a tire.

I ran past the sign that read, "No Entry Beyond This Point," right to where he was working.

When he looked up at me, I asked, "Jimmy, can I buy your race car?"

He told me he wanted $15 for it. What a bargain. I'm sure the tires practically cost that much. I asked him to hold it for me, I'd be back shortly with the money.

Until then, I hadn't even thought about how I was going to pay for it. I just knew I never wanted anything as much as I did that racecar in my entire life. I just had to have it. I had a total of thirty-four cents to my name. I didn't have a paper route. I didn't have any money. There was only one place where I could get it.

Getting money from my mother was like getting blood from a rock. It didn't matter. She was my only hope. I ran back to the house from the Goodyear station. Mom was ironing clothes in the kitchen.

"Mom, Mom," I pleaded. "You got to help me. Please, Please."

Of course, she told me she didn't have any money. And, she just had to let me know how foolish it was for me to buy Jimmy Smith's

185

racecar. It's not as if I was asking her to *give* me the money. I was asking her to *loan* me $15. After awhile, she realized this meant everything in the world to me.

She softened up. I kept the pressure on. I pleaded with her that I needed the money now, before anyone else found out it was for sale. She heard the urgency in my plea.

She finally relented and said the magic words, "O.K."

I jumped for joy as she went to her secret stash to retrieve the money. Before handing it over to me, she made sure I understood that this was a *loan*, not a *gift*. I promised to pay her back by the beginning of September. She recalled I made money racing in Laconia the previous summer. I assured her I would do anything she wanted, just to get that loan.

With the $15 clenched in the palm of my hand, I ran back to the Goodyear station. Number 38 was parked in the back of the station. It was gorgeous. The body was painted a bright yellow, with red lettering. The name "JIM" was painted in red letters on the side of the racecar. Perhaps, that was a signal that someday I would, in fact, bear the name, Jim. Jimmy handed me the rope used to steer the racecar. I handed him the money. The deal was done. I was beaming from ear to ear as I pulled my new racecar into the barn. It was one of the happiest moments of my life. I was so ecstatic; I wanted to sleep in it that night.

A few weeks later, the Soapbox-racing season was underway. Nobody knew who had bought Jimmy Smith's racecar. They soon learned when they saw this scrawny little kid, who had never raced on the steep hill before, pulling number 38 up the hill before the start of the race. The Douglas boys recognized me. I beat them in Laconia the last race of the season. They were the reigning champions in Lakeport.

The Douglas boys were a dynasty in Lakeport Soapbox Derby racing. First, there was Willie Douglas, who graduated with Lorraine. Next, there was John, who was in Claudie's class. Then, there was Donald, who was a year older than I was. He was the reigning champion. And then, there was the youngest brother, Norman, who was my age. This was a tight knit family. The boys helped each other build their racecars as they passed the torch from one brother to the other. Their garage was always filled with racecars. I often played at their house when I lived in Lakeport. We were friends, but we were competitors on race day. We understood that. I had a great deal of respect for them. Now, all I had to do was figure a way to beat them.

We pulled numbers out of Dan Clare's hat to see who would race against each other in the first heat. Wouldn't you know it. I was pitted against Norm Douglas in my first race on Belvidere Street. I was an unknown. The crowd was yelling for Norm to beat me. When our race began, he immediately steered to the center of the street. In fact, he pushed my car to the side to secure the best position. Short of causing a crash, I had to remain to his right. He beat me by a car length. I was done racing for the night. That meant no prize money for me. That's all right. I learned a few things that night. First: Although the course was much faster than the one in Laconia, I wasn't afraid. Second: I needed to steer to the middle as quickly as possible, even if that meant pushing the other racer aside. Third: No doubt in my mind, I had a fast car. All I needed was a little more experience.

Before the next race, I spent every spare moment cleaning my wheel bearings and spinning my tires. It was still too cold to swim in Lake Opoohoo. I didn't want to do anything but prepare for the next race. I raised #38 off the floor in the barn and placed it on top of two wooden crates. Then, I took a towel and spun my tires in a forward direction for hours on end. The more I spun, the longer they turned before coming to a complete stop. I assumed that would make my racecar go faster. That proved to be a good assumption.

Just before the race began, Dick Wells warned me he overheard some of the racers were intentionally going to try to put me in a ditch. Simply, they were going to turn their wheels sharply into my car and force me off the course. I wanted to race fairly. However, if that's the way they wanted to play the game, I was up to the challenge. I may have been scrawny, but it would be a big mistake to assume I wasn't scrappy. I was fearless when it came to racing. For me, it wasn't only about winning. More importantly, it was about making money to support myself. I was already thinking ahead about all the clothes I would need for my freshman year in high school.

Sure enough, in the first heat, the other driver assured his friends he was going to put me in the ditch. When the whistle blew and the race began, I immediately steered right into the other driver's car. I pushed him to the left side. Our tires were locked as we gained speed. I refused to move over, and so did he. I had a faster car. Soon, the sheer weight and speed of my car pushed him away from me. The crowd roared. After all, that's what they came to see. Number 38 crossed the finish line first.

I won my first heat. I won my second heat. The new kid on the block made it to the final heat. People were patting me on the back and offering their congratulations as I pulled my racecar up the sidewalk to the top of the hill. I don't recall who I raced against in the final heat that day. It was a clean race. We were neck and neck clear to the bottom. We were both flying as we crossed the finish line. I didn't know who won until I turned my car around in the wide circle at the bottom of Belvidere Street. It didn't take long to find out.

Dan Clare approached me with that big infectious smile of his, shook my hand, and said, "Nice going kid."

I sensed he was glad that someone new had arrived on the scene to shake up the local racers. I was truly humble. I couldn't tell you the number of times I thought about winning a big race in Lakeport. That was my goal. I reached it that afternoon. Of course, the money helped too. I didn't have to share it with anyone. I won over five dollars. I couldn't have been happier.

That was my focus in the summer of 53.' Every Wednesday night and Sunday afternoon, I could be found racing down Belvidere Street. Soon, I was a crowd favorite. I found my passion. I even thought perhaps racing might be in my future when I grew up. Until then, I had no idea what I wanted to do after I graduated from high school. For sure, I didn't want to work in the foundry or the shoe factory.

What I gained on Belvidere Street, I never got at home. I earned the respect of my fellow racers and even the people in the crowd. They gave me the recognition I yearned for. Maybe it was just for a fleeting moment. However, I got it when I needed it most. I just wanted someone's approval. I got that on Belvidere Street in the summer of 53.'

I heard the thrill of racing gets in your blood. It does. I tried to win at all costs. Other racers learned to stay clear away from me when we raced down the hill. I was a clean racer . . . as long as my competitor raced the same way. Sometimes, accidents just happened. Like the Sunday I had to race against my neighbor, Bobby Johnson. Bobby just finished building his racecar. As I recall, it may have been his first race on the hill. I know he didn't mean to get his wheels stuck with mine, any more than I meant to push him off the street. It couldn't have happened at a worse spot.

Bobby lost control of his racecar as he headed for the wooden fence on the left side of the hill. He crashed through the fence and dropped some 15 feet, head first, into the garden below, while I went on to finish the race. When he hit the fence, his racecar shattered into a million pieces and wooden shards flew in every direction. Unfortunately, Bobby had a serious crash and had to be taken to the hospital in an ambulance. Fortunately, nothing was broken. He dislocated his shoulder and had his arm in a sling for the rest of the summer. That was racing. I always reminded myself that I could be run over by a car crossing the street. I just felt terrible that I happened to be the one he was racing against when it happened.

The final race of the season took place on a Wednesday evening in late August. It was well publicized. The largest crowd of the year was there. Racers came out of the woodwork for that one. Racers I had never seen before showed up for the championship race. Even the state Soapbox Derby champion was there. He had on the championship jacket he wore at the national championship in Akron, Ohio. First prize for the Lakes Region championship winner was a new pair of skis.

This race would be different. A stopwatch would decide it. There would be no one on one racing. Dan Clare stood at the finish line. As each racer went down the hill, Dan clocked their time. After everyone finished their run, two racers were tied with the fastest time: Donnie Harris and me. Donnie hadn't raced all season. He was sixteen and a junior in high school. We each raced down the course in 22 seconds on our first run.

There was a mob at the top of the hill as we prepared for the runoff. I hadn't met Ned Robertson before, but he came up to me, took off his championship jacket, and had me wear it for "good luck" on my final run. We flipped a coin. Donnie Harris went first. He was

189

timed in 23 seconds. It was up to me. I heard the roar of the crowd as I sped down the hill.

After I crossed the finish line, I heard the announcer shout over the loud speaker, "Sonny Virgin wins the race with a time of 22 seconds in his second run."

I held back my tears. I thought for a moment, "The hand of God made all this possible."

I was mobbed at the finish line as I waited for the presentation of the trophy and the award of my new pair of skis. Dan Clare handed me a new pair of Lund skis. They were beautiful, but a bit too long for me. Dan then told me the Douglas's "forgot" to bring the trophy with them to the race. He assured me he'd get it from them and bring it to me in the next few days. I was disappointed. I had never won a trophy. This one was special. I really wanted to have it to take home to show it to my mother.

Claudie wasn't at the race that night, but the word spread like wildfire that her little brother won the Lakes Region Soapbox Derby Championship. Her friends told her I won. She ran home and told Mom and Ben. By the time I got home, in the dark of night, with my racecar and new pair of skis in tow, they already knew. My mother smiled when I entered the living room. I don't think she knew what to say. She probably had never won anything.

Finally, she said, "Good for you, Sonny."

Ben didn't know what to say. He just sat there with the usual frown on his forehead. For all I know, he might have been jealous of me. I was walking on a cloud.

Every time I saw Dan Clare in Lakeport square, I asked him about the trophy. I kept getting the same answer. He kept telling me the Douglas's were supposed to bring it to him. After awhile, I knew they weren't going to give it up. I lost respect for them. If it meant that much to them to keep something they didn't win, then they can have it.

I knew I won. Everyone there that night knew I won. It was even in the Laconia Citizen. The next Sunday, I went to church and thanked God for making that all possible. Summer would soon be over. I earned enough money racing that summer to pay my mother back in four weeks and was able to buy some clothes for school with the rest of my winnings. It was becoming cold at night in late August. My new jacket would soon come in handy.

Before returning to school, I went to visit Lorraine at her new apartment on Arch Street. Ironically, she rented the apartment from Ralph Carignan's dad. I knew Roland Carignan. He was a nice man. I raced his son's Soapbox racer in Laconia the year before. Lorraine was still decorating her place when I visited her. She was as strong and independent as ever, and a bit worldlier. By then, she was into jazz and collecting jazz albums to listen to when she wasn't working. Obviously, Aunt Mildred had been a positive influence on my big sister.

We picked up right where we left off. She was always interested in how I was doing. I told her about my Soapbox Derby escapades. She was delighted to hear I won the big race. Before I left her apartment, she reiterated that if I ever needed help, she'd be there for me. Those words made me feel good. Had she been in Laconia in June, I would have asked her to loan me the money to buy my racecar. I could always depend on Lorraine.

There was just one more piece of business to take care of before heading back to school. It would be a long winter. I didn't have a job. I knew I needed money to go skiing with my new skis. I read in the Citizen that they were holding a talent contest at the street fair in the parking lot next to Laconia High. First prize was $25. I was on a roll. Why, I had just won the Soapbox Derby. The $25 sure would come in handy. Besides, I thought I was a pretty good singer. Time was wasting. I only had a couple of days to prepare for the contest. I picked the popular ballad, "You Belong To Me" to sing in the contest. The song, sung by both Patti Page and Jo Stafford, had been at the top of the billboards for most of the summer and fall of 1952. I knew it well. It was my kind of song.

I must admit, I was nervous the night of the contest. Singing in church, hiding in the choir box, was one thing. This was at night, at a crowded street fair. To make matters worse, I was the first contestant called to perform on the elevated stage. When I got up there, I felt awkward. I made the mistake of looking at the crowd standing below. Suddenly, a blinding spotlight was shining in my eyes. I couldn't think. The words didn't come out. I panicked.

191

I stood before the crowd, totally embarrassed. What seemed like forever was probably only thirty seconds or so. I tried to compose myself and begin the song again. The words just wouldn't come out of my mouth. I felt like I had swallowed glue. I had a case of that entertainer's illness known as "stage fright." The crowd was polite. They must have sensed my embarrassment. Finally, I shrugged my shoulders in defeat and walked off the stage. That was the last time I ever tried to sing in public.

CHAPTER 16

WHAT I LEARNED, I DIDN'T LEARN IN SCHOOL

I vividly recall my first day in high school. I was just another naïve, bug-eyed freshman about to begin a very important chapter of my life. I didn't realize that at the time. I walked into the main building of the Laconia High School complex without even considering the far-reaching implications of the choices I would make that day. Like my peers, my focus was on how I looked and how I'd be accepted in this new fraternity of students.

The students who transferred from the Catholic schools to the public high school were definitely outsiders. Especially those that came from the French school. We weren't accepted with open arms by the other students or the teachers. I honestly felt they resented us. I honestly believed, Protestants saw the French Catholics as inferior working class oddballs.

I felt a strange uneasiness from the minute I walked into the building. I didn't recognize anyone and didn't know where to go. Other kids were talking and hugging each other like long lost friends. The main corridor was blocked by students digesting bits of information on sheets of paper taped to the hallway wall. I overheard someone tell another boy his homeroom number. Soon, I realized there were four separate sections with homeroom assignments plastered on the wall. Above, in bold letters, one of the signs read, "FRESHMAN." We were assigned to homerooms in alphabetical order. I was assigned to one of the S through Z groups. It would remain that way for the next four years.

I pushed my way through the crowded corridor to find my homeroom. On my way there, I noticed the rows of double lockers lining the walls of the corridors. Claudie told me that freshmen had to share lockers. I didn't see anyone's name from the French school on my homeroom list and didn't know how lockers were assigned. The one thing I did recognize on my way there was the basketball court. For some odd reason, it was like finding a familiar friend. I felt comfortable knowing my homeroom was located next to the gym.

Although I had played many basketball games at the high school, I never went into any of the other rooms, except the boy's locker room. That first day in high school, I was in awe, confused, and excited, all at the same time.

There was a flurry of activity when I entered my homeroom. Virtually all the other kids in the room knew one another and were quickly selecting locker mates for the coming year. Nobody spoke to me. They were too engaged talking to their old friends. Soon, I realized all these kids knew each other from junior high and had been going to school in this building for the past two years. Many of them had been together for the past eight years. I was the only transfer from the French school in the room.

I took a seat toward the back and waited for the bell to ring. Finally, I recognized someone from the Irish Catholic School. I played basketball against Paul Slayton before. I liked him then; I liked him even more now. Nothing like a familiar face to make you feel a bit at home. He recognized me too.

He greeted me with a, "Hi Cooz," and we shook hands.

Paul took a seat in the next aisle close to mine. Somewhere in our conversation, he invited me to share a locker with him. I agreed. He told me he'd bring a combination lock to school for us to share the next day. Great! I made a new friend my first day in school.

At St. Joseph's, we sat in the same classroom, with the same students, for the entire year. The curriculum was predetermined. There were no study halls, or library, or industrial arts classrooms. There were no after school activities, except sports, at St. Joseph's. I didn't know such things as a Drama club, Key club, Radio club, Science club, Spanish club, and so on even existed. High school was a whole new experience. I just assumed you went to class, and then went home after school, unless you played on the football team. I was definitely confused. I quickly had to learn my way around the campus.

The Laconia High campus consisted of two buildings. The main building housed the academic classrooms, the school offices, the gym, and the library. An underground tunnel ran between the two buildings. The other building was called the Industrial Arts building. The school cafeteria was in the basement of that building. All the vocational classes were taught in the rooms above. They included such things as Printing, Mechanical Drawing, Sheet Metal, Woodworking, Typing, and the Home Economics classes. Behind the two buildings were the football field and practice field. Parking near the school was reserved for the faculty. Students with cars parked along Dewey Street, adjacent to the rear of the Industrial Arts building. Back then, not many students owned cars, so a student parking lot wasn't necessary.

Oh, if only I could do it over again today. I didn't have any guidance whatsoever in selecting my courses in high school. I didn't know that Guidance Counselors existed. No one told me. They never made an appearance in our homeroom to offer any guidance. Later, I learned that the students who went to Junior High at the high school had already selected their courses. They may have had counseling. Better yet, they may have had parents to help them select their courses and mark a path for their future.

Then, there were the kids like me, whose parents didn't care. I didn't have a human compass to help me through the maze. I was on my own. For instance, I didn't know they taught both college prep English and basic freshman English. In hindsight, I guess it didn't matter. I was from the other side of the tracks and wasn't going to college anyway.

Without any guidance, I signed up for English, Applied Math, Social Studies, and Printing. The only plausible reason I took Printing was that I thought I'd learn how to operate the big printing presses at the Laconia Citizen. The other courses were selected because they were a logical continuation of the courses I had at St. Joseph's. That was it. Nothing too challenging there. I didn't anticipate having any trouble excelling in those classes. Furthermore, I didn't have any idea what I wanted to do after I finished high school. All I knew is what I didn't want to do. I wasn't about to follow in my mother's or Ben's footsteps to work in the sweatshops in Laconia.

The next day at school, I saw Paul in our homeroom. He told me, "Sorry, Cooz, I forgot to bring the lock."

I didn't think much about it, except I just bought a brand new jacket to wear on those cold fall days and nights. I never forgot the time my jacket was stolen at the Opechee Park clubhouse Halloween party when I was seven years old. So, even though it was a warm September day, I carried my jacket around the school with me all day.

My first class of the day was English. That was my favorite subject. I always won the Spelling Bee at St. Joseph's and knew I did well on the Reading and Comprehension section of the exam I took at Assumption a few months earlier. Here was a course I could excel in. I expected to be one of the top students in that class. Unfortunately, as I entered the room, all the seats in the front were already occupied by what I referred to as the "freshman clique," so I had to find a place in the back of the room.

From there, I couldn't read what was written on the blackboard. To complicate matters, the teacher spoke with a soft voice that was hardly audible to those of us in the back of the room. Frankly, I didn't like the teacher. To me, he was conceited and self-centered. He struck me as a misplaced college professor, who probably resented the fact he wasn't assigned to teach one of the college prep English courses.

Even though I knew the answers to his questions, he never called on me. He directed his attention to the first few rows in the class. I usually had to ask someone sitting next to me to tell me the assignment. Even with these disadvantages, I assumed I'd do well on his tests and end up with a good grade in the end.

My next class was Applied Math. To arrive at class on time, I had to run from the far east corner of the second floor to the far west corner of the third floor. Mr. Spurr was a good teacher. He genuinely cared for his students. If I didn't do well in his class, it wouldn't be his fault. Again, I found myself sitting toward the back of the room, barely able to read the blackboard. Applied Math was a snap. What was being taught, I had already learned by the sixth grade at St. Joseph's. Unlike Algebra, this was practical math. Add, subtract, multiply, and divide. How difficult could that be? I saw this as another easy course. Perhaps, I should have signed up for something more difficult. I should have tried to change courses, but I didn't know how to go about doing that.

Those were my two morning classes. Before the lunch period, I had a study period in the school cafeteria. We were told to sit quietly at our assigned table and study. That didn't work well for me. I was a chatterbox. I couldn't sit still in study hall. Looking back, I was immature. My mind wasn't being challenged, so why study? I was genuinely interested in world affairs. So, what I wanted to know, I learned by watching the evening news on television or reading the newspaper. If I ever needed guidance, it was now.

I only smelled the food in the school cafeteria. I didn't have money to buy lunch. At the end of the study period, when the students were forming a line waiting for the cafeteria to open, I either went outside to mingle with the older boys smoking behind the school building or ran to Cyr's Donut Shop to kill time until my next class. Claudie and her friends were crammed in a booth at Cyr's during the same lunch break. Oddly enough, we didn't speak to each other. She was too preoccupied with her friends, or perhaps I embarrassed her.

I went into the other room and watched the upperclassmen play the pinball machine. I wanted to play against them, but didn't. I couldn't afford to lose. Consequently, I went all day without eating anything. It's no wonder I was always hyperactive and couldn't concentrate.

Printing class was a disaster. What a disappointment. I didn't know what to expect; however, I expected more to it than standing for an entire period and placing small metal fonts into a tray, much like aligning the letters on a Scrabble tray.

All they had was one old, antiquated manually operated printing press. That was it. You had to squeeze ink out of a tube onto the press plate and spread it around. Then, you placed your formed letters into a tray and lowered the press. Magically, your letters were transposed to paper and printed. Wow! Now, that was boring. After the first day, I realized this class lacked any substance and I was in for a long, boring year hiding behind alphabet trays, trying to stay awake. The Printing teacher certainly didn't add any excitement to the class.

It didn't take me long to get in trouble at Laconia High. It didn't even take me a week. While, Mr. Volkman was away from the room, the boys in the Printing class were throwing those little metal fonts at each other. Everybody was doing it. About the time I heaved one across the room, Mr. Volkman opened the door and my little font hit him in the head.

"Oh shit," I said to myself.

From that day on, I qualified for Mr. Volkmann's "shit list." I was sent to the Principal's office and had to explain to the Assistant Principal why I was there. In one week, I made the list of "students who needed to be monitored." I couldn't have planned a worse beginning in high school.

My Social Studies class wasn't any better. There were mostly boys in that class. At least there were mostly boys who sat together in the back of the class. We were disruptive. I was as bad as the rest. I sat in the middle of a group of boys who would barely make it through high school, if they didn't quit when they turned sixteen. Unfortunately, I was popular with that group of classmates. I let myself be sucked into being a wise guy. I was warned to keep my mouth shut in class. I didn't listen very well. My report card reflected that.

But, back to the third day of school. My locker mate, Paul Slayton, asked to speak with me outside our homeroom before the school bell rang. I could tell Paul was very uncomfortable talking to me that morning.

He finally blurted it out. "Cooz, I want to be your friend, but my father won't let me share a locker with you," he said.

To that, I sucked in a deep breath and sheepishly replied, "Oh, that's all right, Paul. I understand."

No I didn't. I didn't understand a damn thing. I was stunned. I didn't understand why his father disliked me. Paul's father was Detective Slayton of the Laconia Police Department. I had never been in trouble with the law. Did he not want his son befriending me because of my mother's reputation? I don't know. All I know is that my feelings were hurt. I was dumbfounded. So was Paul. I could tell he was embarrassed and honestly didn't know or wouldn't tell me why his father disliked me. Without any further discussion, we knew we would secretly remain friends. We just couldn't be seen together.

What an inauspicious beginning. In one week, I had fallen from being one of the top students at a rigid private parochial school to one of the bottom students, with a handful of easy courses, at the local public high school. Like a knight, I had fallen off my horse and was trampled by the herd of hoofs passing by. I couldn't help but recall Sister Superior's wise words that I would be "swallowed up like a little fish in a big pond" if I went to Laconia High.

As the weeks passed, I made a half-hearted attempt to improve in school, especially in English. I read my assignments. I did my homework. I really tried, but that didn't matter. In hindsight, I believe I was discriminated against by the teacher. After awhile, I quit raising my hand in class. No matter how hard I tried, I was labeled a "C" student in his class. I was discouraged. Above all, I was discouraged because I didn't know how to fight back.

My pride got in the way. I knew I deserved at least a "B," but I wasn't about to kiss his ass to get it. I simply resigned myself to the fact he favored the cute girls in the "freshman clique," who sat in the front of his class. I also came to believe, for the most part, grades were assigned based on your parent's standing in the community. There were truly some kids that I thought were dumber than dirt that got better grades than I did. I couldn't help but notice that their parents were upstanding leaders in the community or owned a local business. On the other hand, I didn't help my cause by being disruptive in some of my classes. I had some growing up to do. I certainly could have used a good mentor.

When the first report cards came out, I got "Cs" in English and Math and "Ds" in Printing and Social Studies. Not a very good beginning. My Social Studies teacher, Soc Bobotas, warned me to quit disrupting the class. Printing was a given. I could have printed the Guttenberg Bible and still would have received a "D." Frankly, that's what I deserved. Without realizing it, I was slowly giving up.

By December, I didn't even take schoolbooks home. I completed homework assignments sporadically, when I felt like it. Mostly, I relied on tests to establish my grades. I was shutting down. I was rejecting the establishment. Why work hard for a grade and be disappointed when you don't achieve it? Why, I could cruise through high school and get "C"s. Nobody cared about me, but me. And, after awhile, I didn't even care.

*   *   *

However, I soon learned someone did care about me. Much to my surprise, I was approached by the local Veterans of Foreign Wars (VFW) organization. They wanted to sponsor me in the state Soapbox Derby Championship, the following summer. Soapbox racing was at its peak in the state of New Hampshire and Laconia wanted to claim a winner. I was the logical choice to bring home the bacon since I won the big race in Lakeport. You would have expected I would be jumping with joy at the offer. I didn't. It required a big commitment on my part. I wasn't sure I could fulfill it.

It was one thing to win the big race in Lakeport in a racecar I never built. It was quite another to expect me to build a racecar capable of winning the state championship. I was not mechanically inclined. I didn't have a place at home to build a racecar. I didn't have any tools. My old #38 wouldn't work. It didn't meet the official Soapbox Derby requirements. For instance, in Lakeport, I steered by pulling ropes from the outside of the car. The official Derby rules required that I have a steering wheel mounted inside the car. I would have to build a new Soapbox racecar from scratch.

Initially, I declined their offer. They persisted. They were determined to have me race their car in the big race in Manchester. I wasn't naïve, but perhaps they were? I realized the only reason they were courting me was because I won the Lakes Region championship. If I hadn't won that race, they wouldn't give me the time of day. That's how it goes when you're a winner.

Finally, they had the former state champion, Ned Robertson, approach me. His family had recently moved to Laconia from Dover, New Hampshire, the previous summer. Ned was now a senior in high school. I didn't really know Ned, but he offered to help me build it in his basement on Morrill Street. They even assigned a VFW representative to the project to coordinate with me. Sort of like a big brother. What I really needed was someone to guide me step-by-step through the process of building a new racecar. The project didn't quite go the way I hoped it would.

Money wasn't a problem. The VFW even purchased two sets of official Soapbox Derby tires so I could select the best four. I built my racecar in Ned's basement. Initially, that was fine. He gave me good advice and had all the tools I needed. But the honeymoon didn't last long. Within a month, I found myself alone in his basement trying to build a car capable of winning the state championship.

I felt awkward going to the Robertson's after school. Ned's parents worked during the day. I felt like I was breaking into their house whenever I went over there. Nobody was there but me. When they were home, they never spoke to me. They stayed upstairs and I stayed in the basement. It was an uncomfortable situation. I didn't know these people, yet, I was invading their privacy. I am sure they just wanted me to finish what I was doing and get to hell out of their house.

When it was all said and done, it took me seven months to build my racecar. It wasn't nearly as nice as the laminated racecar Ned won the state championship with, but it was the best I could do. I wasn't satisfied with the end product. I envisioned building a car that looked like a bullet that would provide wind resistance. Unfortunately, I didn't know how to round the frame and work with aluminum, so I had to settle for a teakwood "V" shaped racecar. The one thing I did know how to do well was break in the tires. I spent countless hours in the Robertson's basement, spinning and spinning and spinning those tires. If anything, that would be my winning formula.

*   *   *

Besides building my racecar, other things were happening in the fourteenth year of my life. After all, I was a budding teenager too. I looked forward to the high school football games on Friday nights. More than the game, I really looked forward to the dances in the gym after the game. While other kids struggled on the dance floor, dancing came naturally to me. I felt very at ease out there. That was my turf. I was in a world of my own, sashaying and swaying, while leading some cute little freshman girl around the dance floor.

I expressly said "little" for a reason. My freshman year, I was all of 5'1" tall and tipped the scales at a hefty 111 pounds. I had to be a good dancer. I sure didn't have much else going for me. Since I had to buy my own clothes, I was dreadfully limited in the wardrobe department. I didn't have nice pressed khaki slacks, with different colored button down Hathaway shirts for every day of the week, or the preppy white bucks to wear to school or to the dances like many of the other boys in school.

I had three shirts to my name, a pair of blue and a pair of black faded khaki pants, one pair of jeans, and those god-awful stinking high top sneakers I wore every day. The only "cool" thing I had to wear was the red and white nylon jacket I bought a few weeks before school started. I thought it was "cool" because red and white were the school colors. Not to mention, half the school wore one just like it.

Of course, I was self-conscious, but I just figured I wasn't the only one. I knew who to ask to dance and who not to ask. Oh, I would have loved to rest my head on some tall girl's breast, as we waltzed around the floor to some of those popular soft tunes in 53' like, "Till I Waltz Again With You," "I Believe," "Ebb Tide," Nat King Cole's, "Pretend," or "Tell Me Your Mine," by the Gaylords. Both 1953 and 1954 were great years for that nice, slow, easy going, serenade style music. It would almost make me want to have a girlfriend. However, I didn't. I couldn't afford anything like that. All I wanted to do was dance; that didn't cost money.

One Friday night, I didn't make it to the dance after the football game. I vaguely remember going to the football game. Something called "Vat-69 hard cider" got in my way that night. I had never drunk plain cider, let alone hard cider before. One of my friends told me we could buy some at Frank's market in Lakeport to sneak into the game. Why not? I was as adventurous as any other teenager.

Three of us went into the store and we each went to the counter with a quart bottle of Vat-69 cider in our hand.

As soon as we laid the cider on the counter, the clerk informed us, "Sorry boys, I can't sell it to you. It's alcohol."

We left the store and plotted a strategy to buy the hard cider. About an hour later, we returned after a new clerk was behind the counter.

My friend told the clerk, "Hey, I'm looking for Larry's root beer in a quart bottle, but I can't seem to find it."

After going to the shelf where all the soda was displayed, the clerk returned with the bad news we were hoping to hear.

As though he expected we'd be disappointed, he dutifully informed us, "I don't see any there. I'll look out back."

Score one for us. We knew all along it didn't come in quart size bottles. While the clerk went into the back room to search for Larry's root beer in quart bottles, the three musketeers stuffed the quarts of hard cider inside our jackets. To our chagrin, he returned to inform us he couldn't locate that particular brand of root beer in the back room. We left the store with looks of disappointment on our faces.

We giggled and laughed all the way to the game, totally oblivious to the consequences of our transgression, had we been caught. After we bought our ticket to the game and passed through the gate, we made a mad dash to the grass area under the bleachers. Obviously, it wasn't feasible to take jugs of hard cider to our seats in the stands. Sitting under the bleachers, while the Laconia High Sachems were being trounced by a superior football team from Portsmouth, the three of us proceeded to drink all our stolen hard cider as the game played on. I swallowed it like sap out of a maple tree. It had a dizzying effect. After a few swigs of the forbidden drink, it went down ever so smoothly. In no time at all, I was drunk. I could barely stand up. The three of us were laughing and vomiting at the same time.

There's always some creep to ruin a good party. Big sister Claudie was the Captain of the cheerleading squad. She was on the Laconia team sideline getting ready to yell out another cheer, when one of her friends told her, "Claudie, I think your little brother is getting wasted under the bleachers."

Before I knew it, Claudie had her finger in my face, yelling at me to "get your ass home now."

I could barely stand up, so I knew I wasn't going home until I straightened out. However, we had our warning. We had enough sense to realize we needed to get off school property. So, that night, my drinking buddies and I went to Cyr's Donut shop and sat in a booth until the game was over. I was still dizzy and queasy when we walked back to Lakeport.

Those early teenage years were extremely difficult for me. I was struggling to find where I fit in the grand scheme of things. Moreover, I was struggling just to survive. I virtually had to support myself, but never had enough money to buy my basic necessities. I couldn't find a job. I was always hungry. I felt inferior. I could hardly see anything in the distance and squinted all the time. My partial front tooth was barely staying in my mouth. The prongs that held it to the other teeth were broke or worn down. I could flip my false tooth out with my tongue at will. Occasionally, I did that in class, to the disgust of my teachers. I just wanted help from someone, somewhere.

I did manage to make a few dollars every now and then, filling in for Stanley Moulton on his paper route. Stanley was on the high school cross-country track team. When he had a track meet out of town, I delivered his papers for him. Unfortunately, he only needed me four or five times that fall. Even though he was a senior, he didn't want to sell his route. I supposed he needed to make money too. It wouldn't have mattered; I didn't have the money to buy it anyway. I even asked Dan Clare to let me know if he knew of anyone who needed help over the Christmas holidays. He couldn't help me either. Scrawny fourteen year old boys weren't in demand. At least girls made money babysitting on the weekends. I couldn't find anything.

The reality of the situation was that I wouldn't be going skiing again that winter. The snowstorms arrived early. Belknap Mountain was open for skiing in early December. There I was, with a new pair of skis I couldn't even use. That also added to the flames of my burning frustration. Again, I found myself without any money to buy Christmas presents for my family. I just wanted Christmas to hurry by and go away. I would have to be content playing basketball at Our Lady of the Lakes gym. Basketball and dancing, those were the outlets to release my frustrations.

It was Saturday, December 12, 1953. It was snowing when I walked into Mr. Bean's Used Furniture store on Union Avenue in the Busy Corner section of Laconia. I carried the new skis I won in the Lakes Region Soapbox Derby into his store. There was no point in hem-hawing around. My mind was made up.

I approached Mr. Bean at his desk and asked, "How much will you give me for these skis?"

He knew I was desperate. At first, he tried to talk me into keeping them. He told me, "I don't want you to do anything you'll regret. Besides, you might want them a year or so down the road."

I was adamant. He told me he wasn't in the ski business, but agreed to take them off my hands to help me out. I don't think Mr. Bean really wanted the skis. Perhaps he could give them to his son, who was in my class, for a Christmas present? Ten minutes later, I walked out of his store with $15 cash.

With money in hand, I headed for Main Street to buy Christmas presents for my family. I didn't have much, but I had pride. Lorraine was earning good money at the Western Union office. Claudie had a part-time job after school at Lougee-Robinson's furniture store. They knew I needed clothes. I figured they'd buy me a shirt or a sweater for Christmas. I just wanted to get everyone a little something. My $15 didn't go very far. I don't recall what I got my sisters, or Ben, or Pudgie, but I'll never forget what I got my mother. It was a small bottle of her favorite perfume. I went to O'Shea's, wearing my raggedy sneakers, and bought her a small bottle of *"Evening in Paris Eau de Toilette."* How could I forget. She actually smiled and gave me a hug after she opened the beautiful blue box it came in. That made my Christmas.

*   *   *

I played CYO basketball again that winter. I was improving all the time. That's what I liked about the game. There were better players than me, but nobody worked harder at improving his game than I did. Father McDonough let me stay in the gym after everyone else left at closing time so I could continue practicing. I shut off the lights when I was through and walked home alone in the cold of winter, under the light of the moon. I was working on dribbling the ball with both hands, just like my idol, Bob Cousy. Often, after I got home, I lay on my bed, closed my eyes, and visualized myself faking my opponent, dribbling the ball behind my back, and driving in for a lay up. Just like the Cooz.

I don't know if Father McDonough had a special "in" with God, the Boston Celtics, or one of the angels in heaven, but somehow he pulled strings to have the famous Bob Cousy come to the Our Lady of the Lakes gym one night when the Celtics weren't playing. It was on a weeknight in February 1954. I knew Bob Cousy played his college ball at Holy Cross in Worcester. Maybe the church had some influence on him. On the other hand, perhaps he knew Father McDonough from his Holy Cross days. I am sure he had some special connection to get him to come to our gym. No matter, I couldn't have been more excited to see my idol, in person.

The gym was overcrowded with basketball fans that night. It was standing room only. After a brief introductory speech and a little advertising for his summer basketball camp in Pittsfield, New Hampshire, he grabbed a ball and spun it a few times in his hand.

Then, out of nowhere, he said, "I understand there's someone else in the crowd called Cousy."

I was sitting on the floor in the front row. I was so embarrassed. I tried to bury my chin into my chest as though that would make me disappear.

The other kids in the gym were pointing at me and shouting, "There he is."

He came over and helped me up. He smiled at me. I'll never forget it.

He said, "O.K. Cousy, let's play some basketball."

I took my position to guard him. At that moment, he was just another player to me. He dribbled the ball slowly as he advanced toward me. Suddenly, he made a quick step to his left as if he was going to drive by me for a lay up. As he leaned his left shoulder toward me, he tempted me to try to steal the ball from his right hand. As I lunged for it, he passed the ball from behind his back to his left hand. I had made my move. It was too late to change. He had me off balance. He easily drove in for a lay up. To me, it was like a ballet. He was so graceful. I couldn't have been more thrilled. I just guarded the great Bob Cousy on a basketball floor. He brushed my head with his left hand, and then stuck his right hand out to give me a big handshake before sending me back to my seat. I'll never forget that evening as long as I live. I really needed that. What a memory. Somehow, I think Father McDonough and God had something to do with it.

*   *   *

There was still snow on the ground in March 1954, when my mother told me to put my clothes in a box.

What she said in her inimitable no-nonsense fashion was, "We're moving."

That's all she said. No advance notice. No discussion. Again, there was no explanation. That's just the way she was. She always had a hidden agenda. She never told us anything. She wasn't concerned with how her decisions might affect us. We were never part of her plans. What Mom did, Mom did for Mom's benefit.

Thus, on a cold, windy Saturday in mid-March, we moved into our new house on Church Street in Laconia. I didn't complain. Not that it would have mattered. At least this house was better than the rat infested duplex we lived in for nearly two years in Lakeport. And, I was finally going to have my own bedroom. Well, it was sort of like a bedroom. Apparently, it was used for that purpose at one time since it had a sink and toilet in it.

My new bedroom defied description. It was on the second floor in the back of the house. To get there, I went to a door on the first floor in an undefined space behind the kitchen, which led to the barn. The door opened to an attic above the stairs. At the top of the creaky, wooden stairs was the second door to my bedroom. Once inside, my room was the weirdest configuration I had ever seen. The whole room was like an afterthought of space design. The room was shaped like a "T," with walls sloped in three different directions. The ceiling was barely six feet above the linoleum-covered floor. The walls were approximately three feet high before they angled to the ceiling. To lie on my bed, it had to be moved away from the sloping wall. To the left, two windows extended from floor to ceiling. Adjacent to the windows, was the sink and toilet. There was an overhead light bulb, with a drawstring, in the center of the room. At the other end of the room, opposite the door I entered from the attic, was another door that separated my room from another room. Each side of the door had a simple eyehook and latch to secure the door. That door didn't fit very well. The bottom was at least an inch above the floor. An old steam radiator was located on the same wall as my bed. Nothing fancy, but it was my room. Finally, I had some privacy.

The house on Church Street was at least 75 years old. I heard it had been previously used to care for elderly disabled people. That probably accounted for the sink and toilet in my bedroom. Shortly after we moved in, I found several pairs of crutches in the attic.

One thing for sure, the house was in a great location. Grammy and Grampy Garneau's apartment house was across the street from our house. Perhaps she told my mother about the property before it went on the market? Or, perhaps my mother bought it so she could show Grammy Garneau that she could also own a house on Church Street? What mattered to me was that we were close to everything in town.

Undeniably, my mother had an uncanny ability to turn a property into a moneymaker. And that she did, with the house on Church Street.

In the next two years, she totally transformed the place. The first thing she did was tear down all the ugly brown asphalt siding and replaced it with freshly painted white wood siding. Initially, there was a huge porch on the right side of the house. She remodeled the kitchen and converted that porch into an enclosed living room, with a large picture window. She did manage to have a small porch erected in front of her new living room so she and Ben could sit outside and enjoy their cold glass of beer on those hot summer afternoons.

We hadn't been in the house a week before she hung the "Room for Rent" sign in the front window. Ora was back in business! Within a week, she converted what was the front parlor into a bedroom. She closed it off from the kitchen by exchanging the beautiful French doors for two wooden doors with a lock. There were two bedrooms upstairs, besides my little room in the back. Initially, she and Ben slept in one room and rented out the other. They shared the bathroom at the top of the stairs with the renters. I saw my mother coming alive again!

She was on a roll. Later, she added a back bedroom at the end of the downstairs hallway, next to her remodeled kitchen. Oh, it didn't end there. Eventually, she demolished the covered walkway that went from the house to the barn in back. Then, she added two small one-bedroom apartments in that space. I was just waiting for her to convert the barn into four apartments. For a woman with an eighth grade education, she had an amazing ability to turn a property into a gold mine. I'll give her credit for that.

It's unfortunate she was so greedy. To her, money was far more important than her privacy or her quality of life. In my last two years of high school, Ben and Ora actually slept in the living room on a hide-a-bed couch, rather than use one of the five bedrooms in the house. She definitely had a nose for making money, and a hand to cling to every penny of it. What a shame.

Ora always had a scheme to make money. With the two rooms rented, she came up with another way to add to her income. One afternoon, when I arrived home from school, I heard a baby crying in the kitchen.

When I asked who it was, my mother told me it was, "Little Johnny."

It seems that Little Johnny was abandoned by his mother at birth. He was what was called a "failure to thrive child," with multiple birth defects. Nobody wanted him. Somehow, the Social Services people heard about my mother. She willingly took him in. Of course, there was always the money angle. But, what we never quite understood about my mother was her strong affinity toward small babies. She adored babies. It's unexplainable. She loved little Johnny. At that time in her life, he was all she wanted. That was so ironic, considering she basically abandoned my sisters and me with Mrs. Camire when we were young.

It was devastating for Mom when they took Little Johnny away. When Social Services told her they found a nice young couple that wanted to adopt him, Ora tried to stop that. She pleaded with them to let her adopt him. In the end, she had to come to the realization that Johnny would be better served being adopted by the young newlywed couple. That was the one instance I remember about my mother when love triumphed over money.

Another time, she took in a foster child for money. Actually, Diane Yates wasn't a child. She was in my grade in high school. I didn't know Diane very well. Nobody did. You didn't have to know her very well to realize she must have had a very difficult childhood. She was around seventeen when she lived at out house. All she wanted to do was finish high school. She was a Distributive Education student. That meant she only went to school in the morning and worked somewhere in the afternoon. Diane was always working. I saw the weariness on her saddened face when she arrived home at night after working an eight-hour shift at a discount store. I had no right to complain. This girl had a harder life than I did. When I tried to talk seriously with Diane, she'd clam up. She didn't want to reveal anything about her past.

Diane lived with us for nearly a year. I don't know what happened to her after she moved away. She left when she turned eighteen. She simply vanished. I know she didn't graduate in our class. Later, I heard she died at an early age.

There was one more peculiar thing about the house on Church Street. My mother didn't allow me to enter the house from the front door. She had a door put in on the side of the house. When I opened the door, I immediately stepped onto a cellar step. That's how Ben and I had to come into the house. For some reason, only my mother would understand, she actually had the top of this outside door cut to the same angle as the stairs. That definitely drew curiosity from people passing by. After we moved to Church Street, she became fanatically fastidious. She swept the kitchen floor at least three times a day. Ben and I weren't allowed to wear shoes in the house. Of course, it didn't bother her when she and her "new friends" came in the house in their wet shoes after a night of drinking. Fortunately, she didn't have any control over the renters.

Whenever she heard the cellar door, she immediately stopped what she was doing and ran to the door at the top of the stairs to make sure I wasn't wearing shoes in the house. Every now and then, to make her day, I would "accidentally" forget to take off my shoes. The woman would go ballistic. I remember her chasing me around the kitchen with a broom. She tried to whack me with it. By then, I was too fast for her.

Her next recourse was to threaten me with, "Wait until Ben gets home. He'll fix you."

I must admit, that got my attention. Either she didn't tell Ben or he was secretly glad I defied her, but he didn't come after me with a strap. Maybe he was just too tired after another day in the foundry.

My freshman year in school was coming to an end when we moved to Church Street. With all our moves, I had circles of friends scattered all over town. There was my old classmates from the French school, my new classmates from high school, my friends from my days on Winter Street, and my friends from Lakeport. Now, I'd be playing with a new bunch of boys who lived near us on Church Street. I was pleased that the Irish Catholic School, Saint John's, was just down the street from our house. Saint John's had an outdoor basketball court behind the school. I'd be a rich man if I had a dollar for every time I went over there to shoot hoops.

*   *   *

The first few months after we moved into our new house, I didn't play basketball at Saint John's or even bother to meet the boys in my neighborhood. I was far too preoccupied watching the infamous McCarthy hearings on television. The TV was all mine before Ben got home from work. Mom had her hands full with Little Johnny and my brother, Pudgie so she didn't mind if I watched TV. The McCarthy hearings were far more interesting than anything I was learning in school.

McCarthyism was the term used to describe the period of political persecution conducted by Senator Joseph McCarthy of Wisconsin. This self-proclaimed anti-communist chaired the so-called "Senate Permanent Subcommittee on Investigations" in 1953 and 1954. This was the formal name given to McCarthy's nationwide campaign to hunt down communists and communist sympathizers. This was the Cold War. Americans feared communist Russia and were alarmed by the spread of communism in our very own country.

I heard about Senator McCarthy's hearings practically every day from Sister Bebianne when I was in the eighth grade.

She would say, "How can he be wrong?" "Such a patriot." "Besides he's a Catholic." "Even Joseph Kennedy from Boston likes him."

In the beginning, I thought he was the right person this country needed to stamp out communism. However, after awhile I became skeptical. His "investigations" began to look more and more like witch hunts. During his heyday, those who were called before his committee were confronted with circumstantial evidence and intimidation. Many people accused others of being communists or communist sympathizers to save their own careers.

Blacklisting suspected communists ruined many careers, especially in the entertainment industry. That's when I became very skeptical. He even had a Hollywood Blacklist. Suspicions were given credence despite inconclusive evidence. Under the auspices of the "House Committee of Unamerican Activities" (HUAC), many famous well know Hollywood stars, including Charlie Chaplin, John Garfield, Dashill Hammett, Lena Horne, Sam Jaffee, Gypsy Rose Lee, Burgess Meredith, Arthur Miller, Zero Mostell, Edward

G. Robinson, and Pete Seeger, just to name a few, were banished from the industry. Paranoia was rampant. Several celebrities fled the country and went to Europe to find work. Very few dared to speak up against him.

One brave man who did was Edward R. Morrow. On March 9, 1954, on his TV program, he courageously attacked McCarthy and his methods. He portrayed him as reckless, dishonest, and abusive. In his words, Morrow said, "The line between investigating and persecuting is a very fine one and the junior senator from Wisconsin has stepped over it repeatedly." Shortly after that, his credibility began to unravel.

It was during the period from April to June 1954, when McCarthy showed himself to be evil and unmatched in malice. Instead of quitting while he was ahead, he ignorantly chose to clash with the Army in the nationally televised Army-McCarthy hearings. On national television, McCarthy's continued badgering witnesses, exaggerated claims, and showed total disregard of due process. This led to his undoing.

The new media of television captured McCarthy's final moments. Toward the end of the hearings, the Army's well-respected attorney, Joseph Welsh, asked him, "Have you no shame?" Welsh went on to say, "I think I never gauged your cruelty, or your recklessness . . . Have you no sense of decency?"

Hesitant for a moment, the silent gallery broke into applause. McCarthy was stunned. The hearings drew to an inconclusive finish shortly after that.

Senator McCarthy was censured by the U.S. Senate for conduct unbecoming a senator in December 1954. The tide of public opinion turned against him, after seeing him in all his revolting glory. I later learned he died an alcoholic, from cirrhosis of the liver, at Bethesda Naval Hospital on May 2, 1957. What I learned, I didn't learn in school.

CHAPTER 17

BUSY CORNER

As you drive from Lakeport to Laconia on Union Avenue, you reach a fork in the road where you must decide if you want to sway to the left on Union Avenue or sway to the right and proceed down Church Street. In the middle of the fork, stood the aptly named Busy Corner variety store. It was even shaped like the "V" separating the two busiest streets in town.

In the summer of 54,' I was approaching a fork in my life. On one road, I was entering the terrible teen years where I rebelled against authority. On the other road, I was trying to gain the approval of the very adults I rebelled against. Which way would I turn? At the time, even I didn't know the answer to that question. In a physical sense, I took the road to the right by moving to Church Street.

Ben Doucet, the owner of the Busy Corner store, was a formidable influence in the path I followed. His store became my home away from home during my early teenage years. I spent more time in Busy Corner than I did at home. Ben Doucet was a positive influence and helped me make some good decisions in that difficult period of my life. Unlike most adults, he didn't judge me. He treated me as an adult. He also opened the door to his life and let me in.

Busy Corner store was the hub of activity in that part of town. There were three entrances to the store. The door to the main entrance was between the two display windows in the narrowest part of the store. There was a rear entrance from the Union Avenue side and another from the Church Street side. As you entered from the front, the cash register and tobacco products were to your immediate left. The center of my universe, the soda fountain, was also on that side. There were seven round red stools at the soda fountain, where customers sat to enjoy ice cream treats or chat over a cup of coffee.

That's where the neighborhood merchants gathered to catch up on all the latest gossip.

In the back of the store, between both rear doors was a long stretch of racks, filled with magazines and newspapers. On the right side, toward the rear, was a telephone booth. The full length of the wall on the right side was stacked with every non-prescription medicine or drug store device imaginable. Everything from crutches, to hot water bottles, to cough medicines, to baby aspirin. The center of the store was filled with seasonal items. In the winter, gloves, mittens, scarves, deicers and those types of things were on display. In the summer, it was filled with sunglasses, floats, and beach toys and anything else you might need for a day at the beach. By far, the most engaging place in the store was the soda fountain. That's where I closely observed the cast of characters who occupied those spinning stools in Ben Doucet's Busy Corner store.

When we moved to Church Street, I didn't have a job. I didn't have any money. Yet, Ben never kicked me out of his store because I didn't spend anything. To the contrary, he befriended me. He confided with me. He trusted me. That meant a lot to me. I wasn't about to jeopardize his trust. Our friendship didn't happen overnight. I had to earn his respect. For my part, I was wary of most adults. By now, they had taken advantage of me far too many times. In fact, my initial encounter with Ben happened after an elderly woman defrauded me of the money she owed me. This time, the old woman lived on Union Avenue.

That happened in late April. One of the customers in Busy Corner mentioned to me that a woman was looking for someone to hoe her garden. When I knocked on her door, she hired me on the spot. She offered to pay me seventy-five cents an hour to hoe her garden and remove the stones as I hoed. She took a hoe out of her barn and showed me exactly what she wanted done. I told her I'd be back the following Friday during our spring break from school. I showed up at her house bright and early, as promised. As I hoed, I placed the stones in neat piles on the side of the garden, just as she requested.

It took me two solid days, working non-stop, to hoe her garden. I stacked four piles of rocks on the side, near her barn. When I finished late the next day, the palms of my hands were burning with blisters. I don't recall ever working that hard. I was sure she would be pleased. When I rang her doorbell, nobody answered. I thought that was strange. I hadn't seen her leave. Maybe I was too busy working when she left.

The next day was Sunday. I went to her house in the afternoon and rang the doorbell again. No answer. I returned again after school on Monday. This time, she answered the door.

In a stern voice, she asked me, "What do you want?"

"I came for my money," I said.

I couldn't believe what I was hearing, when she told me, "You did a lousy job and I am not paying for that." Then, she slammed the door in my face.

I was stunned. Where do I turn? What can I do to get the money I earned? I thought about it all the way home. I hoped my mother or Ben would go back to her house with me and confront her. I was holding back my tears when I told my mother what happened. My mother could be so callous and uncaring at times.

Her response was, "I have enough problems of my own. You need to learn to take care of your own problems."

After that reception, there wasn't any point in even approaching Ben. I was completely disheartened. Nowhere to turn, I went to Busy Corner store to get away from the house.

Ben Doucet noticed my red eyes and the sad look on my face. I couldn't hide it.

He turned away from the busy soda fountain, put his hand on my shoulder, and said, "C'mon let's go to my office." When we stepped into his office, he closed the door and asked, "O.K., now it can't be that bad. Do you want to tell me what's wrong?"

I was bawling when I told him what the wicked woman had done. He got it. He understood. He genuinely felt sorry for me. That's when we initially became friends. After I wiped away my tears, Ben said, "C'mon, let me make you a nice ice cream soda."

*   *   *

No sooner had I finished my freshman year when motorcycles were roaring down Church Street again. The roar of their engines was as loud and deafening as they were when we lived on Union Avenue. That year marked the 34th annual New England motorcycle Gypsy

Tour. More and more motorcyclists were coming to Laconia every year. My mother had a vacant room to rent. I was surprised when she didn't place her "Room for Rent" sign in the front window. For good reason, that question was answered the first day of the rally.

Out of nowhere, she informed me that Fred Walsh was coming to the motorcycle races. This time, he was bringing another young man with him. She told me he rented two rooms. I needed to vacate mine for his guest. That was fine with me. I enjoyed sleeping outside in the summer. However, I couldn't leave it at that. There were too many unanswered questions. I hadn't seen or heard from Freddy in nearly three years. How did he know we moved? How did he know my mother had a room available for him? Who was the young man he was bringing with him?

My mother simply ignored my questions. They lingered in my mind. I didn't care that he brought a young companion with him. The fact is, I didn't want to ride on the back of his motorcycle anyway. When we moved to Lakeport, I never did find the fluorescent motorcycle hat he had given me.

We exchanged hugs and made small talk after he parked his motorcycle in the driveway. His young friend couldn't have been sixteen. Freddy told us he worked in his motorcycle shop and he brought him to Laconia as a reward. I sensed his young friend didn't like me. He stood back, eyes gazing at me, as Freddy spoke with my mother and Ben. This kid looked like he came from a tough neighborhood in Hartford. Most likely, Fred Walsh bought him the nice leather motorcycle jacket he was wearing.

My, how time changes everything. Fred Walsh looked a lot older. On the other hand, I hadn't grown much in stature in the past three years, but I certainly was a lot wiser. It became obvious my mother had been in contact with him. That's the only way he would have known we moved. Why couldn't she be honest with me? She always had to deceive me. I didn't trust that kid Freddy brought to the races. In fact, I had some serious reservations about Freddy. I began to question his affiliations with boys.

Sunday, the 20th of June, was the final day of the rally. Fred and his "assistant" would be returning to Hartford after the big race at Belknap. Before dawn, I was asleep in my pup tent behind the barn. The pressure of a hand rubbing my crotch awakened me. At first, I thought I was dreaming. Suddenly, I turned to my side and detected a male figure in my tent. I was still half-asleep when I pushed his hand away. Even though it was pitch black outside, I knew it was Fred Walsh. He turned my stomach. I was mad. In an outburst of anger, I pushed him away from me.

I yelled at him, "What are you doing? Get your hand off me. You and your "assistant" friend better leave right now," I snapped at him in a harsh voice.

I was disgusted. He was repulsive. I wasn't only concerned for me; I was also concerned for my little brother. How could I have been so stupid to think this man actually cared for me? He was just another sick whacko, figuring I wouldn't tell anyone if he fondled me.

As it began to get light out, I heard his motorcycle pull out of the driveway. He was gone forever. Good riddance. It wasn't yet seven o'clock when I went into the house. Everyone was still sleeping. Instinctively, I checked on Pudg to be sure he was O.K. As I sat in the kitchen waiting for my mother and Ben to come into the room, my mind relived all the memories I had of Freddy Walsh. The more I thought, the angrier I became.

Finally, my mother entered the kitchen. She was still wearing her bathrobe. I looked directly at her when I told her about the incident that took place that morning. I did that intentionally. I wanted to observe her body language when I told her what happened. Oh, she acted concerned. However, I sensed she might have suspected he was a child molester all along. She wasn't shocked or even alarmed. When I asked her what "we" should do? She offered that "we" should best forget about it.

She said, "After all, you're not hurt."

I ended our discussion by saying, "If you ever let that man in our house again, I'll call the cops." I meant it.

*   *   *

A week hadn't gone by when something odd happened. As I was leaving to play baseball across the street, a black car pulled up to the front of our house. Nobody parked their car on the street. There was too much traffic to do that on Church Street. The driver obviously didn't know. I noticed the car had Massachusetts license plates. I waited to see who stopped in front of our house. Suddenly, two priests came to the door, wearing full-length robes. They asked to speak to my parents. My mother came to the door and invited them in. She sent me outside to play. I went across the street to play baseball with the neighborhood kids, but I couldn't help but peek across the street to see when the black car would leave. The priests visited my mother for quite awhile. They must have been there for nearly two hours.

When I returned home at noon, I asked her, "What did the priest want?"

In her usual response, she told me, "That's none of your business."

I could only guess it must have been about her. Was she getting another divorce? Was the Catholic Church going to annul her marriage? Had she told someone in the church about Freddy Walsh fondling me? Sometimes, I just wanted to help my mother. She just wouldn't let me enter that door.

*   *   *

A few days later, she actually came across the street and interrupted our baseball game. She ordered me to come home right away.

I said to myself, "Oh, oh, now what?"

When I got home, she told me to pack my clothes. She found a job for me working as a dishwasher at an inn on Lake Winnipesaukee. Pack into what? I didn't own a suitcase. So, we went to my room and threw some clothes into a paper bag. No time for explaining. My new boss was waiting for me in his car in front of our house.

He drove about ten miles to the Fairhaven Inn, on the south shore of Lake Winnipesaukee, part way between Laconia and Alton Bay. On his way there, he told me how he and his wife came upon this wonderful opportunity to own an inn on the big lake. The previous year, while on vacation, they stumbled across this great deal to buy the newly named, Fairhaven Inn. It was meant to be. They both quit their high paying, high stress jobs, in New York to follow their dream. He went on to tell me, the building was in need of major renovations when they bought it. They poured all their time, money, and energy remodeling the place. Now, they were ready for the anticipated flood of summer guests, to share the enjoyment and ecstasy of their newly remodeled inn.

I gauged him and his wife to be in their late 30s or early 40s. It was common knowledge to anyone from the Lakes Region that their dream had been recounted time and time again. It was generally known, their dream would likely turn into their nightmare.

I don't recall their name. I didn't work there long enough. I barely lasted a week. As we walked through the dining room to the kitchen, he bragged to me about all the changes they made to the old building. There was something like fourteen rooms at the Fairhaven Inn. As we walked to the kitchen, he told me I'd be working a split shift. They served both breakfast and dinner to the guests. He went on to tell me that was referred to as the "Modified American Plan." I was learning something new every day.

I never worked in a kitchen before. This was my first real job. I didn't know how to run the dishwasher or even clean the giant pots waiting to be cleaned. The cook was peeling potatoes and preparing the dinner meal when we walked into the kitchen. He introduced me to the cook. He was a seasoned veteran of life if there ever was one. He had white hair, a stubby beard and blood shot eyes, and looked to be about sixty. He didn't seem too pleased when he was told we'd be sharing the room off the kitchen together.

My new boss showed me the room I'd be sharing with the grizzly old cook. It was pitch black in there, until he flipped the light switch. There weren't any windows. No ventilation. It was a beautiful June day outside, but the room was hot, stuffy, and moldy. I was assigned a cot, nightstand, and a metal locker to hang my clothes. I was a bit dumbfounded. He could tell I wasn't exactly overjoyed with my new quarters.

He tried to make me feel at home by telling me, "When you're off, you can mix with the guests, use the rowboat, play croquet, swim in the lake, or do whatever you want."

Like most fourteen-year-old boys would do, I went down to the lake and rowed the boat after I hung my clothes in the locker. I thought for a moment, "Gee, maybe this job will be fun."

Even though only half the rooms were rented, the dining room was full for the evening meal. The owners were busily serving the guests, smiling all the while, as if we were all in heaven.

The cook hadn't prepared enough food. He was cussing loudly in the kitchen and arguing with the owner and his wife. I stood by the two large sinks, waiting to be taught what to do. The dishes were piling up. Nobody started the dishwasher. Suddenly, there was chaos. They needed clean dishes in the dining room.

Why haven't you started the dishwasher?" the nervous owner asked.

I looked at his panic-stricken face as I told him, "Nobody taught me how to run the thing." It just got worse from there.

The boss, his wife, and myself, finished doing the dishes at around eleven o'clock that night. They didn't scold me, but I could tell they were disappointed. For now, they were stuck with me.

It wasn't good for me either. When I went into my room, the cook was snoring loudly. There was an empty pint of liquor on the floor beside his bed. The room stunk from the smell of liquor and an ashtray full of cigarette butts. Despite this ominous beginning, I was determined to stick it out and try to be a good employee to the nice young owners of the Fairhaven Inn.

Unfortunately, it only got worse from there. Since there wasn't a window in the room, it was impossible to tell the time of day. We also didn't have an alarm clock to wake us up.

I was sound asleep when the boss flipped on the light and was screaming, "We're late. We're late!"

Guests were already beginning to come down the stairs for breakfast. The cook was still sleeping. I thought the owner was going to have a heart attack.

He was walking a fine line with the cook. He was thoroughly angry, but afraid to push him too far. Cooks were hard to find in the summer around Lake Winnipesaukee. For my part, I jumped into my jeans and tee shirt and headed for the kitchen to help in any way I could.

The boss gave me my first order of the day. "Hurry up and make a pot of coffee for the guests," he demanded. I couldn't help but notice the scowl on his face.

"Great!" "O.K., teach me how," I blurted out.

What else could I say? The whole morning was like a scene out of the Keystone cops. Anything that could go wrong did.

The fiasco didn't end there. The dinner meal went as badly as the morning breakfast. The cook was smoking while he was cooking. He didn't care where his ashes landed. He kept ranting and raving how he needed more help. I offered to help.

His response was, "Just stay out of my way."

Nice guy. Whatever the dessert was suppose to be, the guests didn't get it. I didn't want any part of the dining room. I could hear people complaining from the kitchen. People were becoming hostile, as the owner's wife tried to explain to them that they were short of help. It could only get better.

When I entered my room after I finished washing the dinner dishes, the cook was packing his small suitcase.

Curiously, I asked him, "What are you doing?" Wow! Did he ever lace into me.

He told me, "I'm leaving this fuckin' schlock house. I ain't workin' for no goddamn Jews."

I guess he meant it. A minute later, he slammed the door in my face and headed to his parked car. I watched him drive away from the Fairhaven Inn, in the dark of night. He was gone. He wasn't coming back.

Gee, I didn't know Jews swore. The next morning I learned they did. They're human too. The husband and wife were in the kitchen bright and early. In fact, it was still dark. By now, I knew how to make coffee. Too bad they didn't know how to cook a breakfast for twenty or so people. If they spent as much time cooking as they did hollering at each other, they probably would have been fine. I didn't fault them. They had about as much experience in the kitchen as I did. They sure tried. Before the breakfast meal was over, even I was bringing food to the guests' tables. I survived without anyone biting my arm off. There was a lot of grumbling to be heard that morning.

I was just getting the knack of cleaning those huge pots when the owner told me they would have to replace me. That sounded like music to my ears. I had no idea how much they owed me. We never discussed salary.

He asked me, "Do you mind staying on until we can find extra help?"

I thought that was a bit crazy. I was being fired and asked to stay on at the same time. Heck, I didn't have anything better to do. Besides, in a zany way, I liked working at the Fairhaven Inn.

That afternoon, Mr. Owner drove to Laconia to find a new cook and more kitchen help. I think he was ready to pay anything they asked. I thought to myself, "Maybe a private room wouldn't hurt."

While he was gone, Mrs. Owner was trying to prepare the dinner meal all by herself. I didn't take a break. I stayed in the kitchen and helped her. I really felt sorry for her. I couldn't help hearing her sniffle as she tried to hold back her tears.

The following Saturday, my mother came to the Fairhaven Inn to pick me up. The owners told her how helpful I was. And, that I was "such a nice boy." They handed her an envelope with my pay in it. Big mistake. I never did find out what I was paid. I learned a valuable lesson working at the Fairhaven Inn. Never own a Bed and Breakfast inn.

*   *   *

It's a good thing I was fired. I almost forgot about the state Soapbox Derby Championship. On the way home from the Fairhaven Inn, my mother told me the VFW called about painting my racecar. I returned the call as soon as I got home. Mr. Franks, the VFW coordinator, told me they wanted to take my racecar to Cantin's Chevrolet as soon as possible. He went on to say they needed to keep it there for a week. I met him at Ned Robertson's house the next day. They loaded it onto a pickup truck and hauled it to Cantin's.

The big race was approaching. I hadn't had time to think about it. Fact is I hadn't even test driven my new racecar. Cantin's had it for over a week. After it was painted, Mr. Franks drove me to the Chevy dealership to have a look. I couldn't believe what I saw. It was absolutely beautiful. I don't know who paid for it. That really wasn't my concern. The VFW went all out. I was told it was painted with eight coats of car paint. It was painted dark blue with red and white lettering, spelling out, "Laconia VFW Post 1670."

The state championship race was held in mid-July on a special track in Manchester. It was definitely a bigger event than I had imagined. The racecourse was built exclusively for the state Soapbox

Derby championship. It was only used two days out of the entire year. Saturday was a practice day. Each racer was allowed one run down the course. The course was awesome. There were three lanes, separated by solid white lines. Within each lane, was a striped white line. The objective was to stay as close to the striped line as possible the entire way. At the starting line, the nose of my racecar rested on a ramp that stretched across the three lanes. When given the "GO" signal, the ramp dropped forward, releasing the racecar down the hill.

I was one of the first racers to take a practice run. When the ramp was released, I found myself traveling much faster than I had ever gone before. The 12" official Soapbox Derby tires made a big difference. I had trouble controlling my racecar. As I went down the track, I swerved to the right, and then overcompensated when I turned my steering wheel to the left trying to get back to the striped line. It was not a good run. It was too late to lament that I should have test driven it in Laconia before now.

Because of my poor run, I was given another practice run after all the other racers finished their practice runs. If I didn't improve on the second run, I'd be disqualified. I was a bundle of nerves when I hopped in my car for my second run. I knew the problem. I simply didn't expect to go that fast. I was mad at myself for not practicing while I had the chance. It was too late to worry about it. This was it. I had to improve. When the starting ramp dropped, I held tightly to the steering wheel. I began to swerve slightly, but gently steered back to the striped line. It was a much better run. However, there was no room for error if I was going to win the state championship the next day.

At the end of the practice runs, all the racecars were transported in flatbed trucks to the Chevrolet dealership in Manchester.

An official pulled me aside and told me, "When we get to the shop, you need to tighten your steering cables."

He never physically checked them, so how did he know they were loose? I didn't think they were loose. Usually, this was a two-man operation that would have taken about five minutes. When Ned came over to help me make the minor adjustment, that same man told us I couldn't have any help. As far as I was concerned, I was being harassed. I suspected someone complained about the fancy paint job on my racecar. Finally, after an hour of tugging on the cable with one hand, while trying to tighten the clamp with a wrench in the other hand, an inspector told me it was O.K. Whew. That meant I could race the next day.

The night before the race, I still was mad at myself for not practicing in Laconia. I knew it would have made a big difference. This car was so much faster than old #38.

When we arrived at the track that Sunday, the hill on the side of the track was crowded with people that came to see the state championship. I estimated there were probably sixty cars entered in the derby. Before the race, we drew numbers to determine the starting order.

As luck would have it, I was entered in the first heat. I drew Lane 1 and the racer in Lane 2 just happened to be the runner-up to the state champion the previous year. The three racers shook hands and wished each other good luck before we jumped into our cars.

They announced the racer's names and the town they represented on the loud speaker before each heat. When the starter dropped the flag, down went the ramp, and we were on our way. At the start of the race, I swerved ever so slightly. I soon corrected myself. Midway down the course, I was only a half car length behind the leader. I caught up with him with only twenty yards to go. It all happened so fast. People were screaming. Everybody was standing as we approached the finish line. We were side by side the final twenty yards. Swooooosh. We both went across the finish line at the same time.

The race was delayed for nearly ten minutes. It was a photo finish. It took that long for the officials to determine the winner of the heat. When it was all said and done, they determined the other car went across the finish line about two inches ahead of mine. I saw the picture. I couldn't tell. That was it. My Soapbox Derby career was over. The irony of it was that it was the fastest heat of the day. Not only that, the kid that beat me went on to win the state championship that Sunday afternoon.

Oh, I thought long and hard about that race. If only I hadn't swerved at the beginning, the outcome could have been very different. Or, if the course was just, say, twenty yards longer. Who knows? It was done. Unbeknown to me, until after the race, my mother and Ben were there.

She came over to me and offered her condolences. "Too bad Sonny, you came so close."

Had I won, Ned Robertson, Mr. Franks, all the people from Laconia that were there, and my fellow racers, would have surrounded me in my moment of glory. But, I didn't win. To the loser goes the spoils. Not one single person involved with my racecar came over to offer their condolences. How fleeting victory can be. One minute you're on top, the next minute you're a bum. I never saw Ned or Mr. Franks again.

The next day, I went back to my old stomping grounds at Busy Corner store. The local merchants in the neighborhood all wanted to know how I did the day before. They were all sympathetic. I knew they were rooting for me to win. Their words made me feel better. Mr. Hiltz, who owned the Pontiac dealership in Busy Corner, told me not to worry. He offered to sponsor me the next year. I thanked him, but told him that was the end of my racing career.

Ben Doucet tried to make light of it and told all the guys at the soda fountain, "Hey guys, we couldn't live with him if he won that race." Even I laughed at that one.

Without knowing I was in the store, one of the salesmen came through the back entrance and immediately asked the guys drinking their coffee, "How did the kid do in Manchester?"

That was nice. It really made me feel that some people cared.

*　　*　　*

As the summer went on, I observed how Ben made everything at the soda fountain. Before long, I found myself jumping behind the counter and helping him out when he was swamped. There was more to it than scooping ice cream cones. I learned to be a full-fledged soda jerk. You name it; I could make it. From malted milk shakes, to hot fudge sundaes, to frappes, to ice cream sodas, to banana splits. He was at his store from early morning until he closed at nine o'clock at night. I never asked for anything, but Ben told me to scoop a cone for myself every now and then.

We established a little ritual. King's Chinese restaurant opened that summer. It was way across the other end of town. Every Friday night, Ben Doucet gave me two dollars and sent me to King's to pick up a couple egg rolls for the both of us. That was our weekly treat. When he wasn't busy, we went in the back room and ate our egg rolls. That's the kind of friendship we had.

At other times, if he was suspicious of someone, he'd give me a nod to go in the back room. From there, I watched the person through the two-way mirror. I never saw anyone take anything. That was before hidden cameras, so he told me people stuffed magazines under their jacket or stole candy bars from the candy counter. I was delighted Ben confided with me about such things. He also didn't mind if I sat on the floor near the magazine racks and read my favorite magazines. He reasoned if I was there, people wouldn't take anything for fear I'd see them. That worked out well for me too. I was an inveterate news junkie and spent hours pouring over magazines or reading the out of town newspapers. I was often there with Ben when he closed the store at the end of the day.

*   *   *

Toward the end of summer, Lorraine really surprised me. She probably surprised my mother even more. She returned home. She still worked at the Western Union office, but decided she didn't need an apartment. She had little use for a kitchen and still wanted to fulfill her dream of attending medical school. She could save money by renting a room at home.

Lorraine was a no-nonsense person. She told it like it was. She told my mother that there were stipulations she had to abide by. First, she was a grown-up woman and insisted on being treated as such. She was in control of her life. My mother was not to meddle in her affairs. She was to be treated as any other renter. That meant her room was her private space and would only be entered with her permission. There wouldn't be any restrictions on using the bathroom. I am sure my mother was glad she was back. She respected Lorraine and often confided in her. Above all, she now had one of her kids paying rent.

I was glad she came home. I needed her in my life. Although I didn't see her often, I'll always cherish the fond memories of my visits to her room. She introduced me to good jazz and even some classical music. I sat with her and listened to the great jazz musicians of the day. Names like, Dave Brubeck and Thelonius Monk. He played my favorite jazz song, "But Not for Me." Then there was Chet Baker on the trumpet, and Ella Fitzgerald, and Louis Armstrong. I wouldn't have been exposed to those great singers and musicians if it weren't for Lorraine. She was sophisticated. She wanted the finer things in life. And, she introduced me to those things as well. She was a ray of shining light in a struggling boy's life.

Oddly, I didn't see much of Claudie after she graduated from high school. She worked full time in the office of a local plumbing company. It seemed like the three of us were always going in different directions. We didn't get together like we did when we were younger. My sisters were grown up; I was struggling to find my way.

With my mother finally making money again, she and Ben returned to the Rod & Gun Club on Saturday nights.

Ora didn't ask me; she ordered me, "You be home by five o'clock every Saturday to take care of your little brother."

She didn't have to say it twice. This was how I would compensate her for my room. I was never paid to babysit. That job was just assigned to me. Actually, I was relieved when they went out. I could relax for a while. I watched what I wanted on television. I could even help myself to a couple extra slices of bologna from the refrigerator.

If they said anything the next day, I simply told them, "Pudg was hungry."

I lived for the day when I would eventually graduate from high school and could move away. I felt I was a burden to them. I certainly felt that way on Sunday afternoons. Now that they had extra spending money, they started going to the Red Shanty drive-in restaurant, as a family, for dinner on Sunday evening. My mother loved fried clams. She, Ben, and Pudg, piled into the car on Sunday afternoon, right in front of me, and headed for the Red Shanty. That hurt. They would return home, all smiles, and rave about how delicious the clams were that day. I would get so mad. I would go to my room and bang on my bed. Eventually, I made it a point to spend Sunday afternoon at the Busy Corner store so I wouldn't be around when they left or returned home. I desperately needed to find a way to make some money again real soon.

CHAPTER 18

TROUBLE, TROUBLE, TROUBLE

My luck changed . . . or so I thought. A week before beginning my sophomore year, the lady in the office at the Citizen called. She remembered I had been by there looking for a paper route earlier that summer. She told me one of the delivery boys made the high school football team and wanted to get rid of his route so he could make it to the afternoon football practices.

I didn't give it a second thought. I wasn't in any position to be choosy. I was so desperate; I would have swept the floors at St. Joseph's again. That afternoon, I met Robby at the Citizen office. He admitted he had already sold off the "good" part of his paper route and all that remained was a hodgepodge route, with customers scattered all over town. We went from the Citizen office to his first two customers on Canal Street, right off Main Street. Then, there were three more customers in the apartment house on the corner of Beacon and Church. Next, he made three deliveries on Howard Street, and five more on Davis Place. Then we backtracked to make a few deliveries on Stafford Street.

At this point, I had to ask Robby, "Who delivers the papers too all the other houses we passed on your route?"

It was then I learned that two other paperboys had most of the customers in this part of town. They weren't interested in buying his "leftover" customers. That should have been a clue.

From the end of Stafford Street to the busiest section of my route, I had only one customer on the half-mile stretch of the newly constructed Bisson Avenue. Bob Irwin had just completed building his new Ford dealership on Bisson Ave. Finally, I had about a dozen customers on the lower end of Messer Street. I didn't have a single customer on the mile long stretch from the end of my route to our house on Church Street. From start to finish, I walked over three and a half miles a day for some forty to forty-five customers. That was the lousiest paper route in Laconia. Robby was so anxious to dump it, he actually gave it to me just to get rid of it.

Who was I to complain? I finally had a job. Before it turned cold in the fall, the route was tolerable. It was a known fact that most paper routes were sold in the summer. Winters in New Hampshire were just too brutally cold to be out there braving the elements for a few dollars a week. I knew that all too well. How could I ever forget my old five-mile paper route on North Main Street.

The customers on my new route were very different from my old customers. Many of my new customers lived in rundown apartment houses. Some had lived there forever, others were like Gypsies that vanished in the night, often leaving the paperboy stuck without paying for the paper. They were impersonal and unfriendly. Several of them were barely scraping by to make ends meet. I understood where they were coming from. They were looked down upon, and took their rejection out on me. Often surly and sullen, they constantly complained about the price of the paper, or anything else on their mind. I simply grinned and shared their concern. I understood their frustrations.

Of course, every paper route has unique customers. I managed to pick up a few of the business owners in Busy Corner.

Mr. Truchon told me to, "Go to hell." He wasn't changing paperboys for me.

However, I managed to pick up Shorty's Shoe Repair, Hiltz Pontiac, and Jimmy's Bakery, all in Busy Corner, as new customers. They were more like friends than customers. I stopped and chit chatted with them when I dropped off their paper.

Shorty was my favorite. He was a short Greek with an infectious smile. When he grinned, his face looked like a piano keyboard. His shoe repair shop was on the Church Street side of Busy Corner. I went out of my way so to deliver his paper early in the afternoon. We had a mutual respect for one another. Shorty worked hard so his family could have a better life. I worked hard too, hoping for the day I too could have a better life.

Many a day, I stopped by Shorty's after I finished my deliveries and sat in the elevated shoeshine chair. We bantered back and forth and jabbed at each other with crude little remarks. When he called me a "little shit," or "a little peckha," I took it as a term of endearment.

I would strike back and say something like, "Ah, you sawed off little Greek." or "When you gonna cut the counter down so I can see ya?"

Then we'd laugh at each other. It was always in fun. We understood that. One day, I asked Shorty if he would shine my shoes. In my mind, I thought that was somewhat demeaning to shine shoes for a living.

He looked at me proudly, and in his broken English said, "Of course I shina you shoes. What you think? You as good as anyone else. You pay me, I shine."

That was a lesson in humility for me. Just saying that endeared me to the little man even more.

The first delivery on my route was to the local Red Cross office on Canal Street. The woman at the front desk insisted that I bring the paper to her desk. I resented her. She was surrounded by a cloud of arrogance. She snubbed me as though I was a lowly servant of hers. What really disturbed me was how she paid for the paper. She actually wrote out a check every week for thirty-five cents out of the Red Cross checking account. That took gall. She was too cheap to pay for her own paper.

Conversely, my favorite customer was a young, pregnant woman that lived in the apartment house at the end of Messer Street. She was my last delivery of the day. As I became more acquainted with her, I learned she was married to a soldier stationed overseas. She was from Georgia. She met her husband when he was stationed at Fort Benning. She would have been fine if she had stayed in her small town, but he insisted that his wife move to his hometown while he served overseas.

To her, Laconia was a foreign land. She desperately yearned to be back home in Georgia. She didn't know anyone in Laconia. There was nobody to turn to if she needed help. She didn't have any friends. She told me people made fun of her deep southern accent. She only left her apartment to go to the grocery store.

I took it upon myself to befriend her. She was so lonely. She actually waited at her door to greet me when I delivered her paper.

I'd ask her, "How you doing today?" or, "Do you need anything?"

I tried suggesting a movie. She wouldn't go to the movie theater. Sometimes, I felt like I was nursing a wounded animal. I felt her despair, but I didn't know what to do.

When I collected for the paper, I took the time to listen to her. I knew she felt better once she unloaded her problems on me. She spoke with a slow southern drawl. I never heard such a thing. At times, I just wanted to pull the words out of her mouth. Yet, I found her speech to be divinely charming. It was like talking with a character out of "Gone With the Wind."

She crossed the days off her kitchen calendar to keep track of when her husband would return. He was serving at a remote location on a one-year tour of duty. The baby arrived before he returned. That was a blessing in many ways. Her beautiful little baby occupied all her time. As time passed, her spirits were lifted higher and higher. Finally, her husband returned from his overseas tour and she was off to his next duty station at Fort Stewart, Georgia.

* * *

When I returned to school my sophomore year, I was the same boy I was the year before . . . . with a few exceptions. I wore the same clothes I wore my entire freshman year. I simply didn't have money to buy new clothes. Consequently, I was very self-conscious. I felt inferior to my classmates. Oh, I put on a good front. Always quick with my tongue, ever the class clown. It was just a way to get attention. Or, perhaps it was really a way to deflect people from knowing the truth. I had many friends, but, for the most part, we were the outcasts in school. You know, the ones that wouldn't be going to college. The ones that didn't participate in after school activities. The ones that were usually around when there was trouble. It didn't matter. These were my friends. And if you were my friend, you were my friend for life. That's the way I was; that's the way I am.

There was a part of me that yearned to be accepted. I didn't abandon my old friends at St. Joseph's. To stay in touch with them, I joined Explorer Scouts to be with them and my fellow Scouts that also transferred to Laconia High. That way, we at least kept in touch at our weekly Scout meetings. I needed to reinforce the good values I learned in scouting.

If for no other reason, I stayed in Explorer's because of Cut Fecteau. I was blessed to have Cut Fecteau in my life. Not only as my Scoutmaster, but also as a friend and positive influence. Cut worked at Scott & Williams and had a family. He wasn't paid a cent for all the hours and weekends he unselfishly gave to the boys in Troop 62. His payment was the profound impact he had in molding the young men under his charter into productive citizens after they left scouting. In that difficult period in my life, Cut helped me through the gray area of young adulthood where I could have easily ruined my life.

For the record, I wasn't a bad kid. To the contrary, I was blessed with a good heart. However, like many teenagers, I was susceptible to peer pressure. I sometimes gave in to bad judgment, rather than be called "chicken." That one word affected my decisions more than anything else. Stupid as it was, I refused to be called "chicken." If you wanted to get to me, that's all you had to say. Of course, I kept that to myself. That was my main defense from doing unwise things I knew I would regret.

Sometimes, unfortunately, things happen just by chance. I never intended to harm anyone that Halloween night in the fall of 1954. In fact, I had my heart set on going to the big Halloween dance at the high school gym. My friend, Walter "Wally" Wallette, was going to the dance with me. He came by my house to get me around seven o'clock. As we walked toward Busy Corner, Wally pulled two slingshots from his back pocket. That was never part of any plan. I wouldn't waste a dime on a slingshot.

But, there we were, two teenage boys on Halloween night, on the way to a high school dance, playing with slingshots. We were playing a game with our Wham-O toys as we made our way to the school gym. Wally had a bag of BBs he shared with me. We aimed at streetlights and metal signs on our way. We didn't break any light bulbs or anything. Only a testament to how lousy a shot we were.

As we approached the high school, I took aim at a streetlight on the corner of Gilford Avenue and Dewey Street. Unbeknownst to me, a police car was driving down Dewey Street at the time. It was pitch black out. I didn't see it. The next thing I knew, my shot missed the street light but accidentally hit the side of the police car.

The cop turned on his siren and overhead lights. Wally and I panicked when we heard the siren.

I shouted, "Wally . . . split."

I ran up Union Avenue, heading for the high school. Wally ran to hide behind the Sacred Heart convent. As I was running up the high school lawn, suddenly I was tackled and found myself spread out, face first on the ground. A police officer had tackled me. What an embarrassing moment. All the kids going into the school were gawking at me trying to figure out who had committed a vicious crime.

I was never allowed to offer an explanation. They put me in the police car and drove to the police station. The story was blown way out of proportion when it was told to the desk sergeant on duty. To hear the cop tell it, I was taking dead aim at his police car, fully intending to hit one of the officers.

"Why, I could have blinded them," the officer lamented. "I could have even caused them to crash their police vehicle into an innocent child out trick-or-treating."

I'm surprised they didn't charge me with attempted murder of a police officer in the line of duty. They became extremely upset when I refused to disclose the name of my accomplice. I couldn't violate the code. He hadn't done anything. I refused to implicate my friend.

The police officers drove me home after I was released that night. They couldn't let it go. In the middle of the night, they had to give their version of the event to my mother. She was summoned to appear with me in Juvenile Court the following Saturday. To her credit, she sat calmly in the living room and allowed me to tell her my version of what happened. When I was done, she was angry. Not at me, but at the police. She understood how the police operated in this small New England town. It infuriated her that they were blowing this incident way out of proportion for their benefit. I was just relieved she understood.

The Citizen also blew the story out of proportion. The headline on the front page the next day read, "Robin Hood strikes Police Officer." Oh, my God! They used the exact words the officer told the desk sergeant in their article. "I could have blinded them," it said. The one consolation I had was that they couldn't mention my name because I was a minor.

The next Saturday morning, my mother and I appeared before Judge Jewell in Juvenile Court. To her surprise, the two police officers involved in the incident were also there.

She whispered to me, "Don't they have anything better to do on their day off?"

"Shhhh, Mom," I whispered back.

Next, the Judge asked the police officers to recount the events of the evening of October 31st. By the time they were finished, I had been portrayed as a serious danger to the community. My mother was infuriated. She knew the cards were stacked against me.

When the Judge called me to step forward, he never asked my version of the incident. His only question to me was, "Who was with you that night?"

I replied, "I was alone."

I refused to squeal on my friend. I could tell the Judge was frustrated by my answer.

As the Judge was contemplating what to do with me, my mother suddenly stood up and asked to speak. All her accrued anger from the many years of being scorned and put down by the self-righteous people of Laconia came pouring out. She admonished the police for being hypocrites and liars. She told the Judge there was no justice for the poor people of Laconia that didn't live on the north end of town. She went on to tell him that I was a good kid. That I had never been in trouble. That this whole "trial" was a sham. Wow! She said what most people in Laconia didn't dare say to his face. I was proud of Mom for sticking up for me. However, she didn't please the Judge.

He ordered me to come to the police station every Saturday morning at nine o'clock "Until further notice."

I wondered, "What did that mean? How long is further notice?"

I learned. For the next eight months, until the end of June the following year, I had to go to the police station every Saturday morning and sit with the other social misfits in the main lobby. I assume the idea was to humiliate me in front of every person that came to city hall to conduct business.

Some of my old paper route customers saw me sitting in a chair in the long hallway and inquired, "Sonny, what are you doing here?"

What could I say? Should I tell them I almost killed a cop?

There was no rehabilitation program for us branded juvenile delinquents. That disappointed me. I never saw the Judge again in the next eight months. The police didn't even talk to us. They just went about their business and left us to rot in a chair for some two or more hours every Saturday morning. Eventually, around noon, one of the cops came downstairs from the police station and told us we could go home. That was it. I earned the privilege of sitting with all the other young social deviates of Laconia on Saturday mornings. These kids were constantly looking for trouble. The banded together and plotted their next crime at these weekly sessions. They came from broken homes. Why, I learned their older brothers sat in these very same chairs before they did. A few even graduated to the state penitentiary.

*   *   *

The evening after my mother and I appeared in Juvenile Court, I was about to enter the kitchen when I overheard her telling Ben, "If only I had let him go to Assumption, he wouldn't have got into trouble."

Whoa. I took a step back to digest what I overheard. Was my mind playing a game on me? Certainly, I didn't hear what I thought I heard? Did I hear my mother say I could have gone to Assumption? This needed clarification.

I walked into the kitchen and immediately confronted her. A look of guilt was plastered across her face. I could tell she wanted to clear her conscience.

She began with, "Do you remember last summer when those two priests came to talk to me?"

Of course, I did. I listened intently, as the whole story unraveled. Apparently, I had scored very well on the tests I took at Assumption when I was in the eighth grade. They would have offered me a scholarship then; however, the campus was completely destroyed in the giant tornado of 53.' It took them over a year to rebuild the school and dormitories. They were ready to reopen in the fall of 1954. That's why they came to talk with my parents.

She revealed that they came to offer me a full tuition scholarship at Assumption High. All my mother had to pay for was my books, room, and board. I was shocked to hear this. I was so angry with her. Why didn't she include me in the meeting with the priests? How could she deny me the opportunity of a lifetime? I would have done anything to go to Assumption. If I had spoken to those two priests, I would have asked if there was any way I could work in the cafeteria, or mop floors, or do anything to pay for my room and board.

Her obsessive greed trumped my opportunity for a better education. She denied me the one chance to fulfill my dream. More importantly to her, if I went to Assumption, she and Ben would lose their free Saturday night babysitter. Better to keep me at home, even if I did get into a little trouble every now and then.

I walked out of the room and left her mumbling. I could only imagine how different my life would have been had I gone to Assumption High. I just wanted to run away. The more I thought about it, the more I realized I didn't have any place to go. I was stuck there for three more years.

On two occasions, I was excused from going to the police station on Saturday morning. Once, my sister Lorraine found a job for me giving away free samples of TUMS to the Saturday shoppers on Main Street. A man came to the Western Union and asked her if she knew anyone who could pass out samples of "TUMS for the Tummy." Until then, I had never heard of TUMS. That day, I learned they were chewable antacid tablets that were taken for heartburn relief. The man left several boxes of TUMS with Lorraine. I positioned myself in front of Woolworth's store, at the intersection of Main and Pleasant Street.

As people passed by doing their Christmas shopping, I handed them a free roll of TUMS. As I said before, I enjoyed observing people. The more affluent often refused to take a free sample of TUMS. It's as though it was beneath them to take anything free.

The majority of shoppers approached cautiously to see what I was giving away. Once I assured them they were free and were good for heartburn, they smiled as they accepted the free gift. Then, there were the less fortunate. The poor people on welfare. They not only blatantly demanded more than one roll; they sent their children by four and five times to stock up on a lifetime supply of TUMS.

Strangely enough, I felt I had some special power giving away free samples. I was sort of a surrogate Santa Claus. Everyone was in a festive spirit. Christmas was just around the corner. It was in my power to determine who got what. Here was my opportunity to help the poor. When the children knew I wouldn't reject them, they took full advantage of the opportunity. Why did I care? The more TUMS I passed around, the better it appeared I did my job. By four o'clock, all the TUMS were given away. The TUMS man was pleased, my sister was pleased, and I was extremely pleased. Being paid to hand out free samples. Now that's a job I liked.

A few weeks later, a woman in charge of the March of Dimes called my mother to see if I would be available to collect for them again that year. My mother told her she had to clear that with the police department.

Quite undiplomatically, she told her, "Sonny goes to Juvenile Court on Saturday. You're gonna have to ask the cops to let him help ya."

If it were anyone but me, I doubt the lady would have called the police station. However, I had the reputation of being the best fund drive collector in town. Forget my juvenile record; they needed me! So, I didn't have to go to the police station the Saturday I collected for the March of Dimes.

Oh, those volunteer ladies were so sweet when they needed me to do their bidding. Any other time, if they saw me walking down the street they wouldn't give me the time of day. They were all gathered in the Chamber of Commerce office in the Laconia Tavern building that Saturday morning, sipping coffee, dressed in their finest wool skirts and expensive sweaters from O'Shea's. Their job for the day was to pass me a cardboard cup with a number on it, collect the money I brought in after spending the day out in the freezing cold begging for donations, and adding my tally to the overall count. Whoopee, what a tough job.

By noon, most of the other kids turned in their cups and were through for the day. Not me. I wasn't about to let anyone outdo me. My pride wouldn't allow that. I had a reputation to maintain. So, I collected door to door until after three o'clock. When I came in out of the cold, I sensed that some of these old bags hadn't done anything but talk and drink coffee all day, and were glad that I was finished so they could go home.

When I handed one of the women my cup, she looked at me strangely and announced to everyone in the room that my cup had been tampered with. Essentially, she accused me of stealing money. That really made me mad.

Defending myself, I replied, "Judge Jewell's wife asked for change from a dollar bill so I had to open the box to give it to her". I went on to tell them she donated fifty cents.

Sure enough, when they looked in the box, the dollar bill was in there. The woman offered an insincere apology and said it was "just a little misunderstanding." I was boiling mad. How dare she accuse me of stealing from the March of Dimes. I let her, and everyone else in the room know, I would never steal a penny.

I finished by saying, "And from now on, you get someone else to do your dirty work. Don't ever call me to help you again!"

I was fuming mad. I left the room without taking my prize for collecting the most money for the 1954 March of Dimes drive.

*   *   *

Christmas fell on a Saturday that year. The week before the big holiday, the weather was brutally cold. A Nor'easter had settled in over the east coast, bringing hurricane force winds and heavy snow. Low-level clouds blocked out the sun for nearly ten days. By Christmas week, I was worn out from freezing in the cold every afternoon to deliver my papers. By Tuesday, 21 December, I couldn't take it any longer.

The wind was howling and spitting balls of ice in my face as I made my way to the end of Stafford Street. It was dark out. I could barely make out the smoke spewing from the chimneys as I began to walk the long, lonely half-mile stretch up Bisson Avenue. I was so cold, I couldn't feel my feet. My hands were numb. I couldn't feel the newspaper in my hand when I opened the storm doors to place the papers in a safe place. Something was happening to my body. I was becoming delusional. At the time, I didn't realize I was suffering from hypothermia.

I tried. God knows I tried to finish my route that day. By the time I made it to Irwin Motors, I just knew I'd die in a snow bank somewhere if I tried to continue on. In that instant moment when I came to grips with the gravity of my situation, I turned around and began the long, difficult trek back home. I covered my face with my newspaper bag to keep from getting frostbitten.

There was a large puddle of crushed ice, frozen water, and mud in the road as I approached the corner of Stafford Street. It was a sharp 90 degree turn off of Bisson Avenue. I tried to hug the snow bank on the side of the road as a small sports car came whizzing around the corner without slowing down. Without any regard for me, the driver sprayed me from head to toe with the mixture of cold mud, water, and ice. It burned when it hit me. There I stood, soaking wet from head to toe.

I was crying and sniffling, as frozen tears ran down my face. I seriously questioned whether I could even make it home from there. I was in a very dangerous predicament. The only thing I could think to do was pray to God to please, please, help me make it home.

Out of nowhere, He came to my rescue. It was an epiphanic moment in my life. It was surreal. As I stood there under the street light, ankle deep in frozen slush, I began talking to myself. Either I was talking, or God was talking. All I remember is that I was transformed in that instant moment. I felt like I was gathering strength. I wasn't going to be defeated.

In the stillness of the night, I promised myself, right then and there, that someday, I too would have a fancy sport car . . . and a big motor home like the one I saw in the Weirs last summer . . . . and a beautiful house . . . . and a beautiful wife. My children would have a car when they turned sixteen . . . . and I would never have money problems again. That, I promised myself, on that cold winter night, standing in the slush on the corner of Stafford Street and Bisson Avenue. I now had something to live for.

*　　*　　*

Trouble enters your life when you least expect it. I wasn't looking for trouble that Halloween night. Neither was Lorraine when trouble entered her life about the time it entered mine. Her incident was far more dangerous. It also involved the Laconia Police Department.

One evening, she was busily transmitting telegrams at the Western Union when her boss's wife came into the office. At the time, Lorraine didn't think anything of it. In fact, she was pleased to see her.

She greeted her. "Good evening Mrs. Campbell," she said.

Mrs. Campbell didn't acknowledge her greeting. Instead, she walked right to the counter and reached in her purse. She had a look of despair. Before Lorraine could say anything else, her boss's wife was pointing a handgun at her.

Lorraine was always cool and calm under fire. When Mrs. Campbell opened her mouth, she was hysterically confronting my sister. She began accusing Lorraine of having an affair with her husband. Her accusation was beyond absurd. Mr. Campbell was a middle aged, mild mannered, soft-spoken man, who lacked any distinguishing characteristics, other than the fact he was a chain smoker. He was barely five foot tall and lucky if he weighted 130 pounds soaking wet. If it weren't for the gun, aimed directly at her, this whole fiasco would have been totally ridiculous.

As her voice quivered, she went on to say, "You can have anyone you want. You're breaking up our marriage. Stay away from my husband."

"Oh, no, Mrs. Campbell. You have this all wrong. Your husband loves you and your children very much," said Lorraine.

All the while, Mrs. Campbell held the gun on the counter in her right hand. Lorraine calmly tried to assure her there was nothing going on between her and Roger Campbell.

"Why, Mrs. Campbell, you know I have a steady boyfriend. Your husband is a nice man, but I assure you there is nothing going on between us."

She deliberately refrained from referring to her boss by his first name. She carefully avoided inciting this woman, while hoping that someone would come to her rescue.

It was night. The office was lit up. Anyone passing by could easily observe the two of them talking at the counter. The gun in her right hand was also quite visible.

What seemed like an eternity lasted about fifteen minutes. A police officer happened to be walking by the Western Union on his way to the police station. All the cops on the night beat knew Lorraine. As he passed by the office, he waved to her. She waved back, all the while trying to alert him that there was big trouble in the Western Union. She rolled her eyes and tried to point her waving hand down at the gun to get his attention.

She didn't know if he saw Mrs. Campbell's hand and the gun on the counter. At that moment, it was her only chance for survival. She continued to allay Mrs. Campbell's false aspersion. Now, she applied a bit of reverse psychology. She was telling Mrs. Campbell how attractive she looked. It worked. She could tell Mrs. Campbell was beginning to relax.

The police officer must have spotted the gun. He called for back up. He had his 38 revolver pointed right at Mrs. Campbell as he burst through the door. He hollered at her to raise both hands above her head. She complied. He moved swiftly to grab the gun off the counter, while another officer wrapped his arms around Roger Campbell's wife. The incident was over.

The following morning, police officers were back in the Western Union. They were dusting for fingerprints. Nothing happened to Roger Campbell's wife. My sister chose not to press charges. The only thing she asked was that Gladys Campbell be barred from ever going into the Western Union office again. Lorraine handled the situation so bravely that evening. She was given two weeks off, with full pay, to recover from what could have been a very tragic ending.

*   *   *

Sometimes you can be in serious trouble and don't even know it. Like the time Buddy Shelby came into Truchon's store and asked if I wanted to go to Franklin with him and see if we could pick up some girls.

I didn't know Buddy very well. He was a couple of years older than I was. He wasn't in my circle of friends. He was a loner. It was on a Sunday night. I was hanging out at Truchon's playing the pinball machine. I agreed to go to Franklin with him. There was nothing better to do at the time. His car was parked behind Truchon's store. That was an odd place to park. However, I didn't think anything about it at the time.

The car was nice and warm when I stepped inside. He left the engine running.

"Nice car," I said. I really meant it.

It was a two-year-old Cadillac DeVille. Buddy went on to tell me his uncle owned it. He said he was in Florida for a vacation and asked Buddy to look after it for him. I didn't question that. It seemed plausible to me. We listened to Rock N' Roll on radio station WKBW as he drove down Union Avenue on our way to Franklin.

The girls he had in mind weren't home, so he decided to go to Belmont. No luck there either. We drove around for a couple of hours. It was nearly ten o'clock. I had to get home or I would be in trouble. I asked Buddy to drop me off at my house. Instead, he drove to a Used Car lot on South Main Street.

Naively, I asked, "What are we doing here?"

With a smirk on his face, Buddy told me, "This is where the car came from."

At first, it didn't register. I couldn't reconcile why his uncle would leave his car at a Used Car lot? Then it registered.

For the last three hours, I had been joy riding around in a stolen car with someone I hardly knew. I was still on probation. If the police had stopped us, I would have been in serious trouble. They would never believe me if I told them I didn't know the car was stolen. Nobody is that stupid. I probably would have been sent to reform school. Again, something as innocuous as going for a Sunday drive could have put me behind bars. I dodged a bullet that night. I realized I needed to be more careful with whom I associated. I needed to smarten up. Trouble was everywhere around me. Trouble comes in three's. I hoped that was it for a while.

That April, Claudie left Laconia. Big sister was finally getting out of the house. She earned it. I hated to see her leave, but was also happy for her. She joined the Air Force. She took her basic training at Lackland AFB in San Antonio, Texas. Her follow on assignment was in the medical corps at Hamilton AFB, in northern California.

I couldn't help but wonder, "Maybe, someday, that will be my ticket out of Laconia too."

CHAPTER 19

THESE TIMES THEY ARE A CHANGIN'

The summer of 1955 finally arrived. It not only signified the end of my sophomore year in high school, it also held the promise of a better job. Before school let out for the summer, Wally and I contacted Smith Farms to get our names on the list to rake blueberries in August. Mr. Smith assured us we would be on his crew that summer. That meant I could sell my God-awful paper route just before pickin' season began. My spirits were high. Things were looking up. In a few months, I would be sixteen.

In the morning, I played basketball at the outdoor court at St. John's. This would be the year I tried out for the varsity basketball team. I felt confident of making the team. Some of the boys I played against at St. John's already played on the varsity team so I knew how I stacked up against them. I still delivered the Citizen in the afternoon. Every day, after I finished delivering my papers, I made it a point to drop by Busy Corner store and visit with Ben Doucet or stop by Tony's Shoe Repair to engage in a little banter with Tony Ortakales. Busy Corner was my turf. That's where I grew up.

On Saturdays, after collecting from my customers, I treated myself to a strawberry ice cream soda or a hot fudge sundae at Busy Corner. I looked forward to my special weekly treat. I even contemplated what I'd order while delivering my papers. One time, I was so hungry I skipped my usual treat at Busy Corner and headed for Jimmy's Bakery instead.

The aroma of freshly baked goods was irresistible. The smell in the bakery was enough to make my stomach gurgle. On that day, I ordered a whole custard pie. Then I went to Morin's market on the corner of Winter Street and bought a quart of chocolate milk. With both hands occupied, and my paper bag hanging from my shoulder, I made my way home and carefully opened the side door to the cellar. Ah, what a treat! I devoured the entire pie and quart of milk, while sitting at the bottom of the cellar stairs.

Ora and Ben's summer routine hadn't changed one iota. They sat on the front porch after Ben came home from work, drank their quart of Schlitz beer, and gawked at all the tourists driving up and down Church Street. Now that they had extra income coming in, and a built-in babysitter, they resumed their Saturday night ritual at the Rod & Gun Club.

That was Ora's turf. The dancing and the drinking offered her an escape from the inner demons she chose not to confront. At the Rod and Gun, she escaped from the consequences of her life and miraculously converted herself into the queen of the ball. When a man asked Ben for permission to dance with his wife, that empowered the both of them. Him, by giving his permission, and Ora, by exposing her perceived sexual attractiveness. This was her weekly fix to bask in the adoration and approval she so desperately craved.

I never complained about babysitting my little brother. That would only have incited my mother. She would have readily let me know how ungrateful I was and how much she sacrificed for me. The thing is, she believed it.

Ben and Ora came pouring in, barely able to stand up, around 2:00 a.m. every Sunday morning after their night on the town. Since Pudgie slept downstairs, I had to stay in the living room until they came home. If they weren't too hung over, they repented for their sins of the night before by attending the 11:30 a.m. mass at Sacred Heart church the next day. All too often, Ora was too hung over to get out of bed until late Sunday afternoon. Her false teeth even hurt. We kept a stock of Alka Seltzer and ginger ale around the house to nurse poor Mom back to life so she could return to the sweatshop for her shift on Monday.

That summer, I stopped going to Sunday mass. The smell from all the alcohol consumed by the faithful parishioners the night before was too overwhelming at the high mass. I went once and left the church after fifteen minutes. Moreover, I could just as easily observe all the hung over parishioners ordering Alka-Seltzer's at Busy Corner on their way home from mass. I opted to spend my hour of devotion, scanning the Sunday papers, sitting on the floor in the corner of the store.

Often, I went to the Weirs on Sunday afternoon. I stuck my thumb out at the corner of Union and Gilford Avenue and hitched a ride to the Weirs.

When the MS Mount Washington stopped at the Weirs to board passengers for the two and a half hour ride around Lake Winnipesaukee, I joined the other boys who dove into the big lake from the starboard side of the first deck to hustle passengers before the ship took off.

While paddling in the deep water, we hollered to the passengers, "Toss in a coin and watch the divers go to the bottom."

The surrounding beauty captivated the tourists. While they waited for the ship to leave the dock, they entertained themselves by tossing dimes and quarters at the divers.

The trick was to catch the coin in your hand before it hit the water. Then dive down with the coin in your hand for three or four feet to let the people think you were retrieving their coin. It was a fun way to pick up a dollar or so on a Sunday afternoon. I usually caught enough coins to treat myself to a box of caramel corn and a slice of pizza. At around five o'clock, I stood beside the Handy Landing store at the entrance to the Weirs and hitched a ride back to town from someone returning to town after spending a delightful afternoon at the beach.

*   *   *

If I hadn't liked Ben Doucet so much, I wouldn't have felt sorry for him. Ben was such a dreamer. He was always chasing a star in hopes of striking it rich in one failed venture after another. I was involved with his latest scheme that summer. The big news around the city was that none other than President Dwight D. Eisenhower was going to spend a night in Laconia on his way to the White Mountains. Eisenhower's visit was sort of a payback to his old friend, and Chief of Staff, Sherman Adams. Adams coaxed him to pay a visit to the Granite state as a way of thanking the voters for his 1952 primary victory.

Ben was well aware of my talent for collecting money for whatever cause that came along. He told me about his plan to place a stand right in front of his store. He asked me to operate his booth and sell flags, "I like Ike" buttons, banners, and a variety of souvenirs, commemorating the President's visit. I couldn't turn him down. According to the published schedule, President Eisenhower was staying at the Laconia Tavern overnight on June 23, 1955. The next morning, his caravan would proceed down Church Street, right past Busy Corner store, on his way to the mountains.

I tried to convince him that the President's caravan would be whizzing by his store in a split second. There definitely would be a crowd of locals standing in front of the Store to watch Ike pass by. However, this was Ward 2. This was Laconia. For the most part, these people were hard working laborers. I couldn't see them spending money on banners and coffee mugs. As soon as his caravan drove by, the crowd would quickly disperse and head back home. They wouldn't even come in the store for a soda.

I hated being right. Unfortunately, I was. Ben was stuck with a bunch of useless souvenirs, with the date of Ike's visit imprinted on them. I don't know how much he lost on that venture. Whatever it was, he was quite sullen for a couple of weeks.

On the other hand, I had one of those once-in-a-lifetime experiences when the President came to Laconia. The afternoon the President arrived, Lorraine was mobbed by the press corps sending telegrams at the Western Union. They set up a pressroom in the basement of the Laconia Tavern. She was so swamped; she hired me to run telegrams to and from the pressroom and the Western Union. Now, that was exciting. There I was, in the smoke filled pressroom, with news reporters from all over the country.

Of course, all the state politicians had to amble in and do their share of glad-handing. I took it all in. Miss New Hampshire and Miss Winnipesaukee were escorted into the pressroom. They managed to flash their pearly teeth for the photographers, while gasping for air in this unventilated smoke-filled sanctuary. I couldn't help but notice that typing and smoking went hand in hand, while I watched the seasoned veterans peck away at their typewriters.

Soon, one of them would holler, "Runner," and I was on my way back to the Western Union to deliver their typed copy to my sister.

I was the only kid allowed in the pressroom. I was even issued a badge. By nine o'clock that night, the pressroom was empty.

I don't know what possessed me. Chalk it up to curiosity. I wanted to see the President. He was sitting with Sherman Adams and some other dignitaries in the enclosed porch next to the hotel lobby. The Secret Service was the last thing on my mind as I stepped onto the porch where President Eisenhower was sitting. Just about the time he turned his head in my direction to see who was entering his space, a huge hand grabbed me by my shoulder and pulled me back. Why, I was within three feet of shaking the President's hand!

A couple of Secret Service agents jerked me back into the lobby and asked the obvious question. Once I assured them I meant no harm, they politely told me I couldn't stay on the lobby floor. They allowed me to leave. I left . . . with the memory that I came within three feet of shaking hands with the President of the United States!

By the end of July, I gave my paper route to Bobby LaFrance's younger brother. Actually, I owed it to him for filling in for me a few times, so I just paid him off by handing him the route. I was glad to be rid of it. Earlier that day, Mr. Smith called and told me a truck would pick me up in front of Busy Corner the first Monday morning in August. It was blueberry season.

*   *   *

Early that Monday, a truck picked up the seven boys waiting in front of Busy Corner and drove us to the blueberry fields on the outskirts of Gilmanton. What an awesome sight. Before my eyes, were acres upon acres of blue-coated fields. After a brief demonstration on how to use a blueberry rake, the thirty some odd boys Mr. Smith hired for the season, were assigned areas to be raked. Beginning at the bottom of the mountain, we raked blueberries in a lane about eight feet wide, clear to the top of the field. Once you finished raking the berries in your lane, you were assigned another area to rake. This process was repeated over and over for the entire month of August, until all the fields were completely clear of blueberries.

A low bush blueberry rake is similar to a dustpan with an inverted handle at the top. The rake has some twenty long teeth in the front, with metal sides to prevent the berries from falling out. With rake in hand, you simply flicked your wrist and scooped the berries into the rake. Once the rake was nearly full, you tipped it on its side and allowed the blueberries to cascade into a wooden pint basket. A crate contained twenty-four pint baskets. We were paid $1 for each crate we filled. On a good day, I usually raked seven or eight crates full of blueberries.

It didn't come as a surprise to Mr. Smith that the new hires gorged themselves with blueberries the first day on the job. At the end of the day, my hands and face were smeared in blue from all the blueberries I stuffed in my mouth. That night, when I closed my eyes, a sea of blueberries were ineradicably implanted in my dreams, only to be disturbed by an urgent need to find my way to the toilet. It was like having my first cigarette or jug of hard cider. It was a lesson to remember. For the rest of the month, I don't think I ate another blueberry.

Wally and I pretty much worked side by side. No matter how hard I worked, Wally always managed to rake a crate a day more than everyone else. He just had a knack. Nobody raked more blueberries than he did. Actually, I was glad I worked next to him. He motivated me to work harder; consequently, I made more money.

Raking berries was a fun job. Oh, it was hard work, but we also had fun in the fields. We were never bossed around like migrant workers. Everyone worked at his own pace. Mr. Smith was fine with that. He brought jugs of ice water to the field and even encouraged us to take breaks. It wasn't uncommon to rake up a grass snake every now and then. Some boys were scared to death of snakes. That's when the fun began!

At the end of each day, we reconciled the number of crates we picked with Mr. Smith. On Friday afternoon, we were paid for the prior week's work. I was content to reach my goal of $35 a week, which was slightly above average. By the end of the month, I made nearly $150 raking blueberries.

Things were looking up. I finally had enough money to buy some clothes for school. I also set aside money to buy new ski equipment, and even saved a few dollars so I wouldn't be bumming off my friends all year. I had to budget carefully, knowing it would be a long time before I would get my hands on money again.

*   *   *

In the fall of 1955, there was more going on than deep blue skies, leaves changing colors, and people putting up wood framed storm windows for another harsh winter. There was a storm brewing, but it wasn't about the weather. No, this was about a culture change sweeping across the country. You only had to look around to notice that the new model cars were a lot fancier. They had more style, more chrome, and bigger engines. The new Ford Thunderbird convertible was the rage, followed by the powerful Oldsmobile 88, Pontiac Star Chief, and ever-popular Chevy Bel Air. Those were exciting cars. Those were exciting times.

Communist Russia still had their big bombs pointed directly at the U.S. However, the man everyone feared, Joseph Stalin, was now dead. Nikita Khrushchev was certainly a force to be dealt with, but not to the same extent as Stalin. In fact, he denounced Stalin for his intolerance, his brutality, and his abuse of power. There was hope that perhaps we could reach an accord with the new Russian leader.

In many places, blacks weren't allowed to vote and women were hardly allowed in the workplace, but that's not a problem, right? Many people didn't think so, until a few brave people stood up to speak out for civil rights. The U.S. Supreme Court handed down a landmark decision the year before in a case called *Brown vs. Board of Education of Topeka, Kansas*. In that decision, the high court ruled, "The segregation of white and colored children in public schools was unconstitutional." Courageously, on December 1, 1955, Rosa Parks refused to give up her seat on a public bus to make room for a white passenger. She was arrested, tried, and convicted of disorderly conduct.

Subsequently, fifty African-American leaders gathered and organized the Montgomery Bus Boycott to demand a more humane bus system in Montgomery, Alabama. Ninety percent of the Negroes in Montgomery participated in the boycott. It lasted 381 days until the ordinance segregating blacks and whites on public buses was lifted. That one brave move by Rosa Parks opened many eyes to the injustice and bigotry prevalent throughout the South.

A young Baptist minister, named Martin Luther King Jr., was president of the Montgomery Improvement Association, the organization that directed the boycott. The protest made King a national figure. His eloquent appeals created a positive impression on people both inside and outside the South. This was the beginning of what we refer to as the Civil Rights Movement. Yes, these times they were a changin.'

There was also a changing of the guard taking place in the world of music in the mid-50s. A new style of fast Bebop music was the new rage everywhere. Why is it that change is usually viewed as something bad and threatening? Adults were visibly concerned about this new craze called Rock N' Roll. They were sure it would undermine the morals of our youth. They didn't understand it. They said it had sexual overtones. It was immoral. Why, it even brought people of both races together. Moreover, as a teenager who loved to dance, I couldn't get enough of it.

I don't know of a tecnager who didn't see the movie, "Blackboard Jungle," released in 1955. I walked out of the Colonial theatre with a cocky swagger, snapping my fingers to Bill Haley's, "Rock Around the Clock," after watching the show. I identified with Greg Miller, played by Sidney Portier.

In the movie, Miller tried to get the most out of his education but soon realized nobody really cared, so he succumbed to the frustrations and decided to bide his time until he could legally drop out of school. He wisely stayed out of trouble for fear of being expelled and sent to reform school. I certainly could relate to that. The ubiquitous Detective Slayton seemed to take a special interest in my daily activities. The man simply didn't like me. He would have loved to send me to reform school.

"Blackboard Jungle" was a shocking movie for its time. If students could terrorize teachers in Brooklyn, was it far fetched to believe that the same type of disruption could happen in the far away reaches of New Hampshire?

The trend of the time for a teenager was to be "cool." To be "cool" meant different things to different people. Most of all, it was reflected in the powerful impression the movies of the day had on teenagers. It would be a mistake to discount the influence of the movies of the 50s. Movies such as, "The Wild One," "Blackboard Jungle," and "Rebel Without a Cause," had a profound impact on shaping teenage culture in the mid-50s.

It was reflected in the way you dressed. It was cool to wear 14" pegged pants. You couldn't buy slacks that way. They had to be specially tailored. It was cool to comb your hair in Duck's Ass hairstyle, like the kids in Blackboard Jungle, and later like James Dean and Elvis Pressley. It left a message akin to, look out, or, I don't care. Most importantly, it was about how you carried yourself. It was cool to have that controlled, sullen look, almost as if you were pouting. The look so popularized by the late, great, James Dean. Either you had it or you didn't. Saying words like, "cool man," or "I dig it," and greeting friends with words copied from a movie like, "Dadio," didn't make you cool. The popular farewell words of the day were, "See you later, alligator." That was supposed to be cool? It only went to demonstrate the profound impact music and movies had on teenagers at that time.

This new swing sound called Rock N' Roll certainly captured my attention. This was the music of my day. My *drug de jour* was the steady stream of great hit songs coming at me rapid fire, one right after another. Songs such as, "Tutti Frutti," by Little Richard, "Maybelline" by Chuck Berry, "Ain't It A Shame," by Fats Domino, and La Vern Baker's hit, "Bop Ting-A-Ling." What was so different about these great artists? Simply: they were black. They had soul. Their music was finally recognized and accepted by teenage America. The music of Pat Boone, Eddie Fisher, Tab Hunter, Doris Day, and Patti Page, was quickly going the way of the dinosaur. This was another indication that teenagers had a mind and a voice too. It was our time to be heard. If the world was changing, we were the ones responsible for the change.

For my sixteenth birthday, Danny Matthews took me to the Colonial theatre to see "Rebel Without A Cause." If a movie ever had an impact on my life, that was the one. Oh, how I could identify with James Dean's portrayal of the sensitive high school misfit Jim Stark in the movie. Jim Stark defiantly rejected the values of his parents while desperately aching to "belong" and attempting to find a purpose in life. As with his character in "East of Eden," Dean played a misunderstood outcast desperately craving approval from a father figure.

For God's sakes, that was me! I was that disenchanted, rebellious teenager, desperately seeking acceptance and approval from his mother, who was too self-absorbed in her own quest for acceptance. All I wanted was a little love and attention. Without it, I was left to my own wits to find approval and acceptance whenever and wherever I could.

It didn't matter to me that I didn't have a birthday cake or birthday present from my parents. My birthday hadn't been acknowledged from the day I was born. It was enough that Danny took me to the movie. We substituted the cake with a six-pack of Budweiser he bought from his local "source."

It was after midnight when I quietly made my way to my bedroom. Outside my window, the snow was falling from the sky. As I took off my jacket, I noticed the frost coming from my mouth as I exhaled. It was freezing in my room. When I made my way to the radiator in the corner, I discovered the control knob had been removed so I couldn't turn on the heat. That night, and for the rest of the winter, I slept in the unheated room next to the attic. Happy Birthday, Sonny!

I fell asleep dreaming about the scene in "Rebel Without A Cause" where Jim Stark is playing "chicken" against his adversary, Buzz Gunderson, the school bully. In the scene, the last one to roll out of his car before it goes over the cliff is called "chicken." What I was dreaming wasn't about Gunderson's arm being caught in the door handle, sending him to his death. No, my dream was about someday owning my own car like Jim Stark and visualizing myself rolling out of my car at the last split second like he did.

I wandered from that dream to dreaming about playing point guard for the Laconia High School Sachems varsity basketball team. In that dream, I was making great passes to teammates and dribbling the ball behind my back, just like Bob Cousy, to the roar of the crowd. How timely was that dream. Basketball tryouts were scheduled for the following week.

*   *   *

The varsity basketball tryouts were held the next Tuesday afternoon. After an hour or so of basic basketball drills, it was time to get down to business. The new coach had the returning varsity players guard the non-varsity players in a one-on-one situation. We sat on the sidelines and watched the proceedings, as everyone took their turn to try to impress the new coach.

When it came my turn, Bobby Carter, a returning senior, was sent out to guard me. Prior to that, I watched Bobby steal the ball from one boy as he dribbled toward the basket and block a shot attempted by another player. That didn't faze me. I was ready for him. Starting at mid-court, with ball in hand, I dribbled toward the left sideline. He waited for me to make a move toward the basket. I sensed he thought I would to try to drive by him to make a lay up, so I changed direction and dribbled back toward the foul line. There, I made a quick shoulder fake, like I was going to drive straight to the basket. He reacted by stepping back to block me. When he did that, I immediately stopped, turned, and took a jump shot. Bobby Carter was on his heels. Swishhhhh. All he could do was watch the ball fall through the hoop. The kids sitting on the sideline clapped. I heard one of them holler, "Atta go Cooz." I tried to conceal my grin as I took my place back on the sideline. My tryout couldn't have gone any better.

It was close to 6:00 p.m. when the tryouts were finished. The coach had us wait in the gym until he returned with the list of those who would be cut that night. A few minutes later, he returned with his list. Ten players were cut. As he read the ninth name, I was confident I made the team. Then, the tenth name was read . . . it was my name. There was silence in the gym. You could hear a pin drop. Stunned doesn't begin to express how I felt at that moment. To me, this was a cataclysmic catastrophe of unparalleled proportions.

I wasn't going to let that happen without an explanation. As the other boys showered after practice, I went to see the coach. I pleaded my case.

"What did I do wrong?" I asked. "Didn't you see me fake Carter out and make the basket?"

He just sat behind his desk, with his head down, and simply said, "Sorry, I made my decision."

I headed straight out the school building so nobody could see the anger on my face. I was crushed. My dream was shattered. I had my heart set on playing varsity basketball ever since I was in the sixth grade. As I made my way home, I kept trying to find the answer. It had to be something besides basketball. Was it my Duck's Ass hair cut? The clothes I wore? Or, was he influenced by other factors, like my background?

I was angry. I felt betrayed by an adult again. That night, as I huddled under the seven blankets on my bed, I could only wonder, "When in hell am I ever going to get a break in life?"

The next morning, as I walked toward my homeroom, it seemed like the whole school stopped to ask, "Didja make it Cooz?"

To my credit, I held my head high and responded, "No, I wasn't good enough."

End of discussion. I vowed I would never attend another high school basketball game at Laconia High. I couldn't get the right answer from the basketball coach, but in my heart, I knew that someday he would have to give that answer to a higher power.

I was deeply hurt by not making the varsity team, but I knew there was nothing to be gained by dwelling on it. It is what it is. Some people call it character building. Whatever it is, I had to move beyond it. Besides, it was winter. There was snow on the ground. And, didn't I save money to buy new ski equipment?

* * *

Young Francis Piche had a dream too. His dream was to someday own a prosperous ski shop in Belknap county. He held down two jobs just to save enough money to start his business. I met Mr. Piche when he was just starting out. It couldn't have happened at a more fortuitous time. After looking at all the ski equipment in his store, I had to confess that I only had $55.

He paused for a moment, and then said to me, "Look, I'm going to give you a heck of a good deal, but I expect you to tell all your friends to come and see me."

He did give me a heck of a good deal. For $55, I was able to buy a new pair of skis, with the new step in bindings and a new pair of ski boots. He even threw in a set of ski poles to seal the deal. There was only one thing lacking in my ski arsenal: Money.

That was always the all too familiar story in my adolescent years. I aspired to do all sorts of neat things, but was always denied those opportunities for lack of funds. Funds were limited, but I never gave up. I believed in that old adage: *"When there's a will, there's a way."*

The week after Mr. Piche fit my boots to my bindings, I marched into the office of Fritzy Baer, the General Manager of the Belknap County Recreation Area, and offered my services in return for ski passes. Mr. Baer just happened to need a busboy to clear tables during the peak Saturday lunch period.

While chomping on his cigar, out of the side of his mouth he told me, "Ya, Cousy, I can use you. How bout' seventy-five cents an hour and a ski pass for every day you work?"

I was delighted with his offer. It was a win-win for the both of us. As it turned out, it didn't go quite as I envisioned.

Many of the skiers treated busboys like dirt. They made no attempt to bring their trays to the trashcans. The cafeteria was always packed during the 11:00 a.m. to 1:00 p.m. lunch time, and it was as if it was my fault a table wasn't ready for people to sit at as soon as they got their food. People became angry at me, instead of the skiers who lingered around drinking coffee and talking with their friends, instead of being polite and giving up their table. Hell, yes, blame it on the busboy. It's all his fault!

On Saturdays, caravans of busses made their way from Massachusetts carrying busloads of school kids to the Belknap Area. Some of these kids came from the inner-city areas around Boston, just like in the movie "Blackboard Jungle." Many of them didn't come to the area to ski; they came looking for a fight.

After the lunch rush, we folded the tables and stacked them to the side of the room, leaving the main floor open for kids to dance to the music on the jukebox. On Saturday afternoons, kids came from everywhere in the state to jitterbug and show off their dance steps at the Belknap Area. It was the place to be.

That was a recipe for trouble if there ever was one. This wasn't the movies; this was happening in real time. It wasn't uncommon to see opposing gang members from places like Chelsea, South Boston, and Dorchester, dressed in leather motorcycle jackets, engineering boots, and light blue jeans, circling in their gangs, with switch blade knives in hand, just waiting for someone to say the wrong thing to ignite a brawl.

There I was, on a cozy Saturday afternoon, bussing tables at a ski area full of thugs looking for trouble in the boondocks of New Hampshire. If some of these gang members were in high school, they must have been there on the ten-year plan. They looked to be well into their twenties.

On one particular Saturday, a gang of hoods intentionally poured a strawberry milk shake on a table, allowing it to drip onto the chairs and floor. They laughed at me as I attempted to mop it up, just trying to goad me into a fight. I knew better, but I also knew this could turn into a very violent day at the Area.

Fritzy Baer was sitting at his desk, oblivious to the world, when I barged into his office and pleaded with him to call the state police to the Area. It took a little convincing, but when he saw these thugs tearing snow chains from bus tires to use as weapons, he looked at me and said, "Oh my God, what to hell is going on out there?"

Without any delay, he immediately got on his phone and called the state police. Fortunately, a stream of police cars arrived within a half an hour and a riot squad was on hand to avert any potential outbreak. The thugs were given the option of leaving or going to the county jail. From that day on, two police officers were on duty at the Belknap Area on Saturdays for the rest of the ski season.

*　　*　　*

Many changes happened in January 1956. It would have been a dull evening babysitting my little brother on New Year's Eve had Danny Matthews not shown up, unannounced, with a bottle of vodka. Danny was well on his way to being inebriated when he knocked on the door around ten o'clock that night.

As he stumbled into the house, wet shoes and all, with that silly grin of his, he announced, "Hey Cooz, I knew you were stuck babysitting so I came over to wish you a Happy New Year!"

With Pudg sound asleep and nobody else around, Danny and I proceeded to drink the bottle of vodka. Danny had this uncanny ability to imitate my mother.

In his best Ora act he would imitate her with a line like, "Sonny, you keep that goddamn Matthews kid away from here. I don't want to see him in this goddamn house again. Do you hear me?"

I was almost rolling on the kitchen floor laughing when he did his latest imitation of her. Of course, the more I laughed, the more it egged him on. Finally, a little before midnight, I sent Danny on his way.

My head was spinning, but I managed to wipe up his footprints before they got home. I was sound asleep in Ben's chair in the living room when my mother, Ben, and another loud couple, came staggering into the kitchen, making a beeline to the freezer. Even half asleep, I couldn't help but notice Ben acquired one hell of a big black eye. As the story was related to me, Ben stood up for my mother's honor at the Rod & Gun Club, and the two Bilodeau brothers jumped him. I knew Ben well enough to know he would never back down from a good fight. He was fearless that way, but the Bilodeau boys easily outweighed him by twenty-five pounds each and it took two of them to take him down. He was like a happy prizefighter, getting all the attention, as my mother doted over him and applied a cold ice pack to his eye.

The next morning when I entered the kitchen, poor Ben was sitting at the kitchen table with a towel full of ice covering his left eye. He proudly removed the towel from his bruised face so I could view the damage done the night before. His wounded eye was black and blue, all puffed out, and practically swollen shut. The left side of his face looked like he might have had an encounter with a pit bull the night before.

When I suggested that he go to the hospital and get his eye checked out, he scoffed, and said, "I don't need to go to the damn hospital for this little thing,"

He looked bad, but there would be no convincing the punching Pollock to seek medical treatment. No, he would rather display his shiner like a badge of courage.

Shortly after observing poor Ben's eye, my big sister Lorraine came bouncing into the kitchen, all smiles, joyfully exposing her newly acquired engagement ring, poised on the fourth finger of her left hand. What a New Year's Day dichotomy: Ben sitting on one side of the table, wincing in obvious pain; Lorraine directly across from him, smiling ecstatically, as she pondered a future life of love and bliss; while I sat between them not knowing whether to smile joyfully or show remorse for Ben.

I was able to escape the confrontation of both emotions, when my mother suddenly appeared in the doorway demanding, "Someone, get me an Alka-Seltzer."

When all the questions of the activities of the night before were answered, Ora began to take control of my sister's wedding plans. It's a given she had to be married in the Sacred Heart Church. Lorraine wanted a simple wedding ceremony, followed by a small reception, limited to the immediate families. Oh, no, that wouldn't be right for my mother. Ora had to send out wedding invitations, announcements, and insisted they have a wedding reception at the Opechee Park clubhouse. This had to be a first class wedding. After all, she wasn't paying for it!

Time was of the essence. Lorraine's fiancé, Bill, an Army helicopter pilot, was scheduled to report for additional training at Fort Rucker, Alabama, the following month, before heading off for a tour of duty in Korea. By circumstances, thankfully, sufficient time wasn't available to produce some ostentatious celebration.

A few days later, when Lorraine and Bill's engagement and impending wedding was posted on the second page of the Citizen, ironically, a front page story pertaining to another relative drew far more interest from the local citizenry.

There, in bold black and white lettering was a story about the State of New Hampshire Fish and Game Department catching two men killing a helpless deer in a field north of Sanbornton. According to the paper, they shined their headlights, at night, directly at the poor defenseless creature, blinding it, while they shot at it until it fell to the ground in the snow-covered field.

In a hunting state like New Hampshire, poaching was as dastardly an act as adultery. As hard as I tried to understand why my grandfather, Joe Garneau, would do such a stupid thing, there was no plausible explanation. As far as I knew, my grandfather was not a hunter. I didn't even know he owned a shotgun. To my knowledge, he didn't even like venison. That didn't matter. What mattered was that he was there that night. He pleaded guilty and was fined a whopping $1,500. Worse yet, he lost credibility and standing in the French Catholic parish, where he was a leader in the Knights of Columbus, as well as losing the respect of many of his friends and fellow shopkeepers on Main street. Shame on you Grampy Garneau.

Now he had a little dose of the public sneering my mother had to endure.

*   *   *

As if the first two weeks of January 1956 didn't have enough surprises, the real shocker came on January 12 of that year. Just five days before the statute of limitations was due to expire, the FBI arrested six members of the eleven-member Brinks Robbery gang. Once billed as "The Crime of the Century," the FBI tracked all the pieces of the puzzle to a successful conclusion. The public was as stunned the day they were captured, as they were the day the robbery took place on January 17, 1950. On May 16, 1956, the FBI stormed into the apartment of the last two gang members in Dorchester, Massachusetts, and arrested the both of them. When it was all said and done, one gang member died in prison, one was already dead, and eight of the gang members received maximum sentences of life imprisonment, but were all paroled in 1970. The snitch, "Specks" O'Keefe, only received a four year sentence and was released from prison in 1960. Only $58,000 of the $2.7 million stolen was ever recovered.

*   *   *

Less than a month after the FDI rounded up six of the Brinks gang, on a Saturday morning, on a cold winter day, Lorraine and Bill took their marriage vows in the Sacred Heart Church. Despite the joy of the occasion, my mother was chagrin with the knowledge that her oldest daughter and star boarder would soon be moving. To spend a few weeks together, before Bill had to leave for his next assignment, they decided to rent an apartment from Grammy Garneau, directly across the street from our house. This would afford them a little privacy.

It all happened so suddenly, my sister didn't have time to contemplate the life before her as the wife of an Army officer. There would be the constant moving from base to base, the lonely nights waiting and praying for her husband to return home safely from another deployment, the social demands of being a career officer's wife, and eventually her very own life as a mother and woman in a changing world. Her life would be very different from that day forward. If anyone was up to the challenge, it was my spunky, feisty, sister, Lorraine.

What, with Ben's black eye on New Year's Eve, Lorraine's wedding in February, and the successful capture of the Brinks robbers, it was time to settle down by a cozy fireplace and read a good book. Ah, and such a book resounded all across the country in the winter of 1956, sending shock waves to every living room, and possibly bedroom, in small towns all over New England.

This was especially so, in the town of Laconia, New Hampshire. It was there that Grace Metalious wrote the shocking fictitious novel, "Peyton Place," which was a composite of all small towns where ugliness rears its head, and people try to hide all the skeletons in their closets. It may have been a "fictitious" novel, but to everyone living in Laconia or nearby Gilmanton, several characters and episodes were drawn from events that actually occurred in nearby towns and with people Metalious actually knew.

There sure was a lot of finger pointing going on in Laconia. Of course, it seemed like everyone "personally" knew the controversial author. Even my mother claimed to have drunk with her at the Rod & Gun. What really mattered was that her book was so popular, it sold 60,000 copies within the first ten days of its release and remained on the New York Times bestseller list for fifty-nine weeks.

Grace Metalious wrote very accurately about New Englanders and many in her hometown still remember the scandal caused by the book. Years later, when she died, she was almost barred from being buried in the church cemetery, but the townsfolk in Gilmanton finally relented. I was proud to have met Grace Metalious. She was a rare talent. A breath of fresh air for anyone brave enough to speak the truth and expose the hypocrisy so prevalent in our society. With writers such as Grace Metalious, Jack Kerouac, Norman Mailer, and Ayn Rand questioning contemporary values, these times, they were definitely a changin.'

CHAPTER 20

MY FIRST LOVE

Mom refused to rent a room to a woman, other than my sister Lorraine. She said they were too much trouble, stayed in the bathroom too long, and always left a mess. As a consequence, she would always have to pick up after them. She much preferred men. They were quiet, didn't linger in the bathroom, paid their rent on time, and never gave her a problem. Since we only lived a block away from the Scott & Williams factory, she rented to a steady entourage of foreigners, mostly from South America, who came for a six to eight week training program at Scott's to learn how to use the big knitting machines. The foreigners were exceptionally quiet and polite, paid their rent on time, and we hardly knew they were living in our house.

However, one day when I came home from school she was sitting in the living room absorbed in what seemed like a serious conversation with a woman I had never seen before. She introduced me to Elizabeth and told me she would be occupying the room adjacent to mine. Elizabeth looked at me with a half smile and extended her right hand, while staying seated. I was instantly preoccupied trying to analyze this new stranger in our life who would be living one latch click away from my bedroom. She looked frail, almost hungry, as my eyes tried to capture the physical features of our new tenant.

As she stood up to leave, I noticed she was tall, about thirty years old, and appeared to have a bruise on her left cheek. She was well dressed, probably in her best outfit to impress Ora Novak, and arrived with only one small suitcase. Elizabeth appeared to be shy by nature and desperately needed a place to stay. There was something sexy about her. My, my, how the imagination of a sixteen-year-old boy, exploding with newly discovered testosterone, could fantasize encounters with a seductive older woman.

As soon as Elizabeth left the living room, I launched a cascade of questions at my mother. "What was she doing here? Where did she come from? Why is she renting a room to a woman?" And on and on.

Oddly, my mother was willing to share what she knew about her new boarder.

Mom readily told me, "Elizabeth came from Connecticut and took the train to Laconia to get away from a man who abused her." Her confidence shattered, her self-esteem low, she couldn't take the daily pounding of his fist any longer.

My mother went on to tell me, "She arrived in Laconia around noon today, stumbled into Freddie's Café, and was sent here when she asked Freddie if he knew of a good place to stay." Broke, no job, and no place to stay, my mother took her in. Not only did my mother allow her stay with us, she coerced Freddie into giving Elizabeth a job as a waitress, loaned her money to buy food until she could get back on her feet, and became her confidant and friend. Certainly, Ora identified with her. She felt her pain. She knew misery and understood Elizabeth's suffering. In her past, Ora had also suffered indignity and abuse. This encounter was as therapeutic for Ora as it was for Elizabeth.

In a matter of a couple of weeks, Elizabeth was smiling and enjoying her new life in the bucolic town of Laconia. She made friends at work, paid her rent on time, and was eternally grateful to my mother. In the afternoon, during her shift break, she often came by to talk with her friend, Ora, before going to her room. In one of those conversations, Mom learned that Elizabeth had a new boyfriend. His name was Norman.

Norman was also a stranger who wandered into town and met her at Freddie's Cafe. My mother didn't know Norman or anything about him, that is, until Elizabeth told her that Norman was recently released from the State Penitentiary.

All the right alarms went off. My mother tried to convince her that she was playing with dynamite again. Poor Elizabeth, with her low self esteem, she desperately searched for love and accepted it anywhere she could find it. Unfortunately, she wasn't particularly attractive. She had one of those long horse faces with drooping eyes and a gangly figure. She was vulnerable to any man looking to take advantage of her. Regrettably, she was cast in that mold. Nothing my mother would say could change her mind about her new ex-con boyfriend. She fearlessly defended her Norman.

"Oh, no, Ora, you don't understand. He's paid for his crime. He's a new man. He's kind to me," she told my mother.

Why, she even brought him to the house one afternoon to meet her friend, Ora.

I didn't want to miss the opportunity to size up Norman either, so I came directly home from school that day just to meet the love of Elizabeth's life. He was as phony as a three dollar bill. He went overboard trying to win my mother's approval, but I could tell by the tightness of her jaw muscle that she wasn't the least bit enamored by Norman. Elizabeth was on cloud nine as the con held her hand, while she extolled how wonderfully he treated her.

I didn't get it. Norman didn't have a job, mooched beers off her when she was working, sponged money from her, and soon became upset when she smiled at any of the regular customers. He freeloaded off her until the bar closed at 9:00 p.m., and then walked her home every night. She was now living life in a new fish bowl.

Within a month of meeting the "love of her life," Elizabeth confided in my mother that Norman was very jealous and twisted her arm the night before when he walked her home. She was becoming disenchanted with Norman. The magic had worn off. She didn't know what to do. He hadn't hit her . . . yet, but she was scared of him. All my mother could tell her was that she had to end their relationship now.

This is how it ended. One night, when I went into my freezing bedroom, I thought I heard a noise coming from Elizabeth's room. I knew she was still at work, so I disregarded it. Later, I was awakened by the sound of scuffling coming from her room. Her lights were off, but I heard her crying as Norman told her to "shut up."

She was too scared to scream for help. Then, Norman threw her onto the bed and was tearing her clothes off. I just had to help her.

A hundred thoughts entered my mind at the same time. She desperately needed someone to help her. I thought of busting through the adjoining door and pulling him off, but I didn't know if he held a knife on her. Besides, he was much bigger than I was. In desperation, I opened the door to the attic and rushed down the stairs to get Ben's help.

Barging into their room, I pleaded, "Ben, Ben, wake up. Norman is in Elizabeth's room right now and he's hurting her."

Ben took the matter into his own hands. He bolted from their bedroom in his pajamas and was at the top of the stairs before I could make it around the corner. It all happened so suddenly.

Ben flung Norman down the front stairs, while telling him, "You get your sorry ass out of here," and "I'll kill you if you ever come in this house again."

Norman was cowering and apologizing as he quickly made his way out the front door. He was pleading to Ben, "Please don't call the cops."

I don't know if Ben or my mother called the cops on Norman that night. I do know he left town and was never seen again. When I went back to my room after the big confrontation, I heard Elizabeth crying, as she tried to muffle her sounds in a blanket.

"Are you alright, Elizabeth?" I asked.

She responded from the other side of the door, "I will be, Thanks."

The events of that relationship seriously rattled Elizabeth. She was embarrassed to have been duped again. I could only wonder how many times she would allow herself to be victimized before something seriously harmful happened to her. A few days later, she and my mother were both in tears as she made her way out the front door, suitcase in hand, heading for a new destination. Ben drove her to the train station on his way to work that morning. We never saw Elizabeth again.

*   *   *

Now that I was sixteen, I desperately wanted to learn how to drive a car. I knew better than to ask my mother or Ben to teach me. We had an unspoken understanding between us. She wanted me to drop out of school, work at the shoe shop or someplace . . . anyplace . . . and pay her room and board. That wasn't going to happen. I was determined to graduate from high school, just like my sisters had done. By now, she was resigned to that fact. She had to settle for my free babysitting service on Saturday night, while I had to settle on the fact the heat wouldn't be turned on in my room until I paid for it. We both held our ground.

Ronnie Timmons already had his driver's license and his father let him drive the family car occasionally. Ronnie wanted to teach me, but his parents wouldn't allow that. All he could do was tell me when he was shifting gears and letting the clutch out. I signed up for Driver's Ed at the beginning of the school year, but wasn't accepted for the fall session because I wasn't sixteen at the time. However, a break came my way when I was selected for the spring session. I don't know how the school selected students for the course. The driving instructor, Socrates (Soc) Bobotas may have had something to do with it. Driver's Ed was in demand. Some thirty students applied for the class; only five were selected.

As my History teacher, I respected Soc Bobatas, but more importantly, regarded him as a friend. Having had him as a teacher for three years, we knew each other quite well. Soc once told me I was wasting my time in school and was capable of earning much better grades. He was correct. However, at that time in my life I was preoccupied with my own survival, let alone learning about the history of Western Civilization.

The Driver's Ed course lasted twelve weeks. The five of us met Soc in the school parking lot, three days a week, for driving lessons. By the end of the twelve week session, we all mastered the skills needed to take the state driving exam . . . with one exception: Me!

With a wink, Soc Bobotas told me, "I think you'd benefit from a little more "one-on-one" personal training Cooz. Don't you think?"

He had a slight grin on his face when he suggested that. The fact is he told me I drove very well and really didn't need any additional driver training. Later that day, after we hopped in the car, Soc confided with me that he'd have to monitor a study hall during that period unless he happened to have a student that needed additional training. He didn't want to spend that hour in a boring study hall any more than I did sitting there passing notes and doodling on a notepad.

Besides, it was spring, the snow was almost completely gone and we finally had great weather to drive around and kill an hour, three times a week. Most of all, it told me that Soc Bobotas trusted me enough to allow me to share this little secret.

Some days, I drove Soc to the Laconia Country Club and waited in the car while he checked out the latest golf equipment in the Pro Shop. On other days, we drove to the Weirs or out toward Gilford . . . whatever we could squeeze in during that hour.

I wasn't allowed to use the school Driver's Ed car to take the driving test, so it took some conniving and creative thinking to convince my mother it would be in her best interest if I had my driver's license, just in case I had to take her or Pudgie to the hospital in an emergency. With conviction, I assured her that would be the only circumstance in which I would ever drive their car. She bought into that line of bullshit.

It was on a cold, rainy day in late April when Ben came home from work early to drive me to the police station to take the driving test. I passed the written portion with flying colors. Next, came the eye exam. That's when I learned I needed glasses. I flunked the eye exam. End of test. There would be no further examination until I got glasses. I knew I squinted when I read. Maybe that's why I had trouble seeing the blackboard in school?

Two days later, the school nurse arranged for me to have a free eye examination at a local optometrist's office. What I discovered that day was that my vision was 20/200 in my right eye and 20/400 in my left eye. When I asked the optometrist how long my eyesight had been that bad, he informed me that most likely I was born that way. To think, all those years I struggled trying to read the blackboard in school and finally learned all the while I had terrible vision. Not only could I not qualify to drive a car, now I needed to earn money to buy a pair of glasses. My woes never seemed to end.

*   *   *

Spring break finally arrived. It was an absolutely gorgeous day outside as I walked down Merrimac Street, on my way to a friend's house when I came upon a fellow Explorer Scout, Richard Charon, playing with visiting relatives in front of his house. He called me over to meet his cousin.

Suddenly, before me, stood the most gorgeous girl I had ever seen. My heart was pounding, my knees were weak, and I was speechless for a moment as I gazed at this beautiful girl approaching me in the street. Richard's cousin, Nancy Cleary, was visiting from Manchester. Words can't describe the energy flowing through the both of us as we met in the middle of the street. It was a magical moment. I don't know where she came from. God must have brought her to me. It was love at first sight. I was instantly in love for the first time in my life.

I don't know what came over me. I held her hand, right there in the middle of the street, gazed in her eyes, as we both grinned and stared at each other. Chills were running through my body. Nancy was barely five foot tall, shiny brown hair, huge brown eyes that twinkled when she looked at me, dimples on both cheeks, and the cutest shaped body of any girl I had ever seen. But, it was the energy, the mutual attraction we shared, that took control of me. It was as though we waited our entire brief lifetime to meet.

For the next few days, we couldn't see enough of each other. Richard told her that I was "the Cooz," his friend, a good basketball player, and a "real cool cat" on the dance floor. I didn't know Richard very well, but I certainly agreed with anything positive he had to say about me. In the course of our conversations, I learned that Nancy went to the largest high school in the state, Central High in Manchester, had very strict parents, that her father owned a small grocery store near their house, and that she didn't have a steady boyfriend.

Richard played the drums, so I suddenly acquired an interest in his talent as an excuse to see Nancy every day during her visit. We didn't have any time alone, so we mostly grinned and stared at each other and talked about all the little things we had in common, like music and dancing. Oh, how badly I wanted to squeeze this girl on a dance floor. Her aunt finally agreed to allow her and Richard to go to the dance at the high school gym on Friday night, the day before she was to return to Manchester.

I wore the only good clothes I had to the dance. The same shirt and pants that I wore at my sister's wedding three months earlier. I waited nervously inside the school gym for her to arrive.

Finally, Nancy came into the room in a stylish khaki skirt, pressed pink blouse, and brown penny loafers.

She spotted me standing in a corner, came over to me smiling, and said, "C'mon Cousy, let's dance!"

That was one of the most memorable nights of my life. We moved on that dance floor as if we had been dancing together for twenty years. And when the new Elvis Presley song, "I was The One" played, she pressed her body even closer to mine, rested her head on my shoulder, as we squeezed our joined hands together in an embracing caress. I wasn't dancing; I was waltzing on a cloud.

Here I was, dancing with the most gorgeous girl in the room, and all she wanted was to be with me. Me, the sawed off little runt, with the bad eyes, the missing front tooth to complement a mouth full of cavities, not a dollar to his name, not a car to drive her home, and no prospect for a brighter future.

"What did I do to deserve this girl? What could she possibly see in me?" I wondered, as we walked together in the rain, holding hands, on a cold April night. Richard trailed behind, finally allowing us to be alone.

As I held her hand on the way back to her aunt's house, I told her, "I've never felt this way before. I think I'm falling in love with you. You're the best thing that's ever happened to me."

We stopped walking for a moment. Gently, she squeezed my hand, looked at me with those big brown eyes of hers, and said, "I've never met anyone like you. You're just so sweet. I think I'm falling in love with you too. Here we are, soaking wet, and I just want to stay out here with you all night,"

I was touched. No, I was thrilled! We felt the same way. There I stood, with this beautiful girl beside me, who only wanted to be with me. After awhile, Nancy told me she overheard Richard's mother telling her mother bad things about me on the phone. Something about me being "trouble" and "wild." Nancy wasn't influenced by her aunt's gossip. They weren't about to change how she felt about me. Where we left off that night was that we would write to each other. She would write first and give me an address where I could send my letters to her.

I desperately wanted to press my lips against hers, as we stood in front of her cousin's front door saying our goodbyes. I didn't though. I would save that for another special moment. I detected a small tear running down the side of her face, as I smiled, turned, and waved goodbye . . . . for now.

* * *

Teachers seemed to have a way of finding out everything that was going on at the school. Back in school the next week, Soc Bobotas saw me in the hall and asked me who I was taking to the Junior Prom?

I looked at him, smiled with a befuddled look, and said, "Soc you don't get it. Kids like me don't go to the Junior Prom."

I saw the sadness come over his face as he realized he just put his foot in his mouth. I knew he didn't mean any harm. He really thought I would go to something like the Junior Prom. He didn't hurt my feelings, because the Junior Prom was so far removed from my thought process, there is no way I could be disappointed. I couldn't even begin to dream of going to my Junior Prom with Nancy Cleary. All I could do was hope that someday, somehow, I would make it up to her. For now, I didn't have a car to drive her to the big dance, didn't even have a suit, and couldn't afford a corsage or a dinner at a fancy restaurant, so I reasoned they would just have to crown some rich shmucks in my class as the king and queen of the Prom for 1956. Cousy didn't live in that world.

My world was hanging out at the Nut Shoppe across from Scott & Williams, next door to Freddie's Café. The Nut Shoppe was formerly St. Jacques little grocery store where we went for ice cream cones in my younger days at St. Joseph's. The original Nut Shoppe was on Main Street. The owner was an elderly lady, named Doris, who had to relocate when her landlord raised her rent. Moving across the street from Scott & Williams was not the answer. First off, there was no place to park your car on busy Union Avenue. Secondly, everyone still did their shopping on Main Street. Besides that, the Busy Corner store stocked everything people might need in that neighborhood.

Little did Doris realize her new customers would primarily be the teenagers from the French Catholic high school and my friends

269

from Laconia High, who dropped by on their way home from school for a soda, a little gossip, and to listen to the jukebox.

At first, Doris was concerned that teenagers would be bad for her business. In time, she knew everyone by their first name and looked forward to the kids coming by in the afternoon. We respected her, supported her, and helped her little business succeed. Fighting or swearing was off limits in the Nut Shoppe. She wouldn't make a fortune there, but it was better than she expected.

She knew she took a big chance turning her business into a teenage hangout, but, like I jokingly told her once, "Doris, you got to risk it, if you want the biscuit!"

She gave me that knowing smile, to let me know she understood.

The crowd seemed to vanish from the Nut Shoppe a little before four o'clock in the afternoon to make their way to Dale Abbot's house to watch American Bandstand, live from the WFIL studios in Philadelphia. Dale and Frankie Sharp were high school sweethearts. Dale lived with her father and Aunt Cecile, affectionately called, Aunt CiCi, who allowed their living room to become a gathering place for some eight to ten teenagers every afternoon.

Actually, American Bandstand wasn't shown to the national television audience until August 1957, but it was shown locally via a television station in Boston. It was all about Rock N' Roll in 1956, as we watched the Philadelphia teenage celebrities show us the latest dance steps and the new Rock N' Roll artists perform their latest hits live on television. Often, Frankie and Dale practiced the latest jitterbug steps in the living room as we watched the show.

I carefully avoided dancing at Dale's house. I intently watched every move the Bandstand stars showed off, but I wasn't satisfied copying someone else's dance tricks. I wanted to develop a few surprises of my own. Alone, in the privacy of my bedroom, I created a few steps I planned to introduce in the first citywide Jitterbug contest to be held in the high school gym at the end of May.

By this time, Wally Wallette had a job detailing cars at night at Hiltz Pontiac, across the street from the Busy Corner store. Often, I stopped by and visited Wally while the shop radio was tuned to WKBW in Buffalo, New York. Oh yes, the Hound was around! Mr. Movin' was groovin,' way up there in the stratosphere where the weather was cool and clear! We would simultaneously bellow out a big "Ah-whoooooo" cry, imitating a barking hound, in unison with our favorite disc jockey. After he finished work, we often went by Truchon's or the Nut Shoppe to play the pinball machines, where I helped my friend part with some of his hard-earned cash.

I consciously chose to go anywhere but home until after Ora and Ben were asleep. The pressure was mounting for me to move away or pay rent to stay there. By some twisted quirk of my imagination, I reasoned that the more I stayed away from home, the faster time would pass and the sooner I could completely move away. In my sophomore year, my mother punished me by not allowing me to go to the high school dances on Friday night. I was much wiser now and figured out a solution to that problem. I simply didn't go home after school on Friday afternoon. You can't "ground" me if I'm not there!

Friday's were my party night. If one of my friends had a car, we cruised around town after the dance and ended up at Weeks Dairy Bar or Bill's Diner. Mostly, we were just hangin' out, scheming and dreaming, and every now and then, knocking down a few beers to validate our teenage macho virility.

Finally, the day of the first citywide Jitterbug contest arrived. Oddly enough, I didn't even have a dance partner until the day before the contest. A few girls came right out and asked if they could be my partner, but I respectfully declined. Sorry, I reasoned they just didn't know how to dance with "soul." Nancy would have been my choice but she wasn't available. I just would have to go out there and win it for her.

After considering my options, I asked a quiet girl from school that I had danced with a few times before to be my partner. Frances, wasn't in our clique, didn't hang out at the Nut Shoppe, and had never been to Dale Abbot's house, but I knew she could follow me and would complement my dancing style.

Before the contest began, I took Frances to a corner of the gym and showed her a couple of the moves I planned to pull off so she wouldn't be surprised and thrown off guard.

There were approximately twenty couples in the contest. As the music played, the judge tapped contestants on the shoulder to signal they were eliminated. By the time the third song played, there

271

were only two couples left standing: Me and Frances and Frankie and Dale. No coincidence there, these were my close friends, and I knew what they could do. The crowd on the sidelines was frantically cheering us on. I couldn't help but hear my old friend, Paul Slayton, holler out, "Go Get Em' Cooz!"

With the crowd cheering, I went for the kill to Fats Domino's, "Ain't That A Shame." Frank and Dale were limited to doing what they saw on Bandstand. I devised a little step where I actually got on my tiptoes like a ballet dancer, while making a move around my partner. It worked. The place went wild. When it was all said and done, "Cousy" won the first ever Jitterbug contest held in Laconia, New Hampshire.

The Judge presented us a small trophy, which symbolized that Frances and I were the winners. More importantly, we earned bragging rights as the "best dancers in the city." Again, I proved to myself that I was a winner. As Elvis said in his song, *"you can knock me down, step on my face, slander my name all over the place, but, uh, huh honey"* . . . . you won't keep this kid down.

I was born to win and nobody was going to take that away from me. The dance contest was another opportunity to validate myself, to prove my worthiness, to gain my own approval. I so desperately needed that. After thanking Frances for helping me win the contest, I hurried home to write to Nancy to let her know I won.

I thought to myself, "Maybe she'll like me even more now," as I turned off the light, exhausted, fulfilled, and soon asleep.

*   *   *

When June arrived, Lorraine was loading her car and heading to the Medical College of Virginia, in Richmond, Virginia, to study to become an X-Ray technician. There was no keeping my sister down. She was determined to be in the medical field in one way or another. With her husband stationed in Korea for a year, this was her opportunity to attend medical college. With Claudie in the service, Lorraine off to medical college, that just left me at home. Well, almost, at home.

I landed a summer job working as a soda jerk at the Knotty Pine restaurant in the Weirs. As soon as school let out, Frankie Sharp and

I would be moving into a cabin behind the restaurant with two other boys from Franklin, who also would be working in the kitchen with Frank at the Knotty Pine.

There was just one more piece of business to attend to before I began my summer job. It had been nearly two months since I last saw Nancy. Those two months seemed like forever. I thought of her every day, practically every moment. We conspired to meet in Manchester on a Saturday before I had to go to work for the summer.

Bright and early on a Saturday morning, I hitchhiked the 50 miles to Manchester. It took three and a half hours to get there. Over an hour of that time was spent walking the streets of Manchester, just looking for her house. By then, it was 11:30 a.m. She was patiently waiting in the lower right corner room of the three-story brown house on Valley Street when I knocked on the window. She came out the back door and met me in the alley behind her house. There wasn't any hesitation. We were in each other's arms before we even said "Hello."

We had to move away from her house quickly, lest her mother catch her cavorting with that forbidden, nefarious boy from Laconia. Hand in hand, we went to the woman's house where I had been sending my letters.

Nancy's friend greeted me with, "So this is the boy with the dreamy bedroom eyes that I've been hearing all about."

I didn't know what to say. I didn't know what she meant by "bedroom eyes." I was self-conscious enough. The last thing I needed was to have something else wrong with my eyes.

She and Nancy laughed as she explained, "You've got sexy eyes that could tempt a girl to follow you to the bedroom."

I guess, in some ways, I was still quite naïve. I blushed, while a bit embarrassed that I wasn't familiar with the expression.

There wasn't anywhere we could go to be alone. We walked the streets and confirmed how much we missed each other while we were apart. I told her about my summer job in the Weirs. She promised she would try to have her older sister drive her there to see me. I assured her I'd look at her picture every day and stay faithful to her while we were apart. It was 2:30 p.m. Time to leave. I had to get home to babysit my younger brother.

A block from her house, she began to cry. I held back my tears, and before I realized what was happening, our lips bonded, and I felt goose bumps running up my arms. Our lips locked momentarily, confirming Nancy Cleary as the first love of my life. Soon after, I was on the highway leading out of Manchester, hitchhiking my way back to Laconia.

CHAPTER 21

SUMMER IN THE WEIRS

I joined the repetitive chant of "See ya next year," "Ya, see ya next year too" "Hope you have a good summer," which really sounded like "summah," heard throughout the halls of LHS on the last day of school.

My focus was on getting to the Weirs that afternoon to begin my summer job at the Knotty Pine restaurant. When the bell rang to release us from school, I pushed my way out the front door with all the other students and hitched a ride right in front of the high school from a motorcyclist heading to the Weirs. By the time we crossed the bridge over the canal that separated Paugus Bay from Lake Winnipesaukee and turned onto Lakeview Avenue, a few hundred motorcycles were already parked along the busy main drag of the Weirs, gathered there to join the party for the 36th Annual New England Motorcycle Gypsy tour. By the end of the three day event, some 40,000 or so motorcyclists would find their way to the Weirs. Motorcycle Week unofficially signaled the beginning of another busy summer at the ever popular Weirs Beach resort.

Business owners were still busily washing windows and placing their "Welcome Motorcyclists" signs in front of their restaurants and arcades as we cruised our way to the front door of the Knotty Pine restaurant. I went inside, met my new boss, George Casana, and his wife Rhea, and took a quick tour of the restaurant. It was appropriately named, Knotty Pine. The entire décor, from the walls, to the booths, and even the rest rooms, was overwhelmingly decorated in knotty pine wood. I surmised this probably gave the visiting tourists the feeling they were dining in a rustic lodge. Booths were lined along the front wall, aside large windows facing the street, where people passing by could look directly into the dining area before entering the restaurant. By the front entrance door, Rhea observed everything, while serving as hostess and cashier. She was a very private person, rarely spoke in her broken English accent, was not particularly friendly, and was the self-appointed supervisor of the employees that worked in the front area of the restaurant. George, an amicable man, and a tireless worker, was in charge of the kitchen. He actually was the owner and responsible for the entire operation.

As was common at the time, most of the businesses in the Weirs were only open for a brief ten-week period, from mid-June to Labor Day. In that ten-week span, the owners worked endlessly to gross enough money to last until the following year. Many of them also owned businesses or homes in Florida and headed south after Labor Day, back to their winter residences; a sort of gypsy, nomadic life that appealed to them.

After touring the restaurant, George walked me to my new "summer home" behind the restaurant. It was a converted World War II style "Dallas" hut he probably bought very cheaply at a surplus auction. It was even painted in a military brown color. The four wooden flaps were raised to allow fresh air to enter the cabin. The cabin became the summer home for the four boys who worked at the Knotty Pine. The waitresses rented rooms in nearby boarding houses or stayed at the Lakeside hotel, directly across from the restaurant.

Frankie Sharp was already in the cabin talking with Dave and Dennis, the Hoffman brothers, from Franklin, when we walked in. Instantly, I liked the both of them and knew we'd get along just fine as roommates and coworkers. After placing my belongings on top of my bunk, the four of us headed to the kitchen for a briefing from George. The other boys worked in the kitchen, while I was assigned to the soda fountain in the dining room. My experience helping Ben Doucet at the Busy Corner store proved invaluable in landing this job. I briefly looked at the dessert menu and knew I wouldn't have any difficulty concocting anything that was ordered from the fountain. However, things didn't go quite that smoothly my first day on the job.

As the dinner crowd arrived, I quickly put on my white jacket and apron, typifying my role as the "soda fountain attendant." While I was rearranging cups and saucers, one of the waitresses ordered four glasses of ice tea. Rhea pointed to the large metal ice tea container, as she rushed by my station on her way to the door to greet new arrivals. Simple enough. I filled four glasses with ice, cut a lemon, put a slice in each glass, then pushed down on the spigot to allow the tea to flow into the glasses.

Soon, all hell broke loose. Apparently, in the rush to close the restaurant the previous year, the former soda jerk failed to empty the ice tea container. The four customers were drinking tea that had been left in the pot for over nine months! Immediately, Rhea was at their table trying to mitigate their complaint. Obviously, the tea was rancid, if not downright disgusting. It didn't come as a surprise that they stormed out the door before ordering their meals.

Rhea and I had a bit of an argument, as though it was my fault the teapot hadn't been emptied and cleaned in nine months. I defended myself and told her she should have checked it before opening for business. The blame game didn't resolve anything, except she learned that I wasn't about to let her push me around.

I took the teapot to the kitchen and scrubbed it out, while one of the waitresses made a small pot of tea. That was the only incident that day. Ironically, that was the only tea ordered for the duration of the evening. All is well that ends well. The restaurant was full with hungry motorcyclists from five until after nine o'clock. I survived my first day on the job. Other than the teapot incident, Rhea and George were pleased with the way I handled the soda fountain orders. Before going to the cabin, I helped myself to a large portion of blueberry pie a-la-mode. That was the only chance I had to eat anything that first day on the job.

I enjoyed working at the Knotty Pine restaurant. From the soda fountain, I observed all the happy faces enjoying their summer vacation, getting their fix of fried clams and French fries, and stuffing themselves with milk shakes, hot fudge sundaes, or, if they dared, my Mount Washington special banana split. I worked a split shift, from 10:00 a.m. to 2:00 p.m. and 5:00 p.m. to 9:00 p.m., six days a week.

The Weirs was a buzz of activity. There was a steady stream of vacationers coming and going every week. During my afternoon break, I met new friends practically every day. One of the favorite gathering places for visiting teens was Tarlson's arcade, in the heart of the Weirs. I spent many afternoons there that summer playing Ping-Pong or miniature golf with newfound friends vacationing in the Weirs with their parents. There was a steady parade of cute teenage girls looking for a little action while on vacation. Oh, I quickly let them know I had a girlfriend in Manchester, while they told me about how they missed their boyfriend back in Massachusetts or Connecticut, or wherever, as we held hands, walking in the sand on the beach, enjoying an evening stroll under the stars.

Life was good. I was making money, meeting new people practically every day, and thoroughly enjoying living away from home. Relationships were ephemeral in the Weirs. There wasn't any time to get serious. You simply passed the time of day, playing and partying with new friends at one of the arcades, or along the beach at night, or at a party at someone's rented summer home. There was always something to look forward to after I finished my night shift at the Knotty Pine.

*   *   *

The summer tourist season was well underway by the beginning of July when I woke to the sound of fire trucks arriving in the Weirs from all directions. The area was notorious for fires. It was not unusual to have three or four major fires every summer. This time it was the newly constructed restaurant directly across the street from the beach. Rumor had it the mafia owned it. Who knows? What was certain is that it had a minimum charge of $5.00 simply to get in the place. I didn't know anyone willing to pay the $5.00 minimum for a cup of coffee. Word around the Weirs was that the new restaurant wasn't doing that well. The fire was quite suspect.

All four boys in our cabin jumped into our clothes and ran to the fire to help out. While the firefighters were containing the blaze, some dozen or so people were helping to remove contents from the kitchen and the bar. It was dark outside when I accidentally bumped into Chuck Jameson. I had seen Chuck in the arcades before, but never made his acquaintance.

As it happened, he and I were taking bottles of liquor from the bar area and carrying them outside when I came up with the bright idea that we should reward ourselves with a bottle of liquor apiece for all our effort. We each hid a bottle of liquor under a bush and retrieved it a couple of hours later, after everything capable of being saved was removed from the smoldering restaurant. The new restaurant was burned to the ground.

It was after 2:00 a.m. when Chuck and I walked the back streets of the Weirs to his cabin behind the Lakeview hotel on Tower Street. He was actually shorter than I was, had gorgeous blond hair, and a tanned, muscular body. Chuck was the short, light, and handsome, quintessential all-American boy in every teenage girl's dreams. Chuck Jameson lived in Manchester, was the captain of the gym team at Central High, was very popular and well liked in school, knew Nancy Cleary, and was saving his money to go to college. His mother was a nurse, divorced, and raising Chuck and his younger disabled brother.

We became very good friends that summer. That first night, I finally fell asleep on the floor of his tiny cabin that barely had room for a single cot. We talked until dawn and laughed about our new acquisitions. I looted a bottle of something called Drambuie that had sort of a licorice taste, while Chuck ended up with a bottle of some fancy orange tasting drink called Grand Marnier. We only took a few sips of each bottle, and couldn't understand why people would spend good money on that stuff, before we hid our stash under his cabin. From that day on, we were pretty much inseparable.

There was another fire on the outskirts of the Weirs that summer. Fortunately, Chuck wasn't with me that night. I was playing a pinball machine in the Half Moon arcade when some friends came by to pick me up to go to a beach party at the highly private Governor's Island on Lake Winnipesaukee. I never gave it a second thought as I hopped in someone's car and drove off to the beach party.

When we arrived at a deserted lot on the edge of the lake, some 15 to 20 people were already gathered around a bonfire. I wasn't about to ask who owned the property. I didn't even know whose car I came in. However, I did notice piles of lumber and trusses stacked adjacent to the lot. Obviously, somebody was planning to build a house.

I was drinking my second beer, when suddenly someone shouted, "Fire!" Sure enough, the trusses were going up in flames.

"Oh shit," I exclaimed. Now I knew we were in deep trouble.

Kids were jumping in cars to make it out of there as fast as they could, while the flames kept soaring higher and higher.

In a matter of minutes, fire trucks and police cars were swarming the private island community. I didn't leave in a car. I chose to run through the woods and lay low in the brush to avoid being apprehended by the police. I saw flashing spotlights shining in the distance looking for suspects. Sirens and horns were blasting in the still of the night. This was serious trouble.

I finally found my way off the island in the dark of night, about two hours later. Cautiously avoiding being spotted, I made my way to the Weirs on busy Route 11B. I ran through the woods and behind houses, on a three-mile wild odyssey that night. God definitely sent one of his special envoys to help me make it to my "summer home" safely.

It was daylight when I told my roommates, "I spent the night at Chuck's cabin."

The morning after the fire, everyone was talking about the big fire on Governor's Island. All the trusses and framing were burned to ashes. Rumor had it that the police apprehended two cars full of "suspects," ranging in age from 16 to 25, but nobody questioned knew how the fire started. For my part, I kept my mouth shut. I wasn't there. I didn't know anything. I laid low and stayed away from the arcades for a few days. Fortunately, I was never questioned by the police. Needless to say, I dodged a bullet and counted my blessings on that one.

*   *   *

Next door to the Knotty Pine restaurant stood a small pizza stand. I don't recall if it even had a name. It didn't need one; the aroma from the freshly baked pizza could be inhaled from a half a mile away. You're talking pizza, you're talking Italian. Tony, the owner of the small pizza stand lived in an Airstream trailer with his very pregnant wife, parked about twenty-five yards from our cabin. He was operating his little business on a shoestring budget. Gas to heat the pizza oven was supplied by a 100-pound propane tank, standing outside the back door of his stand. He ran an extension cord, on the ground, from the pizza stand to his trailer for lighting. I don't recall ever seeing a hose connected to a septic system to dispose of waste matter.

The reason I'm telling you about Tony is because we had to put up with his complaining wife all summer. Right after we moved into the cabin, he was knocking on our door pleading with us to keep the noise down. Even when the cabin was empty, she still complained to her husband that we were making too much noise. We didn't have a radio, seldom were in the cabin except to sleep, never ever had a single beer in there, and were very careful to avoid disturbing his sickly pregnant wife. I believe the woman created the term, "morning sickness." Whatever it was, she had it 24/7 the entire summer.

When I was in the cabin resting during my afternoon break, I could hear her constantly complaining without any justifiable reason. After his admonishment, Tony would walk the beaten down path from their trailer to our cabin to convey his wife's latest message. I actually felt sorry for the guy and always assured him we would do our best to "keep it down."

Over time, her incessant complaining for no justifiable reason was causing too much friction between us. One afternoon, Dave Hoffman and I decided to do something about it. We went to the pizza stand to have a heart-to-heart talk with Tony.

He conceded that her complaints weren't warranted but asked us to "be patient and understanding." "After all," he added, "We didn't know what it was like to be seven months pregnant." Now, that certainly was enlightening!

I suggested to Tony that perhaps his wife would be more comfortable staying in South Boston with her parents for awhile? He got my drift.

Again, he pleaded with us to be "more understanding."

We weren't getting anywhere in our conversation, until I asked, "Hey, Tony, do you need a permit to keep your propane tank standing outside exposed like that?"

He looked at me as if he was just caught with his hand in the cookie jar. Suddenly, Dave and I were eating free pizza, and Tony assured us he would handle his wife. He acknowledged we were "good boys." He never complained to us the rest of the summer.

* * *

I'll never forget the night Louis Armstrong and his All Stars played at the Winnipesaukee Gardens. All the parking lots were full and the sidewalks were jammed with people who came to hear "Satchmo." People were standing in line for nearly a block, waiting to eat at the restaurant. We normally closed at nine o'clock; but that night we didn't finish serving tables until nearly eleven. From the soda fountain, I saw people walking in the street to avoid the crowded sidewalk.

Out of the corner of my eye, I spotted the Bobotases, and their friends, the Noucases, walking by the restaurant to join the long line. That gave me the opportunity to do a big favor for my favorite teacher.

Claire Bagley, one of the waitresses, was cleaning off a table when I said to her, "Claire, stay cleaning this table until I bring some friends here."

Then, I ran outside, took Soc by the hand, and told him and his friends to follow me through a side door to the "reserved" table. Soc didn't even know I worked at the Knotty Pine, but was grateful to learn that I did. They avoided an hour wait to be seated and were able to make it to the Gardens before the band began to play.

We could hear Louis Armstrong's band playing from Lakeview Avenue, as Frankie and I ran from work to sneak in behind the bandstand where the band was playing. The dance hall was actually built over the water and a walkway was constructed behind the bandstand to be used as an exit in case of a fire. Very few people knew it was there. That was one of the little secrets reserved for the people who lived and worked in the Weirs.

As we were watching Louis Armstrong through the screen window behind the bandstand, he suddenly turned away from the crowd in the middle of playing "*When the Saints Go Marching In*," wiped the sweat from his brow, while catching his breath from blowing his trumpet, and gave a wave with his handkerchief and flashed his famous smile at us, before turning back to the crowd. Wow! Simply amazing! The great Louis Armstrong waved at me. A tribute from one former paperboy to another!

*   *   *

Every day brought a new adventure that summer in the Weirs. I'll always remember the time I "almost" bought my first car. Byron was a couple years older than I was. In fact, he graduated from high school with my sister, Claudie. He was a loner, didn't have any friends, and had a reputation for being a troublemaker. He suddenly appeared in the Weirs one evening. He told Frank and me he was going into the Army the following month and asked if we knew anyone that might be interested in buying his car. He told us he just wanted to dump it before he left for basic training.

I was excited at the possibility of owning my very own car. I became even more excited when Byron told me he would let me have it for only $50.

He said, "That's just because I like Claudie and you're her brother." Such a deal. Frankie came with me as we took a test drive around the Weirs. It was an old black coupe but it purred like a kitten. I was ready to hand over the $50 when Frank reminded me I should have a clear title before I handed over my hard-earned money to Byron. His reputation preceded him.

Good old Byron then informed us he was working on a construction crew, building the new Interstate 93 in the White Mountains. He went on to say, the title to the car was at the rooming house where he was staying, near Lincoln, some fifty miles away. We agreed that Frank, Dave, and I, would drive there in Byron's car. He would get the title and sign it over to me. I would then pay him for the car and we would drive it back to the Weirs that night. That was the plan.

It was after eleven o'clock when we reached his rooming house, where the new highway was being constructed. We got out of the car, and waited for Byron to come back with the title. And we waited, and waited, and waited. The sonofabitch pulled a fast one on us. He went into the rooming house and never returned with a title. There we were, in the middle of the night, fifty miles from the Weirs, with Frank and Dave having to be at work by seven o'clock in the morning.

The nights are very cold in the White Mountains, anytime of the year. We were shivering as we walked in the dark, barely able to see the road, with no sign of life anywhere. We walked and walked and walked for four straight hours, just to keep moving. By 5:00 a.m., we were shivering and desperate. We saw a light go on at a house along the highway. This was not the time to be shy. Desperate times call for desperate measures.

I told my friends, "The worse thing that can happen is the guy will shoot us."

I must say, he looked quite concerned as he stood by his front door listening to our tale of woe.

He pondered our story for a moment, and then finally, in that familiar deep New Hampshire brogue, said, "Well, you fellas seem to be in a little bit a trouble. Reckon' I could getcha to the Weis after I have my coffee."

Those words were music to our ears. As daylight came over the surrounding mountains, we hopped in the back of his pickup truck and were on our way to the Weirs. We were both shivering and smiling as we opened the cabin door to wake Dennis up for work. It was nearly seven o'clock.

As Dennis rubbed his eyes, he asked, "Where you guys been all night?"

I replied, "Oh, we were just out buying a car."

*　　*　　*

The days were shorter and the nights were colder as we closed in on Labor Day weekend. It was only a week or so before the summer season would end at the Weirs when I was struck with the Asian flu. I recall that Sunday afternoon quite vividly. I was playing Ping-Pong at Tarlson's arcade during my afternoon break when I suddenly became dizzy and began to sweat profusely. I was playing against Bobby Gilbert, an acquaintance I knew from high school, whose parents owned a cabin colony on the highway heading toward Meredith. My knees gave out from under me so I braced myself against the table. Bobby noticed I was pale and sweating. He suggested that I go home immediately.

I recall telling him, "I can't go there, I don't have a home."

He helped me get in the front seat of his car and drove me to the first place that entered his mind . . . . his house. When Mrs. Gilbert met me, I was becoming delirious. She and Bobby immediately put me on a bed in one of their vacant cabins. For the next six days,

I wandered in and out of a coma. Mrs. Gilbert nursed me back to normal from the dreadful Asian flu that recently began to spread around the world in the summer of 1956. I was one of the first people to contact the virus. By the end of 1957, 70,000 people in the United States died from the Asian flu.

Looking back, I am sure I teetered on the edge of death those six days. I didn't know I had been in and out of a coma all that time. I recall perspiring constantly, getting chills, and being wrapped in warm blankets. I was told that Mrs. Gilbert spent many hours wiping the sweat from my brow, while caring for me that week.

When my fever finally broke the following Saturday, Mrs. Gilbert was holding me up, as I sat up feebly in a bed, while she fed me chicken soup. She was the angel God sent to save me from nearly dying.

Dazed, I looked at her with a confused look and asked, "Where am I?"

Mrs. Gilbert answered, "My son Bobby brought you here. You were a very sick boy. Now you just take it easy and rest. You're going to be all right now. I'll be back in a little while."

She left me alone for awhile. I was weak, but I didn't want to fall back to sleep. I got up, made my way to the sink in the corner of the room, splashed cold water on my face, and slowly tried to reconstruct what happened to me.

Later that day, Bobby and his mother recounted everything that happened. They didn't know why they didn't take me to the hospital. They were just too preoccupied caring for me at their place. All they knew is that I was running a very high fever and they assumed it would break in a day or so. Later, we learned about the Asian flu pandemic spreading across the globe. When I got it, there wasn't a vaccine available to counteract it.

I was so sick, I didn't even remember what Mrs. Gilbert looked like. Bobby told me he went to the Knotty Pine and told George Casana that I was extremely ill and was being cared for by his mother. The next day, still very weak, but on the road to recovery, I made my way back to my cabin and returned to work at the Knotty Pine. To this day, one of my biggest regrets in life is that I never returned to visit Mrs. Gilbert to thank her properly for saving my life.

As the summer season ended, Chuck Jameson returned to Manchester. He invited me to his house for a visit. I promised to take him up on his invitation. Nancy Cleary didn't have the opportunity to come to the Weirs. That summer, her father sold their house and his corner grocery store and they moved to a farm in the country outside the town of Derryfield. That would make it even more difficult for me to see her.

Chuck told me he would "Give her my love" for me. He was a good friend. I knew I'd miss him.

As was the tradition in the Weirs, all the businesses closed early on Labor Day and held employee appreciation parties. The Knotty Pine was no exception. The "closed" sign was placed in the front window at six o'clock and George grilled succulent T-Bone steaks for everyone. He even had a couple bottles of wine available for our party. After our delicious meal, George thanked everyone for making it another very successful season. It was noteworthy to mention that not one single employee quit or was fired from the restaurant that summer.

Frank and I agreed to reunite with Dave and Dennis at the Franklin versus Laconia high school football game in October. The waitresses hugged us as they said their farewells and I even managed to get a little kiss from my favorite waitress, Claire Bagley, the reigning Miss Winnipesaukee, who was returning to the University of New Hampshire for her junior year. I exchanged a firm handshake with George as we were leaving the restaurant and thanked him for being such an understanding boss. Why, I even got an awkward hug from Rhea on my way out. Before I left the building, I made sure to empty and clean the ice tea container . . . for next summer.

My Senior Graduation Picture - 1957

CHAPTER 22

MY SENIOR YEAR

No matter how hard I worked or how much I saved, I never seemed to have enough money. All the money I saved working at the Knotty Pine restaurant was gone by the end of my first month back in school. Before I returned to school for my senior year, I bought myself those much needed eyeglasses. Oh, I could have probably bought a cheap pair of plain vanilla frames, but that wasn't like me. I had to have the latest fashionable dark horn-rimmed glasses, with a tint of multiple hues in them. I had to be cool. Then, of course, I needed to buy a suit for my graduation class picture. Not just any suit. I chose an off-white wool sport jacket, with a pair of matching black wool slacks, a wide collared white Van Heusen shirt, and a preppy looking dark maroon tie with black diagonal stripes. I wanted to look my best for my graduation photo. After all, that may be my first and only formal picture.

I was bombarded with one expense after another. More clothes, class pictures, class ring, class yearbook. Poooof, it was all gone. This graduation ritual would have been fine had I not been the one to have to pay for it all. I probably could have skipped the graduation ring, but why?

I reasoned, "Couldn't I at least have what everyone else that was graduating has?" I couldn't deny myself a class ring. Like the formal picture, I convinced myself this would probably be the only ring I ever owned.

By the end of September, the LAKON staff was busily collecting information to complete the 1957 LAKON. One of those girls, with five lines of accomplishments listed below her name in the yearbook, came to our homeroom to gather all the particulars to put in the LAKON, such as, our activities, accomplishments, future plans, and anything else that might be of interest. There was a considerable amount of chatter in the classroom when it came time to list "Future." I suspect half of us didn't have the foggiest notion what we'd be doing after we graduated, but felt we needed to put down something impressive.

If I were being honest, I probably would have put, "Towel boy in Miami beach." After all, that's what I really wanted to do after I worked another summer in the Weirs. I wasn't sure about the "towel boy" part, but I heard it was a great way to meet girls, tanning in scrimpy little bikinis, while hustling some fairly decent tips. Who knows? I had no idea what I wanted to do. For certain, I knew I wasn't going to college or working in the shoe factory. Stumped, I finally asked Ronnie Timmons what he wrote down. Ronnie told me he filled the blank space with the word, "Service." Now that sounded downright noble and patriotic to me, so I put "Air Force" in the blank beside the word "Future."

My immediate future was established within a week after completing the LAKON questionnaire. I was hired on a part-time basis, working after school and on weekends at Lee's Cut Rate store on Main Street.

Initially, it sounded like an ideal after school job, but within a week I realized that nothing I did would satisfy the owner. I was hired to operate the cash register and serve customers; however, I spent more time unloading boxes and stocking inventory in the dingy, dirty basement of the store. Yet, I was required to wear a button down shirt, necktie, and clean khaki pants at work. By the end of the day, my clothes were always soiled, and I looked like I spent my shift kneeling on a dirt floor.

When I wasn't working in the basement, he had me haul furniture, clothes, and other goods, to the second floor of the store. I never could work fast enough to please Freddy Rosenbloom. When I did work on the main floor, he insisted I "find something to do" all the time, as he constantly peered down at me from his glass office, situated on the stair rise between the first and second floor. One minute, the irascible owner would send me to one corner of the store to wipe dust off cans of baby powder or some other product that hadn't sold in years, while in his next breath he would holler at me to attend to a customer who just walked in the store.

I was determined I wasn't going to let this big blowhard get me down. I refused to allow his bellowing management style bother me.

To the contrary, I simply would ask him, "What do you want me to do next, boss?" and allowed him to set my priorities.

After a month on the job, I really thought he was backing off and I was meeting his expectations when suddenly, out of nowhere, he told me he was "cutting back," and I was fired.

Initially, I took it personally until I learned nobody ever pleased him, and his store had a reputation as a "revolving door" for eager high school kids that needed to work. By mid-October, it was too late to find another part-time job. All the grocery stores had staffed up for the year. I was in for another long winter, hanging out at the Nut Shoppe, watching American Bandstand at Dale's, going to Explorer Scout meetings, and hitchhiking to see my girlfriend, who lived way too far away.

*   *   *

Columbus Day was observed on Monday, the 8th day of October, in 1956. Probably nobody remembers that but me, but if you love baseball and are still breathing, you'll always remember it as the day Don Larsen pitched the only perfect game in World Series history.

That afternoon, we were off from school and I went to get a haircut at Tony Lyman's barbershop, downstairs in the Laconia Tavern. It was a slow day in the barbershop. Nobody was there but Tony and me. His small television was on as we watched the fifth game of the World Series between the cross-town rivals, the Brooklyn Dodgers and New York Yankees. When he finished cutting my hair, it was the bottom of the fourth inning and the Yankees were ahead 1-0.

We were watching a heck of a pitching duel between Sal Maglie of the Dodgers and Don Larsen of the Yankees. Tony invited me to stick around and watch the game with him. I told him I'd watch it until the Dodgers scored a run. In the fifth inning, Gil Hodges hit a long line drive into left center that looked like a guaranteed double, when, out of nowhere, Mickey Mantle snared the ball in his glove in a spectacular catch to deny the Dodgers a hit. Mel Allen and Vin Scully were doing the TV broadcast for NBC that day. As each inning passed, the excitement in their voices increasingly resonated from their microphones.

By the top of the ninth inning, everyone in the stadium was standing, cheering Larsen on with each pitch, as he completed his epic masterpiece. When it was over, I was hoarse from cheering. Tony and I were grinning and shaking our heads in amazement. Together, we witnessed a piece of baseball history, October 8, 1956. Again, the dreaded Yankees went on to win their seventeenth championship in a seven game series. The Dodgers left Brooklyn and moved to Los Angeles shortly after that.

*   *   *

Later that week, my mother received a telephone call from Mrs. Jameson, inviting me to stay at their house for a weekend visit. Apparently, the call caught my mother off guard. She didn't have time to think of a reason to refuse the request. Nobody had ever asked her for permission for me to stay overnight before.

She graciously told Chuck's mother, "That would be fine with me."

The next Saturday morning, with my overnight bag in my left hand, I stuck my right thumb out to catch a ride from someone, anyone, going to the big city to do a little Saturday shopping. Hitchhiking was a much more acceptable method of getting around in the 1950s than it is today. Generally, I didn't have a problem hitching a ride during daylight hours. However, the practice became proportionately more difficult as the evening darkness settled in. Many times, I walked for several hours at night before anyone stopped to give me a ride.

After sticking my thumb out for a few years, I had it down to an art. I made it a point to always wear nice clothes when I hitchhiked and carried a switch blade knife in case some weirdo tried to do something to me. I also made up a story about being a boxer training for a big fight, should some queer start moving his hand toward my leg. Furthermore, I learned to stand and wait under a streetlight with easy access for a car to pull over, rather than walk some lonely road in the dark of night. The fact is I learned more from people I met hitchhiking during my travels across the state of New Hampshire than I ever did in school.

On this particular windy, rainy, Saturday morning on my way to Chuck Jameson's house, I quickly got a ride from an elderly couple on their way to Manchester to do a little furniture shopping. In our conversation, they asked where I was going in Manchester. I told them I didn't quite know and gave them Chuck's address. They knew exactly where he lived and went out of their way to drop me off a block from his house.

The Jameson's lived in a modest apartment complex near the south end of Valley Street, fairly close to Nancy's old house. Ruth Jameson happened to be unloading groceries from her car when I knocked on their door. She stopped what she was doing, came over and gave me a warm welcome and a hug, and we were soon sipping tea at her kitchen table, sharing stories as though we had known each other our entire life.

Once I met his mother, it was easy to understand why Chuck was so well mannered and polite. Ruth Jameson was absolutely charming. She didn't prejudge me, she wasn't a malicious gossip, and I found her to be a very caring person. I just felt very comfortable and at home around her. She candidly told me about some of the difficulties she had to deal with, raising two boys on her own, while working as a nurse on the night shift at a local hospital. She wasn't complaining, just talking to me as an adult, sharing some of her wisdom and knowledge.

Rain poured down heavily that day and the next day also. I hardly noticed it, as I was happily playing card games on the kitchen table with Chuck and Ruth Jameson. On Sunday afternoon, as much as I wanted to stay longer, I knew when it was time to leave.

Chuck and his mother drove me across town to my favorite spot to catch a ride back to Laconia.

On the ride there, Mrs. Jameson startled me a bit when she said, "You know Cooz, I know your girlfriend's mother." That was a surprise. She then told me, "Pauline Cleary told me you're not 'the type of boy' Chuck should hang around with." She went on to tell me that she asked Nancy's mother if she had personally met me.

"Well, no, but my sister in Laconia told me all about him," Nancy's mother replied. What her son told her about me, and what Mrs. Cleary told her, didn't correspond. For that reason, Ruth

Jameson invited me to Manchester that weekend to form her own opinion.

As we parted, Mrs. Jameson gave me a warm hug and told me she would be calling Nancy's mother to "set the record straight."

Her parting words were, "Cousy, you're welcome at our house anytime, and don't be a stranger."

As they drove away, I couldn't help but think; my, what a small world we live in. I never would have thought she knew Nancy's mother, and now she was about to "set the record straight."

That she did. Nancy was all excited when she called me long distance a few days later to tell me her mother let her know it was O.K. for me to come to the house in Derryfield to see her. I told her as soon as we had a day off from school, I would be there. It had been over four months since I had seen her. Not only was I dying to see Nancy again, I also wanted to meet her mother and gain her approval.

It seems I was always being prejudged and talked about by people who didn't even know me. Once people came to know me personally, I usually was able to dispel any disparaging rumors they may have been told. Unfortunately, all too often, people resented me because of my mother's past wanton behavior. That wasn't fair to her either, but I didn't have it in my power to change that.

* * *

On a clear, crisp, fall day in late October, Ronnie Timmons and I hitchhiked to Derryfield. The truth is I didn't want to hitchhike alone, so I told Ronnie a lie that Nancy's sister was dying to meet him. I was hoping he could borrow his father's car that day, but that didn't happen, so we were stuck hitchhiking. At least I had someone to pass the time with while waiting for a ride. We didn't have a problem hitching a ride on U.S. Route 3 to Hookset, but walked a long way on a back road to Derryfield to make it to Nancy's farmhouse in the country. It was such a gorgeous fall day, we didn't think much about it at the time.

I met Nancy's mother, but never did have the nice long chat I was hoping to have with her. Before I could sit down, Nancy was pushing me out the front door to go for a walk on an old dirt road on their farm.

"After all, you came to see me, not my mother," she uttered with a smile.

We kissed and hugged, as we whiled the afternoon away, walking down that old dirt road. We were having so much fun just talking and being together again, I lost track of time until the afternoon shadows began to surround us. I knew it was time to leave, but allowed my emotions to take over and didn't leave her house until her father called her, right before dusk, to come in the house for supper.

When the sun went down, suddenly it became cold awfully fast that time of the year. Ron and I walked in the dark of night, shivering all the while, in our light fall jackets. It must have been twenty miles from her house to U.S. Route 3, of which, we probably walked five of those miles that evening. If it hadn't been for a farmer picking up his wife in Hookset, most likely we would have walked the back road the entire way. The temperature was dropping by the minute, as we stood shivering under a streetlight on Route 3. Car after car passed by us, but nobody would stop to give us a ride.

Finally, it was after ten o'clock when an old black coupe, kind of like the one I tried to buy from Byron the previous summer, slowly drove by us, kept going for another 100 feet or so, then finally came to a stop. We both ran as fast as we could, hands swinging wildly above our heads, as we made our way to the car stopped on the side of the road.

To my surprise, a black family occupied the car. I was surprised, because very few black people lived in New Hampshire back then, and, because I had never been given a ride by a black person before. The lady opened the door on the passenger side and got out of the car. Her husband, who was driving, smiled at us and told us to get in the back seat.

Certainly, apologies weren't necessary, but his wife apologized to us when she told us, "I'm sorry, but you'll have to put our two girls on your laps if you want a ride."

The young ones were just as cute as can be, as we woke them from their sleeping state and set them across our laps. The little girl in my lap looked to be about three. She stared at me with her big brown eyes, as the car pulled back onto the highway. Before the car regained full speed, she rested her head on my shoulder and was soon sound asleep again. The warmth of her little body soon took the chill of the night away from mine. It was a surreal moment. A moment I'll never forget. The racial barrier definitely came down for me that night.

They were only going as far as Concord, but went way out of their way and drove the extra thirty miles to Laconia, so we wouldn't freeze on the side of the road. Heaven knows, nobody else would have given us a ride. When nobody else would stop to pick us up, a black family, in a crowded car, was the only ones who came to our rescue in our time of need. That gesture of kindness would never be forgotten.

*   *   *

As winter arrived, it became too cold to hitchhike anywhere beyond a 10-mile radius of Laconia. Nancy and I continued to write to each other and I even drove to Manchester to see her one night when she was babysitting for a doctor on North Elm Street. Correction. I didn't drive. Ronnie drove his father's car that night. He, another friend called "Jug," and I, went there together. It was in late November. There was snow on the frozen ground.

The visit didn't go well. I am sure the doctor wasn't aware that three teenage boys were coming to see his babysitter at his house. Then, there was the little matter of drinking his liquor. "Jug" was being a macho jerk and helped himself to a few drinks out of the doctor's liquor cabinet. Nancy was trying her best to be graceful but I sensed she was quite uncomfortable with us there.

Even I felt uneasy. I don't know what I was thinking that night, other than I wanted to see her. It was awkward. We couldn't be alone, my friends were acting like jerks, and the children she was babysitting were surely going to tell their parents about our unapproved visit. We might have cost her a job. Fortunately, we didn't stay there very long. Ronnie and "Jug" waited in the car, as I kissed Nancy goodbye out on the freezing front porch. Parting was always such sorrow. This time, I knew we wouldn't have a chance to see each other again until next spring.

That winter, I settled into my old pattern of babysitting my younger brother on Saturday night. That was the one rule in our house: Be home at 5:00 p.m. on Saturday to babysit Pudg. That was it.

Since I moved away the past summer, it was as though I was on my own. Oh, I still had my room in the frozen tundra upstairs by the attic, but since I was free to wander about without any curfew, I chose to stay away from home as much as possible. That may shock some people; however, you have to realize, I pretty much supported myself since I was ten, so my being extremely independent shouldn't surprise anyone.

That winter, I spent many nights at Stu White's house. It was a matter of convenience. Stu's mother worked the night shift at Laconia hospital and they had an extra bedroom. Stu's older sister had moved away and Mrs. White felt Stu was safer at home with me there. Besides, the vacant bedroom was heated. Wherever I stayed, I was careful not to eat their food, unless it was offered to me. Food cost money and I didn't want to upset anyone.

It's strange how things work out sometimes. I wasn't looking for pity or a handout from anyone, but my friends sort of looked out for me. I never asked for anything, but Stu's girlfriend, Connie, often came by with a sandwich or fruit. She came from a wealthy family and was sure her parents wouldn't miss the food. That's just how things worked out for me my senior year in high school.

*   *   *

I was still active in Explorer scouts and hardly missed a meeting. In fact, I played basketball for our Explorer scout team. It was at a basketball game at the old St. Joseph's gym when misfortune struck again. We were playing an Explorer scout team from Rochester and were getting an old fashioned butt kicking when it happened. As I was driving for the basket, their center stuck his elbow out intentionally and smacked me right in the face. He hit me so hard, I fell backward onto the floor from the blow.

When I slowly gathered myself to get up, blood began to trickle from my nose. My glasses were shattered in pieces, scattered all over the floor. Instinctively, I put my hand to my mouth to check if my partial plate was still intact. It was. I was too dizzy and stunned to fight.

I could only wonder, "What did I do to make that guy want to hit me like that?"

The real pain was that my only pair of glasses was broken. Now, I was without glasses again until I could afford to buy another pair. I wanted to cry, but I held back the tears as I walked off the court.

My night was done. I just wanted to get out of there. My jacket was stored in the closet upstairs by the meeting room. As I walked in the dark hallway approaching the lighted meeting room, I stopped in my tracks when I heard a scouting committee member talking about me. Unbeknownst to me at the time, they were selecting an Explorer Scout to attend the summer Scout Jamboree at Valley Forge, Pennsylvania.

It was all somewhat vague, but the gist of what I overheard was that because of Ora, I wasn't "representative" of the kind of scout that should be selected for that honor. Another outstanding member of the committee commented that I looked like a "punk" with my hairdo. I couldn't believe what I was hearing from the dark of the hallway. Without knowing I was there, Cut Fecteau strongly defended me.

What I heard Cut say was, "Listen I wouldn't have nominated Cousy, if I didn't think he deserved it. He's a damn good kid."

I didn't want to hear any more trash talk about me or my mother. When I walked into the room on my way to the closet, everyone was staring at me. Some of the men looked embarrassed and lowered their chins, while others looked at me defiantly. Cut saw the blood running from my nose.

He immediately left his chair and came to me, put both hands on my shoulders and looked directly at me with sad eyes, and asked, "Are you alright?"

I replied with a slight nod. What could I say? The blow I took in the room that night, hurt more than the blow I took on the basketball court. I grabbed my coat and left the building.

As I walked past the Nut Shoppe I noticed it was unusually crowded in there for a school night. I didn't want to go inside and have to tell everyone what happened. I just wanted to be alone. My cousin, Lou, came running out the front door when he saw me walking by and told me that a bunch of cute girls were in there. It seems they came all the way from Rochester to see Cousy play against "their guys."

Then it hit me. A couple of weeks earlier I met some girls from Rochester High at the Belknap Recreation Area. It was on a Saturday. I did recall dancing a couple of dances with a cute blonde that day. I never imagined they would come to Laconia to watch "their guys" play a basketball game against Cousy's team. Hmmmm, now that might explain why I got smashed in the face.

*   *   *

Another winter finally passed. In a few months, I would graduate from high school. One positive thing that happened that winter was that the Boston Celtics finally won the NBA championship in their 11th season in the NBA. My man, Bob Cousy, was selected as the Most Valuable Player in the NBA. Things were looking up.

When the weather finally became bearable again, I hitchhiked to Manchester to visit the Jameson's. After catching up on all our winter activities, I had to leave early to return home to babysit. As I mentioned, I learned more from people while hitchhiking than I ever did in school. On my way back home, I had a great life lesson in the art of salesmanship. I learned more in a one-hour drive with a salesman going to Laconia than I could have ever learned in a college course.

The first thing I noticed when I opened the door to his car was how well dressed and groomed he was. He wore brown slacks, a blue long sleeve shirt, with a diagonal striped tie that complemented his shirt and slacks. For no particular reason, we immediately got into a conversation about his profession: Sales.

"First of all," he began, "to be successful, you have to love what you're doing. Next, you have to believe in the product you're selling. If you don't believe in it with a passion, you can't sell it." "And, above all," he went on to say, "You have to believe in yourself." By then, I was on the edge of my seat, intently listening for more.

His one-sided conversation continued. "You see, son, you're selling more than a product. When your mother goes to the grocery store to buy a can of soup, she has several choices, right? There's

Campbell soup, Heinz soup, Del Monte soup, and so forth. To be a successful salesman, I have to build a good rapport with the store manager. I need to earn his trust and confidence. How do I do that?" he asked.

Like a dumbbell I answered, "I don't' know?"

He went on to tell me, "I earn it by listening carefully to him, by giving him the best possible service I can, by remembering little things like his anniversary, his kid's birthdays, and anything else he may have told me. In return, that just might give me the edge I need. Like, stocking my soup in a preferred spot, or even ordering more from me than my competitors." "So, you see," he said, as his voice rose with enthusiasm, "You're not selling soup, you're selling yourself!"

I was fascinated by this lesson in salesmanship. As we continued the drive to Laconia, I began to visualize myself as a salesman. With the knowledge I gained that day, I was given a head start in a possible career.

As I closed his car door, his final remarks to me were, "You're a bright kid, and I think you've got what it takes to be a salesman. Learn to listen carefully, take good notes, and remember, the customer's always right."

Walking down Church Street, I was absorbed in deep thought. "What should I sell? Cars? Houses? Insurance? Lumber? Clothes?" I didn't know the answer, but I believed I had what it took to be a salesman.

In April 1957, I was given that opportunity. I landed a job as a door-to-door salesman selling magazines for an outfit called the "Civic Reading Club," out of Boston. The plan was to have me go door to door throughout Laconia, soliciting people to buy "the package." Once we finished with Laconia, the Regional Sales Manager and I would drive to the outlying towns around the Lakes Region to do the same thing. I was paid solely on a commission basis. Likewise, the Sales Manager's pay was based on closing my sales with the customers. Basically, his salary was dependent on how many subscriptions I sold.

At first, I did very well selling magazines. I really believed in the product and the word "NO" was not in my vocabulary. I was as persistent as I was when I was selling chances on that dumb plastic clown for my mother or collecting for the March of Dimes. Except now, I wasn't hustling drunk people in the bars on Main Street.

Without too much elaboration, my spiel was that I wasn't selling magazines, I was giving them away!

I would tell potential customers, "You'll receive Look magazine every week, the Saturday Evening Post twice a month, and any two other magazines of your choice," selected from a large list of available magazines, like, Popular Mechanics, Good Housekeeping, and so on every month.

I went on to say, "That's eight magazines a month and all we ask is that you pay the mailing cost of only twenty-five cents a week. That's what it costs us to mail the magazines from the publisher's house directly to your door. Not only that, you'll receive your magazines one day before the stores get their copies."

I was prepared for the next sentence to come out of their mouth, which was, "O.K. what's the catch?"

If I got that far, I showed them the back page of Look magazine. The entire back page was an advertisement paid for by Camel cigarettes. I would pause momentarily, and then share the hidden secret of the magazine business with them.

As I gauged the level of interest on their face, I proceeded to tell them, "You don't pay for magazines; the advertisers do. You see, if we can double the number of readers looking at this Camel ad every week, we can double the cost they have to pay for the ad. Now, you know why we can afford to make you this offer."

I could tell by their body language before I even finished my pitch if I sold a subscription. Oh, there was nothing wrong with my delivery. The plain truth was that people didn't want to buy magazines. They were skeptical, or they didn't read, or they were broke. I heard every sad story imaginable. I used every trick of the trade and even made up a few of my own to make a sale. One time, I became so exasperated trying to sell to this lady, after forty-five minutes of pleading, I sarcastically told her, "Look, if you don't want to read the magazines, you can always use them to start your fireplace in the winter."

She actually thought I was serious and said, "Ya, that's a good idea!"

In the first few weeks on the job, I was selling three or four subscriptions a day. My first paycheck arrived within a couple of weeks after I began selling. I understood there would be a two-week delay in receiving my checks. I was pleasantly surprised to learn that I made over $80.00, working part-time, my first week on the job. With that, I immediately bought myself another pair of glasses.

Unfortunately, I began to count my chickens before they hatched. I opened a charge account at O'Shea's and was spending money on clothes before I earned it. Joe, the Sales Manager, asked me if I knew anyone else that might want a job selling magazines. I made the mistake of bringing Danny Matthews onboard.

Danny couldn't have cared less about selling magazines. He just wanted to hang out with me after school. As the weather turned warmer, we were inclined to want to join other kids playing baseball or to hang out at a drug store munching on an ice cream cone. Meanwhile, it became obvious to us that our Sales Manager had a bit of a drinking problem. While we were banging on doors, he was off on some side street sipping on a pint of whiskey. As time went on, we spent more time on the road traveling farther and farther away from Laconia, which meant less time spent knocking on doors trying to convince people to take our magazines at "no cost whatsoever." By the middle of May, Joe was practically begging us to increase our sales. Frankly, I simply wasn't motivated to sell magazines any longer. I could only take so much rejection. My heart wasn't in it.

The clincher came when I didn't receive my paycheck one week.

Joe kept telling me, "The main office told me they sent it."

I never got it. Next, he admitted he may have forgotten to send in the required paperwork. That didn't make sense to me. I quit the job around the end of May. By then, I was owed three weeks pay. I was mad at Joe, the Civic Reading club, and myself. Now, I owed money at O'Shea's and didn't have a job. I waited long enough for my pay. It was the right choice to quit. To this day, I never received the money I was due. However, in that job I learned that I could really sell . . . . when I wanted to.

$*$ $*$ $*$

Finally, after four difficult years, and a lot of perseverance, I made it! My graduation ceremony was held in the high school auditorium, on Monday, June 10, 1957. The week before graduation should have been a happy time, but it turned into the saddest, most unforgivable time of my life.

Oh, that week began well. My courses were completed and I spent most of the week roaming the corridors, collecting farewell entries in my yearbook. Flattery will get you everything, as classmates I hardly knew were telling me how much they'd miss me and wishing me profound success in the future.

Only Billy Metcalf had the nerve to write, "To my buddy, Cooz. If you lay off the women and the booze, you might grow a couple inches taller!"

Usually, the entries told how much I livened up the class, or that I was a cool cat on the dance floor, with an occasional reference to my deficient physical stature. It didn't matter to me what they said. There was just something nostalgic about completing a phase of education with the same collection of people. It's as if we were bonded in a friendship that would soon dissolve, as we went our separate ways.

There were a few graduation parties at different places, and even one held at someone's summer home on Paugus bay. Of all the parties, that's the only one I recall. Perhaps that's because I got so drunk, I fell face first into the lake that night. I must have been a little carried away with the euphoria of graduation.

The one party that everyone looked forward to was the graduation banquet at the Belknap Recreation Area. It was held the Saturday evening before we graduated. By then, I was so acclimated, I didn't even ask my mother or Ben for a ride to the Area. My pride wouldn't allow me to give them the satisfaction of turning me down. That evening, I put on the nice suit I bought for my graduation picture, was getting ready to go out the door to walk to Gilford Avenue and hitch a ride to the Area, when I remembered, I needed to pay five dollars to get in the banquet.

I was certain one of the parents driving a classmate there would pick me up. I was also confident my mother would loan me the five dollars until I earned my first paycheck working in the Weirs. I honestly never thought for a moment she wouldn't loan me a lousy five dollars. Many times in the past, I borrowed money from her and always paid her back. Why would I expect this time to be different? Besides, I wasn't asking her to GIVE me $5.00, I was asking her to LOAN me $5.00. That's all I asked for.

There I stood, all dressed up in my nice suit, standing before her, pleading, practically begging, for a five-dollar loan so I could attend my graduation banquet. In her cold, cruel, heartless manner, she steadfastly refused to loan me five dollars. She gloated in her power to deprive me, but I found her rejection disgusting. Ben just sat in his chair and watched us argue. He never got involved with me, one way or another. I wasn't his kid, I was Ora's problem.

I couldn't reconcile what I had done to deserve this punishment. I felt the anger gnawing at my body as I kept begging. The rage of years of pent up emotion were burning inside of me. I wanted to throw the kitchen chair right through the damn bay window in the living room.

No, I wouldn't give her the satisfaction of showing her how much she hurt me. I was baffled. Anger consumed my whole body. I just had to get out of that miserable house. I went to my room, tore my clothes off, put on an old pair of jeans, a T-shirt, picked up a jacket, and stormed out the side door onto the street.

I don't know where I was going. I was just walking the streets in a daze, as I wondered, "How could a mother be that cruel?"

I was walking on Winter Street when my cousin Lou saw me, while driving around with some of his friends. He knew it was the night of the graduation banquet.

He got out of the car and asked, "Cooz, what to hell are you doing here? Aren't you supposed to be at your banquet?"

I couldn't hold it inside me any longer. My cousin held me up, while I cried like a baby in front of him and his friends.

As I wiped the tears from my face, I told him, "Thanks, Cuz. I'll be fine." I just wanted to be alone.

It was past six o'clock, the banquet had already begun when Aunt Evie, Lou's mother, found me aimlessly walking the streets. She got out of her car, came over to me, and apologized for my mother's behavior. She sincerely was overwhelmed with sadness for me.

She handed me five dollars and said, "C'mon Sonny, you get in the car, I'll take you to the banquet."

"No thanks, *Matante*, it's too late now," I replied.

It was too late. Besides, I didn't want to be seen looking like I did. After trying to console me, she had to rush back to work at her busy restaurant. Of the 181 seniors in the graduating class of 1957, I was the only one who didn't attend the graduation banquet.

I walked the streets until after midnight, trying to compose myself, trying to understand why my mother was so cold-hearted. Why did she want to hurt me so?

Yet, on the other hand, how could I overcome the hate burning inside me and somehow forgive her? For now, I couldn't. Tomorrow's another day. Tomorrow, I'll search for another way to lift my spirits again. That night, I became impervious to her selfish, heartless ways. I reasoned that someday, she'll look back on her life and regret the way she treated me. Also, that night I made a promise to myself that, as soon as I could, I would always carry a fifty-dollar bill in my wallet. And, never, ever, depend on anyone but myself again.

*   *   *

I left the house the next morning before anyone was awake. I didn't want to face Ora. I caught a ride to the Weirs. As we were crossing the bridge, before heading down Lakeview Avenue, I noticed a few cars parked in front of Howard Johnson's restaurant. It looked like it was already open for the summer season. I thanked my ride for bringing me to the Weirs, got out of the car, and curiously walked over to HoJo's. Within five minutes, I was clearing tables in the dining room. That was the beginning of my new summer job as a busboy at Howard-Johnson's.

I thought to myself, "Clearing tables, not a bad gig for a high school graduate," as I quietly laughed at myself. Soon, I would have money in my pocket again.

As I sat in the auditorium with the rest of the graduating class, listening to boring testimonials about how we are the future, I was thinking, "What to hell did I accomplish in school these past four years?"

Well, I learned how to drive a car, even though I still didn't have a license or a car. I learned to type my senior year. By then, I realized I wasn't born with an ounce of mechanical ability. I managed to type at a rate of 60 words per minute. Not bad, I thought. For sure, I was more the administrative type, than the mechanical type.

Academically speaking, I probably knew as much when I graduated from the 8th grade at the French school as I did when I finished high school. But, I acquired an education through my experiences that nobody in that class could match, taught by people whose paths I crossed, delivering papers, hanging out at Busy Corner, hitchhiking all over the state, and spending my summers in the Weirs. In the words of C.S. Lewis, the English author, *"Experience. The most brutal of teachers. But you learn, my God do you learn."* I was more than ready to make my way in the so-called cold, cruel world that lay before me. I was looking forward to continuing my education in the "school of hard knocks!"

When my name was called, I walked across the stage, was handed my diploma, and walked back to my seat. Shortly after that, I silently made my way through the smiling faces, proudly hugging their offspring, and sharing the happiness of their accomplishment.

No, my mother and Ben weren't there. I didn't invite them. I well remembered they didn't attend Lorraine or Claudie's graduation either. I didn't want to be disappointed like my sisters were. Ora never even gave her daughters a graduation present, so I certainly didn't expect one. How sad is that?

My mother was always quick to point out how well her children turned out to her friends at the Rod & Gun Club. Why, she would tell them, her kids all graduated from high school, as if she encouraged us to complete that phase of our education. Now, she could brag that Lorraine was attending medical college in the south somewhere, Claudie was also in the medical field in the Air Force, and Sonny just graduated too. In truth, I honestly believe she resented the fact we completed high school and she didn't.

The next day, I went to the Weirs to find a place to stay for the summer. I lucked out and rented the last room available at Mrs. Roubo's summer house on Doe Point, near the edge of Lake Winnispesaukee. As luck would have it, Mrs. Roubo was a former customer on my old paper route on North Main Street. She recognized me immediately. When I asked her if she would hold the room for me until I was paid, she said I could move in right away if I wanted and we'd settle up later. I was glad to see Mrs. Roubo, and she was glad to see me. That afternoon I returned to Church Street, packed my few belongings, and moved to the Weirs . . . without saying goodbye to anyone.

CHAPTER 23

THE FINAL SEASON

Major league baseball teams hold spring training in March to prepare ballplayers for the regular baseball season. In the Weirs, restaurants hold their version of spring training in early June, just before Motorcycle Week, to prepare new hires for the busy regular tourist season. Before the summer rush begins, owners are busily staffing up, training and evaluating new employees, and striving to get the cooks, kitchen help, receptionists, waitresses, soda jerks, and busboys to work together as a smooth, cohesive unit.

What I quickly learned was that Howard-Johnson's restaurant was unlike any other restaurant in the Weirs. For one thing, it was the only franchise-operated restaurant in the area. It was twice the size of the other restaurants, was extremely well organized and managed, and did an incomparable volume of business. Fact is it was the busiest Howard Johnson's in all of New England. People flocked there because of its reputation and familiarity. When you ate at Ho-Jo's, you knew what to expect. The level of service, the décor, the menu, and the quality of food was consistent at all their restaurants on the East Coast. Moreover, its location at the entrance to the Weirs, with ample parking for the daily onslaught of tourists, ensured it would receive a steady stream of hungry customers from opening to closing, all season long.

The owner's of this particular Howard Johnson's were Charles, and his wife, Avis Baroody. The Baroody's spent their summers in the Weirs and their winters in Florida. I didn't see Mr. Baroody very often, but Mrs. Baroody definitely was the linchpin that managed the entire operation. A tireless worker, she personally oversaw every facet of the business and ran the operation as smoothly as any big league manager. When I was hired, I applied for a position working at the soda fountain. At the time, they didn't have any openings at the soda fountain. Mrs. Baroody assured me that when an opening became available, I would have the job. However, she was quite desperate for busboys, so that's where I started out.

Looking back on it, there was an unwritten hierarchy at the restaurant, much like a pecking order or a pyramid. Mrs. Baroody was at the top of the pyramid, followed by the temperamental cooks, conceited waitresses, on down to the lowly busboys. In that environment, even the lowly dishwasher thought he had the right to boss me around.

When I began working there, he took great pleasure barking orders at me when I unloaded the large trays of dirty dishes and glasses on the metal tabletop by his station. In no kind manner, he shouted at me from behind his sink, "Put the glasses there," "You didn't scrape the junk off that plate," "Stack the dirty dishes over there," "Separate those cups from the saucers." Bark, Bark, Bark. It's as if he waited for me to come through the swinging door to the kitchen so he could repeat his rant.

Oh, and the haughty waitresses were every bit as bad. Many of them worked at Ho-Jo's for years and made the annual pilgrimage from Florida to the Weirs to ply their trade every summer. A few of them regarded me as their personal servant. To make matters worse, some of my pay came directly from a portion of their tips. So they felt entitled to boss me around. For the first month, I was beginning to think my name was "You."

All I heard was, "You need to clean table #6," "You left some crumbs on that chair," "You need to move faster, I have customers waiting," "You've got a table in the corner that needs to be cleared." "You need to put some plates on that table."

It was crazy. If they didn't have a good night making tips, they'd lament to Mrs. Baroody that the busboy was too slow.

Oddly enough, I was so busy clearing tables and running back and forth from the dining room to the kitchen, I didn't have time to think. I just let their ranting and raving go in one ear and out the other. It didn't go unnoticed by Mrs. Baroody. She carefully observed everything. Ironically, she became my one ally and supporter. She'd stop me in the middle of unloading a tray in the kitchen and tell me to slow down or not to carry so much. She was genuinely concerned that I was going to hurt myself. I never gave that much thought, although I didn't weight 130 pounds soaking wet.

One thing for sure, by the time I finished busing the dinner meal, I was exhausted. Unlike the previous summer, I had to walk about a mile from the restaurant to Mrs. Roubo's cottage on Doe Point. I was perfectly content to take a warm shower at the end of the day, then sit out on the screened porch in the still of the night and listen to the waves pounding against the stone wall at the end of the street. Peace and serenity, away from the constant hustle and clanging sound of dishes, was what I wanted most at the end of the day.

*　　*　　*

I'll never forget the famous entertainer I met one night during "training season" after I finished my shift at the restaurant. There was a cold chill in the air as the rain saturated clear through my clothes that night, while I plodded my way down Lakeside Avenue. I looked like a drowned rat when I walked into the Half Moon arcade to wait out the heavy rain. I smiled and waved hello to Mrs. Ames, the owner, before heading back to a far corner of the arcade to play a few games on my favorite machine. I had the entire arcade to myself. Nobody in their right mind would be out in this miserable weather. For a few minutes, I was alone in the brightly lit arcade, working those flippers in my own little world, when suddenly, I hardly believed who was walking toward me to watch me duel it out with a pinball machine.

I recognized him immediately. I had seen him on television before and was mesmerized by his over the top combination of gospel singing, moans, and screams, as he worked himself into a frenzy, belting out songs like, "Tutti Frutti," "Long Tall Sally," and "Lucille," while banging away in his boogie woogie rhythm style on a piano. Unbelievable. Richard Wayne Penniman walked into an arcade in a little hick town in New Hampshire, on a cold, rainy night in June 1957, to watch me do my brand of music on a pinball machine!

Why, he looked like he came from another planet, as he approached me with his wild pompadour hairdo. He was wearing a striking purple zoot suit, with baggy pegged pants, and a black silk shirt, with a matching black silk scarf wrapped around his neck. He looked downright funny to me. His wild eyes were popping out of his head and he looked like he had just been electrocuted.

When he extended his hand to shake mine, I was smiling and laughing all the while, as I said, "Man, you're Little Richard. What are you doing here?"

He never did give me a straight answer. He said something like, "Came to see you play the machine."

He and his three friends, who were dressed just as peculiarly as he was, stood by the machine and watched me play my "concert." When I hit a magic number on the machine, it burped out a series of five loud beeps, signifying I had just won five free games.

"Man, you're good," he told me, as I proudly turned toward my new visitors.

After a few games, one of his entourage asked me, "Say, where can we get a bite to eat?" I jokingly said, "This time of night, the only place open is the Drive-In Theater next to Howard Johnson's."

They must have taken me seriously. They looked at one another and then made their way out of the arcade.

When I was leaving, Mrs. Ames asked me, "Who were those funny looking colored guys?"

It would have been too hard to explain. I just told her that she had three records on her jukebox, sung by the little guy in the crazy purple suit. The next day, when I told anyone and everyone that would listen, that I met Little Richard the night before in the Half Moon arcade, one of the waitresses piped up that maybe he was in town to watch his movie, "Don't Knock the Rock," which just happened to be playing next door at the Weirs Drive-In Theater. Strange coincidence. Certainly, a strange encounter.

*   *   *

I had been working at Howard Johnson's about three weeks when Nancy and three of her friends showed up at the restaurant for lunch one Sunday afternoon. It had been nearly seven months since I had seen her and at least a couple of months since I had written to her. She tugged on my arm, as I walked by their table, and asked if I could talk to her. I told her, I didn't have time to talk right then, but agreed to meet her at the Half Moon arcade at two o'clock.

During my break, I hurried down Lakeside Avenue to meet Nancy. While jogging there, I was trying to think what I would say. I realized it was unfair of me to string her along any longer. I couldn't make a promise I couldn't keep to satisfy my personal ego. I thought the world of Nancy, but also realized the futility of our relationship. It was time to let this little butterfly out of the jar.

I had a lump in my throat, and was quite nervous, when we met in front of the arcade. Her friends, another girl and two boys, waited in the convertible parked in front of the arcade. She was as nervous as I was as she began to speak. She immediately put me on the defensive.

"You haven't called, you didn't write, I haven't seen you since last November," she said. What could I say? She was right. I realized it just wasn't fair to ask her to be patient and wait for me.

"Wait for what?" I asked myself.

No, it was time to break up. She went on to tell me that the "friend" behind the steering wheel wanted to date her. He even drove her to school. She told him she needed to end our relationship before she would date him.

I respected her for being honest and loyal. The bottom line here was that I didn't have a car, was planning to go to Florida or somewhere south after Labor Day, and wasn't ready to make a long-term commitment with her or anyone. I assured her, there wasn't another girl in my life. I just didn't have anything to offer her.

That was the end. We parted as friends. I told Nancy she was free to date anyone she wanted. In fact, I encouraged her to do so.

"You've got too much to offer to waste your life sitting around waiting for me," I told her.

She needed to find her way in life, just as I needed to find mine. We hugged, right there in the middle of the crowded sidewalk, looked at each other, as I forced a smile when I let go of her hand. She got in the car with her friends. I watched her leave, as they drove down Lakeside Avenue on their way back to Manchester. I let out a deep sigh. Strange, I felt like a weight had been lifted off my shoulders.

*   *   *

By the 4th of July, the restaurant was insanely busy. Mrs. Baroody knew better than I did that I couldn't keep working at such a frenzied pace. She was very willing to hire another busboy. I told her I'd ask my friend, Danny Matthews, if he wanted a job. Danny was odd. He didn't care if he worked or not. He didn't have a lot of money, but he was never broke.

When I enticed him with, "All the fun we could have working together," he bought right into it. Danny was a good worker. He didn't take any crap off the dishwasher or any of the waitresses and went out of his way to lighten my load. One thing about Danny, he was always there when I needed him. He was viewed as a crazy guy to some people, but as a good, loyal friend to me.

About that time, Mrs. Baroody asked me, "Do you still want to work at the soda fountain?"

The next day, I found myself scooping ice cream cones and making sundaes for a few hours in the afternoon . . . before I began the night shift as a busboy for the dinner meal. Now, I was working in a dual capacity, as a soda jerk and as a busboy. It didn't matter that much to me where I worked. I just wanted to help in any way I could. Before long, I was working in the restaurant from early morning until closing time without a break.

Two weeks after beginning my afternoon stint behind the soda fountain, Avis Baroody called me over to the front register.

With a serious look on her face, she proceeded to tell me, "I want you to know, you're the only person working at the soda fountain whose receipts always match with the cash register." In other words, I hadn't made a single mistake.

She was quite taken by that. I didn't see that as a big deal. To my way of thinking, I couldn't understand why they shouldn't match. The underlying message that day was that I impressed my boss. I didn't expect any more would come of it, but she had different plans.

It wasn't even six o'clock in the morning, when Mrs. Roubo was standing at my door, telling me that Mrs. Baroody needed me to come down the stairs right away. I didn't have any idea what she wanted.

When I walked out on the porch, still half asleep, Mrs. Baroody immediately apologized and, in the next breath said to me, "We're really in a bind. I need your help."

"What's wrong?" I asked, with a worried look on my face.

She went on to tell me that the breakfast cook didn't show up for work, so she was in a real pickle. Then, she said, "I need you to be the breakfast cook until I can find another one."

"Why, Mrs. Baroody," I pleaded, "I don't even know how to fry an egg."

She had to be desperate to need me to cook breakfast. I tried to convince her I was the last person she should want frying eggs. That fell on deaf ears. Avis Baroody wouldn't take "No" for an answer. So, there I was, in the kitchen at Howard Johnson's at six in the morning, frying bacon and eggs, making pancakes, and praying that I wouldn't screw up all the orders. Oh, I made plenty of mistakes that day, but with the help of the waitresses, somehow I survived without too many returned plates. Fact is I was quite proud of myself.

For the next week, Mrs. Baroody personally picked me up in the morning, in her pink Cadillac, and drove me to work. It didn't go unnoticed. I was the rising star at Howard Johnson's. Now, everyone was smiling at me and treating me with a newfound respect.

For awhile, I was working in the kitchen, working at the soda fountain, and clearing tables during the dinner rush hour. The difference now was that the waitresses weren't complaining. In fact, they pitched in and helped me out.

As the days of summer passed, Mrs. Baroody became more of a friend and mentor. Without coming right out and telling me, she was teaching me the restaurant business. When word got out that she was teaching me how to make the waitresses' table assignments, an amazing transformation of personalities took place. Suddenly, I was getting little pats on the back and nice compliments from the same waitresses that derided me before.

When she made her weekly run to pick up supplies in Laconia, she invited me along. On one of those trips, we happened to be driving down Church Street when I spotted my mother and Ben having their little Happy Hour on the front porch. I asked Mrs. "B" to honk her horn as we drove by. It probably took awhile for my mother to realize it was her son that drove by in that big pink

Cadillac. When Mrs. "B" asked whom I waved to, I told her it was my mother. Until then, we never talked about my childhood.

One late afternoon, in August, Mrs. Baroody and I had a serious heart-to-heart talk about my future. I didn't know about her past. I didn't know if she had children. Maybe, it was wishful thinking on my part, but I felt a close bond between us. She was my mentor; I was her pupil.

During our conversation that day, out of the clear blue sky, she said, "I want you to come to Florida and work for us next winter." She went on to say, "You don't have to worry about money or a place to stay. Don't worry; you'll be taken care of."

A college education never entered my mind before, until she told me, "If you want to go to college, I'll pay your college expenses, as long as you major in Hotel Management."

Just like that, I was offered a potential future in the hotel and restaurant business. The more I thought about it, the more I realized this was an opportunity of a lifetime.

Knock on wood; I could see light at the end of the tunnel. I had just been offered a job and an education in Florida, when my world unexpectedly came crashing down on me again. Literally crashing down on me. I should have seen it coming. I had been working twelve-hour days. My back was sore from carrying those heavy trays of dirty dishes.

On a busy Saturday night, I was carrying a tray full of dishes to the kitchen when my back snapped. A sharp pain, like a knife thrust in me, struck my lower lumbar area. The next thing I knew, the tray was flying in the air, I was falling to the floor, and broken glasses and dishes were scattered everywhere. I sat on the floor, in the middle of all the broken dishes, unable to move.

Someone hollered out, "Call an ambulance, the kid can't move."

I was embarrassed, in pain, but refused to be carted off in an ambulance. Finally, Danny and one of the cooks helped me up. Even though I was in a lot of pain, I tried to assure everyone that I was all right.

One of the waitresses gave me a ride home. Mrs. Roubo helped me up the stairs to my room and fixed a cold compress for my back. In no time, I was sound asleep. The next morning, my back was sore but I felt somewhat better. Later that day I spoke with Mrs. Baroody.

My career as a busboy, soda jerk, and cook was finished. It was two weeks before Labor Day. She offered to pay me for the remaining two weeks, and told me to forget about work, rest up, and take care of my back. I took her advice.

The following week was wonderful. I did nothing. No pressure, no heavy trays to carry, nothing to do but enjoy a nice week's vacation in the sun and sand at the Weirs, just like all the other tourists. I didn't realize how much I needed that break. It's just what the doctor ordered. I dropped by the restaurant once and spoke with Mrs. "B." She gave me their address, phone number in Florida, and reiterated that a job was waiting for me, right after Thanksgiving. She suggested that's when I should head south. That was fine with me, but one question crossed my mind. What was I going to do for the next three months? The question was answered the following Sunday.

*   *   *

Wally Wallette came by Ho-Jo's to show me his new car. He heard about my back injury and was waiting on the front porch of the rooming house with Danny when I came strolling in from the beach. Of course, he was eager to show me his car, fill me in on all the latest gossip, and tell me what he'd been up to all summer. Since I saw him last, he quit school and was working at the Laconia Shoe Company. None of what he told me came as a surprise. Wally was a fun loving guy. He enjoyed working with his hands, getting into mischief, and would never be mistaken for a rocket scientist. He lived in the moment, and school was not in his plans. For now, he wanted a car, to have some fun, and make a little money. In the words of Mileti, *"If you can have some fun, make some dough, and leave your footprints in the sand, you are a lucky guy."* In a way, I was a bit envious of my friend's carefree attitude.

We were driving around that afternoon when the conversation turned toward work. Wally told me about an opening in one of the departments at Laconia Shoe.

At first I said, "Are you crazy, man? I ain't working in no damn shoe shop."

He kept badgering me to give it a try. After awhile, he assured me it wasn't a sweatshop at all.

"I'm telling you, Cooz, it's not like when your mother worked there. Hell, I wouldn't steer you wrong. You're my buddy."

That was enough to get me thinking. The more I thought about it, the more I convinced myself that might not be a bad gig for the next three months. I needed to do something now that I was out of school. Furthermore, I could use a little more money for my trip to Florida. I needed to leave the Weirs in another week anyway.

My mother was glad to see me when I walked in the house. Actually, I was surprised she was glad to see me. I let her know I didn't come home to babysit. I kept my plan to go to Florida to myself, but told her I was applying for an opening at Laconia Shoe the next day. Why, that was like announcing it was Christmas in August to her. She couldn't have been happier. Her Sonny, finally saw the light. Now, he was going to have a good paying job and pay his mother room and board. She was beaming, when I offered to pay rent for my room. Ora was thrilled. I was returning home, paying her rent, and working in the shoe shop. Her wish for my future was fulfilled. St. Jude must have answered her prayers. She could be downright pleasant, when she was being pleasant!

Wally picked me up early the next morning and we were off to Laconia Shoe. I filled out some forms, met the company president, Mr. Brandeis, and was hired on the spot. My new Supervisor, John Hebert, came to the office to get me and escorted me to my workstation on the second floor.

The shoe factory wasn't at all like the false premonitions I imagined the place to be. Maybe it was because I didn't need the job to support a family or wasn't resigned to doing the same boring, repetitive job for the next forty years. For what it's worth, I was one of only a handful of workers who had a high school diploma, had a good work ethic that fit well in a factory environment, and, above all, knew I would be leaving in a few months.

My Supervisor impressed me from the moment I met him. He was a soft-spoken man who didn't intimidate me or manage by fear, as I had falsely expected. He made me feel welcomed from the beginning and left me alone to do my job, but was always available to answer a question or offer advice if I asked for it. I couldn't have asked for a better boss. Mr. Hebert stood out among his peers. He was well groomed and always wore nice slacks, a dress shirt, and a tie at work. Obviously, I made many false assumptions about the shoe factory. It wasn't a bad place to work at all . . . for awhile.

I worked as a sole press machine operator at the plant. Just as it sounds, there were racks of shoes that had to be fit with corresponding soles. The soles had notches on the side that matched with the shoe sizes. For example, a size 6 shoe would be matched with a sole with one notch on the side; a size 7 shoe with a sole with two notches on the side, and so on. I carefully aligned the matching sole under the shoe, and then placed it on a platform on my machine. With my left foot, I pressed on a bar at the bottom of the machine, which sent the upper plate down to squeeze the sole to the shoe. This simple process was repeated over and over again.

The hardest part of the job was to stay alert while operating the machine. It was a challenge to avoid looking out the window by my station to watch the afternoon sun, shining on the Winnipesaukee River flowing below, while trying to concentrate on the boring, repetitive task at hand.

Even though I could have earned extra money by increasing my production, Mr. Hebert never pushed me to work harder. On my first day on the job, he introduced me to Annette, who also operated a sole press. Annette had a personality like a pile of crap. Tough, dirty, bitter, all those words describe her. She resented me very much, as if I posed some sort of threat. Annette had a nasty disposition and wasn't nice to anyone in the department.

I didn't take it personally. I soon realized she hated everybody. She looked to be about thirty-five and probably had been working there for twenty years. She never spoke two words to me during the nearly three months I worked there. The woman was obsessed with making piece rate, so she took all the easy racks of shoes and soles to her station and left me with the more difficult soles to press.

John Hebert knew it, I knew it, and he respected me for not saying anything about it. He carefully avoided showing favoritism, while dealing with a bunch of temperamental misfits, scattered throughout his department. After laying the soles, the shoes were taken to the next station, where excess material was removed before the soles were stitched to the shoes.

Most of the craftsman who worked there had been doing the same repetitive job all their working life. They sat quietly at their machines, grinding away, hour after hour, day after day, without any disruption, completely void of any emotion. I felt I was working in a land of zombies.

A few girls my age worked in the department next to mine. A couple of them were somewhat cute and Wally soon informed me they were interested in meeting me. I quickly learned that you had to be careful with these girls. They fell in love way too easily. They didn't come from the privileged class, and longed for someone, anyone, to treat them nicely and pay them a little attention. For the most part, they were hopelessly doomed for a life laboring in the mills. A little harmless kissing in the back seat of Wally's car provided a pleasant escape from the monotony of working in the shoe factory. I didn't give any of the girls false hopes. I made it perfectly clear that I had a steady girlfriend in Manchester. That line saved me more than once.

Wally was a good worker, but I never understood just what he did. He seemed to spend his day roaming around the second floor, joking with everyone, having a good time, while I diligently worked at my machine. He was just a big kid at heart. It wasn't uncommon to be hit in the head by a sole thrown across the room. It helped snap me out of my hypnotic state. Suddenly, Wally would pop up from behind a scrap heap to let me know he was the culprit.

It was a beautiful Indian summer day. I had been working at the shoe factory about six weeks when a group of high school students were taking a tour through the factory on a field trip. When they came to our department, John Hebert brought them to my station to explain what I was doing. One of the kids on the tour was actually a friend of mine. Ronnie Chumley was shocked when he recognized me.

"Cooz, what are you doing here?" he said with a look of disbelief.

Ronnie came from a well-to-do family and I am sure he harbored the same misconceptions I had about the shoe factory. To his way of thinking, I was doing humiliating work, far below the expectations of a high school graduate. I knew he wouldn't understand, so I made light of it.

I told him, "Well you see, Ronnie, they're grooming me to be the President here, so I have to familiarize myself with all the equipment."

How naïve can you be? He looked at me seriously, and said, "Ohhhh, I get it," before moving on to the next station.

Even Mr. Hebert couldn't contain his sullen composure when I broke out with that one.

*   *   *

One Saturday morning, Danny came by my house all excited about something. We sat out on the front porch, where he told me, "Listen Cooz, I spoke with the Air Force recruiter. Right now, they're running a special program where they'll guarantee to keep us together through basic training. It's called the "Buddy System.""

I'll admit, I thought about joining the Air Force before, but dismissed it after I got Mrs. Baroody's offer.

"Danny, it sounds good," I told him. "But, I'm really planning on going to Florida to work for Mrs. Baroody."

Danny was rather persistent that day. He said, "So what?" "Why not have a backup plan, in case she doesn't come through?" He had a point. Adults had let me down many times before. "Besides," he went on to say, "The recruiter filled his quota and we wouldn't be going to basic training until the end of November anyway. A lot can happen between now and then."

I told Danny I would think about it and let him know in a few days. The more I thought about it, a backup plan wasn't a bad idea. It wouldn't hurt to talk to the recruiter. My sister liked the Air Force and I really wasn't committed until I was sworn in. Not a bad idea at all.

A few days later, I spoke with the Air Force recruiter. I recall asking him dumb questions like, "Can I get free glasses in the Air Force? Would they fix this messed up front tooth of mine?" Everything he told me was quite positive.

He assured me, "You're not "committed" until you're sworn in. But, if you want a slot in the "Buddy Program" with Danny, you need to take the test and fill out the necessary paperwork today."

"Why not?" I asked myself.

It was a good backup plan, and you never know what can happen. Danny was thrilled that I signed up. I had to plead with him to keep it to himself. I was still working at Laconia Shoe and I didn't want anyone to know my future plans. I would let my mother know when the time was right.

*   *   *

The cold, dreary days of November welcomed the mass of freezing air making the annual slide south from the barren fields of Canada to the leafless neighborhoods of New Hampshire. I hated that time of year. I couldn't leave soon enough. All the while, I bided my time and patiently waited for Thanksgiving to begin my journey to Florida. I planned to take the train from Laconia to Miami, right after Thanksgiving. It didn't work out that way.

Ronnie Timmons was home on furlough from the Navy. Danny told him I was planning to go to Florida. Well, Ronnie happened to have a relative driving there who was looking for some people heading that way to share expenses. That's how I hooked up with Bruce McCarthy. When I contacted him, he told me he was leaving in two days. That was on a Saturday. It all happened so quickly, I didn't even have a chance to tell Mrs. Baroody I was on my way.

That Monday, November 11, I went to work. I don't know why. I probably felt guilty leaving my job without giving the standard two weeks notice. I know I felt badly leaving Mr. Hebert like that. Bruce told me he would come by my house and pick me up at seven o'clock that night. When I got home from work, I broke the news to my mother and Ben that I was leaving for Florida. I didn't have time to explain what was happening. They just had to accept that I was leaving . . . . possibly forever.

Right before I left, I called Mr. Hebert at his house. I apologized for not giving him more notice, but explained this all happened in the last two days. He wished me luck and assured me he would smooth things over with Mr. Brandeis.

Promptly, at seven o'clock, Ben told me, "A car is parked in the driveway waiting for you."

Bruce McCarthy was driving; I sat in the middle in the front seat, and Ronnie Timmons sat on the passenger side by the front door. Danny Matthews sat alone in the back seat next to a chilled tub full of beer. We were on our way.

Yes, we were stupid. No, we shouldn't have been drinking. At least not the driver. Why didn't we wait until daylight to begin this long trip? Or at least until it stopped raining? It was a disaster just waiting to happen. And did it ever happen.

Some three hours later, in the dark of night, the driver fell asleep while driving the car. It all flashed before me as we were heading for a sharp curve, at an excessive speed, on the outskirts of Clinton, Massachusetts. He never turned the steering wheel. He was asleep, traveling at 80 miles per hour. We were flying in the air, as the car crashed through a guardrail and made its way down a steep slope, eventually crashing into a huge plate glass window that housed Government tractors.

At its high point, the car was probably ten to fifteen feet above the ground. When the car finally hit the ground, midway down the slope, the impact was so intense it literally blew the three of us in the front seat right out the passenger door. For a brief moment, I laid somewhere in the field on my back.

I recall Danny telling me, "You're gonna be alright, Cooz. I hid the beer under a tree!" Then I passed out.

Later, I learned that he and Ronnie were O.K. They had a few scrapes and bruises, but were none worse for the wear. They dragged Bruce and me to the side of the road. We were unconscious. A passerby called an ambulance, and we were transported to a hospital in Clinton, Massachusetts.

The accident happened on a Monday night. I don't recall anything until the following Friday. When I awoke, I was on a hospital bed and two nurses were gently cleaning road burns from my back. I didn't know where I was and didn't recall what happened. A nurse came into my room that night and told me what she had heard.

She also told me, "From what I heard, you're lucky to be alive."

"Where are my friends?" I asked.

She let me know the hospital released Danny and Ronnie the day after the accident, but they didn't know if Bruce was going to make it. She went on to tell me, he had a broken spine and may never walk again.

I was banged up, with a few cuts and scrapes, mostly from sliding across gravel, and my head was throbbing painfully, but, as the nurse said, "I was lucky to be alive." It was a miracle I didn't suffer from a permanent loss of memory.

The next day, Saturday, November 16, happened to be my 18th birthday. I was truly grateful just to be alive. I guess it simply wasn't my time. God had other plans for me. It was also the day of the big Notre Dame vs. Oklahoma football game. A nurse pushed me in a wheel chair to another room in the ward so I could watch the game with another patient. Nobody gave Notre Dame a chance of winning, except maybe me. Oklahoma, under the tutelage of the great Bud Wilkinson, had won forty-seven straight games. I watched their winning streak come to an end that day, sitting in a wheel chair in a hospital room in Clinton, Massachusetts. The final score was 7—0.

I suspect I was still in somewhat of a shock, as I pushed myself mentally, trying to reconstruct what happened. I had a clear vision of the car going through the guardrail and flying in the air. After that, everything went blank. By Sunday afternoon, I was allowed to walk the corridor with a cane. My back hurt, I was limping, and my head was sore, but my brain was intact, and I knew I was going to be all right. I always was a quick healer.

That afternoon, Ora and Ben came to the hospital to take me back to Laconia. This time, they were generally concerned for me. I assured them I was O.K. There was a little business to attend to before we could leave Clinton, Massachusetts. The Clinton Police Chief accompanied them to the hospital.

He also confirmed, "I was lucky to be alive." He went on to say, "If you boys hadn't been drunk, you probably wouldn't have survived the accident."

The Chief led us to the lot where the car was impounded. I could hardly believe what I saw. To this day, I have never seen a car that badly wrecked. It was compressed, as if it had been crushed like an aluminum can. The roof barely came up to my waist. Whew! He was right. It was a miracle I was alive.

Somewhere in the conversation, the Chief mentioned that we were each liable for $1,600 for the damage caused by the car going through the plate glass window at the Government building.

My mother wisely asked, "Doesn't the driver's insurance cover that?"

He didn't know, but he told her, "Someone is liable for it."

For the next three days, I never left the house. My mother nursed me back with ice packs and chicken soup. I was in a contemplative mood, probably even a bit depressed. I was afraid to get in a car. A few friends came by to see me. I felt like a big failure and didn't want to see anyone.

*   *   *

I still wanted to leave Laconia. I was ready to start a new life. The answer was right before me. It was time to grow up and make something of myself. If I could patch myself together and walk without the help of a cane, I decided to join the Air Force with Danny Matthews on Thursday. That was to be my ticket out of Laconia.

"Good backup plan," I thought to myself.

I was feeling somewhat better by Wednesday when I told Ora and Ben I was leaving in the morning to join the Air Force. I could tell my mother was confused by the announcement of my sudden departure, less than a week after bringing me home from the hospital. I spent a quiet night at home playing games with my little brother the night before I left.

The next morning, Ben drove me to the Federal Building on North Main Street, where I joined the other recruits for the ride to Manchester to be sworn in. Ben wasn't one to show his emotions, but, surprisingly, he was a little chocked up as he squeezed my hand goodbye.

"You do good. Make your mother proud," were his parting words.

It was 8:00 a.m. when I reported to the recruiter. He asked, "Where's your buddy, Danny?"

I didn't know. I hadn't seen Danny in a couple of days. We were ready to leave. No Danny.

It was after nine o'clock when a police officer came in the room to speak to the Air Force recruiter. I soon learned that Danny Matthews was not joining the Air Force with me. The stupid jerk. He was sitting in a jail cell in Boston. The night before, he went on a little farewell spree and was caught rolling a queer in South Boston. In hindsight, that was probably a blessing. I may have continued on a path of self-destruction hanging around with him.

At 3:00 p.m., November 21, 1957, my life changed forever. I was sworn into the Air Force with some twelve other boys who came from all over the state of New Hampshire. After taking the oath, we were loaded on a bus and taken to Grenier Field on the outskirts of Manchester to begin the long plane ride to San Antonio, Texas.

My emotions ran the gamut from joy to sadness, as I stepped into the giant twin prop driven Douglas DC-7 aircraft for the first plane ride of my life.

The sun was disappearing in the distance, as the big metal bird began its journey down the 1,800 foot asphalt runway. The sound of the engines was deafening, and the whole plane vibrated as thought it was coming apart, as it gained speed while roaring down runway #2.

Both hands clung to my armrests. I wondered for a moment if this heap of metal would ever get off the ground. As the plane approached the end of the runway, the vibration subsided and the big bird climbed into the evening twilight. I released the deep breath I had been holding inside of me and looked out the side window as the plane gained altitude.

It was an unforgettable moment. I saw the lights of Manchester below. Smoke was bellowing from the mills along the Merrimack River and the chimneys of the tiny houses below. Streetlights formed rows of paths for the workers driving home from the factories. Lights appeared in houses, as people arrived home from work. It was a beautiful sight to see, while our plane climbed higher and higher above the city.

A million thoughts were running through my mind as we flew over Manchester. "Was that Nancy I saw with her boyfriend down below? Did we just fly over Chuck Jameson's house? Could that dark, ominous building without any lights on be St. Vincent de Paul?"

We were somewhere over water when the bell sounded, allowing us to unfasten our seat belts. I took a deep sigh, closed my eyes, turned off my brain, smiled a bit, and listened to the droning sound of the engines carrying me away.

My final thought was, "Last week was almost the end of my life; this week was just the beginning."

I Believe

"That our background and circumstances may have influenced who we are, but, we are responsible for who we become."

Anonymous

EPILOGUE

On this mild November day there would be no fire drill in the middle of the night, endless hours marching on the drill pad, or afternoons spent picking up discarded cigarette butts along the roadside. This would be the first day I marched to the mess hall with my fellow airmen without a drill Sergeant reminding us how stupid we were. That was Thanksgiving Day, November 28, 1957, exactly one week after I joined the United States Air Force. The aroma of freshly cooked turkey, stuffing, gravy, apple, and pumpkin pie, overwhelmed the chow hall on this festive day. It was in that dining hall that I enjoyed the best Thanksgiving meal of my life.

`If I had died and gone to heaven, I couldn't have asked for a better meal. For this meal we were allowed to speak with the other airmen at our table, stuff our stomachs with as many servings as we could hold, and walk back to our barracks without marching in formation. I don't believe anyone in that dining room enjoyed that meal more than me. More enjoyable than the scrumptious meal, I was able to enjoy it without my mother's peering eyes gazing at my every bite as if I were plunking her money in my mouth. Until now, I had been afraid to put butter on a slice of bread or dare ask for more than one scoop of potatoes for the guilt I was made to feel. For that reason, I dreaded eating at home when I was growing up.

But the Air Force was different. I devoured the daily regimen of military life and took to it like a duck to water. At Lackland Air Force base in San Antonio, Texas, I found myself and a life I learned to love for the next 23 years, 7 months, and 10 days.

Sometime, during my fourth week in the Air Force, Squadrons of airmen waited outside the "Green Monster" to be called forward to select their chosen career field. When my turn finally arrived, I approached the desk of the awaiting Personnel Sergeant. The first words out of his mouth were: "What do you want to be, boy?"

Until that moment, I had never even considered what sort of job I would be doing in the Air Force. I didn't have any idea what "career field" was even available or the impact of the test scores from my entrance exam. As I pondered the Sergeant's question, I quickly came to the conclusion that, with my poor eyesight, my new employer wasn't about to let me fly a plane or even allow me to get near a runway. As he cocked his head, looking back at the long waiting line of troops, his patience grew weary.

"O.K., boy, what did you do before you joined the service?" he asked.

"I was a short-order cook at Howard-Johnsons, Sir"

"No, boy, your scores are too high for that. You can't be no damn food service cook. You understand?"

I said the first thing that came to my mind, "O.K., How about a tail gunner than?"

"Are you crazy, boy? You ain't gonna be no tail gunner, either." By now, the Sergeant was really getting pissed off with me. His patience had worn thin. I had to quickly come up with an answer. "O.K., Sarge, what career field are you in?"

Why, he looked at me rather proudly, as if he were inviting me to join his fraternity, and said: "I be in "Poisonel." I assumed he meant: "Personnel."

I sarcastically replied, "O.K., Sarge, put me in Poisonel too!" And that's how my Air Force career began in the Personnel career field.

There must have been a drastic shortage of Personnel clerks in the Air Force that year because I received transfer orders to report to the Personnel Technical Training School during my 6th week of basic training. I packed my duffel bag and made the long one mile journey to the other end of Lackland AFB to begin the 20 week intensified course. Now I was in the "real" Air Force, living in a new modern air-conditioned barracks, while learning the various tasks of my new career. At the end of the 20-week course, I graduated second in my class, with orders to Incirlik AB, Adana, Turkey.

By the time I arrived at Incirlik AB, in May, 1958, the Air Force had replaced my worn out partial tooth, performed two root canals, and completed nineteen fillings to my rotting teeth. Before heading overseas, I shed the embarrassment of my former name, and replaced it with the new chosen name of this author. In six months, my new "family" provided all the health care I desperately needed and I gained the comfort and confidence to be able to introduce myself to people without bowing my head and mumbling my last name.

I certainly could fill the pages of a book with tales of adventures of an eighteen year old boy, stationed on the highly classified Turkish installation from which Gary Powers was captured flying over Russian territory in a U-2 spy plane. However, since this chapter is an epilogue, let it suffice to say I grew in leaps and bounds in my initial assignment: physically, mentally, and emotionally. I distinguished myself in my military career and performed in the only way I know how: — to the best of my ability. An innate work ethic to excel was molded in me at an early age, and would signify my identity for the rest of my life. Any lingering doubt was dispelled when I was promoted and selected as the Squadron "Airman of the Month" for Detachment 16 in that initial assignment.

My follow-on assignment was at James Connally AFB, in Waco, Texas, where I met and married my wonderful wife of 32 years. Together, we had three beautiful daughters, who make their home in Austin, Texas. I applied for an assignment to Pease AFB in Portsmouth, New Hampshire, on my first reenlistment in the Air Force. The Air Force kindly obliged and stationed me as close as they could when they transferred me to Mather AFB, California!

I've always been a "take charge" kind of guy and rank never fazed me. If there was a job to be performed, I was the right man to give it to. I had a mindset that said, "Get out of my way; let me do it. With that gung-ho type personality, I achieved the highest score possible on the Personnel Supervisory exam, was promoted to Staff Sergeant while at Mather, and so impressed an inspection team from Headquarters Air Training Command (ATC), that I was reassigned to HQ ATC, Randoph AFB, Texas, and became a member of the Command Personnel Inspection team.

While I enjoyed every minute of my time served in the Personnel field, after eight years in the service, I came to the conclusion there was no demand for forty year old male typists in the civilian world after I retired. After scouring all the military classifications for which I was qualified, I admittedly pulled strings to retrain into the Procurement field.

The Vietnam conflict was in full swing when I retrained in 1967. College students joined the Air Force to avoid the draft, and only the cream of the crop were chosen for the Procurement field. Every Airman in my class at Procurement school had completed at least two years of college. I was proud of the fact that I was the top graduate in my class. From there, my follow-on assignment was at none other than back home at Randolph AFB in the Base Procurement office. With less that one year's experience, I was selected to be the buyer for Air Force One, President Johnson's plane, when it landed at Randolph. Yet, another testament of my "Can Do" attitude.

With only one year's experience in the Procurement field, in my next assignment I filled a Major's position as the Chief, Contract Administration in Bangkok, Thailand. What an experience it was, negotiating with the Chinese and Thais in this most sensitive position, where I learned to deal with the oriental culture, while maintaining the objectives of the U.S. Forces. Notably, I was responsible for administering and negotiating the contract for operation of all the power plants in Thailand. I must have impressed someone while in that capacity. With barely ten years of service, and only two years in grade, I was one of only two Non-Commissioned Officers in the entire country to be selected for promotion to Master Sergeant during my year in Thailand.

The breaks always seemed to come my way during my Air Force career. While in Thailand, my family remained in San Antonio. My follow-on assignment happened to be at Headquarters ATC again . . . this time on the Command Headquarters Procurement staff. Having experience at the base level in both purchasing and contract administration proved invaluable. Whenever there was a disaster, such as a tornado, at one of the ATC bases in the Command, it was MSgt Novak that was called upon to travel to the base to manage every facet of the Procurement support.

I'll never forget the night that Major Mert Baker and I were having a few drinks at the former Green Bay Packer, Donny Anderson's bar, on a cold, stormy night in Lubbock, Texas. In the course of discussing the day's inspection of Reese AFB, Major Baker blurted out, "Jim, why don't you become an officer? You know, you're doing all the work on this trip and all I have to do is take your report and give an out briefing."

He caught me off-guard. I had never thought of being an officer before. In fact, my goal was to become the youngest Chief Master Sergeant in the entire Air Force. The damnedest thing is, I was on track to pull it off! I fully had a goal to make CMSgt at the age of 33, with the minimum required fifteen years of service. That was my goal, until Major Baker, who went on to become a two-star General, started talking some good sense in that pea brain of mine.

"You know, Jim, you'll make Chief Master Sergeant. No doubt about that. But the day you leave the Air Force, there's not a damn soul that's going to remember you after you walk out the front gate." He went on to say, "As an enlisted man, your opportunities are limited. You'll never have the opportunity to work in Systems Command at the Boeing's and Lockheed's of this business. And furthermore, if you look at what your retirement pay will be as a CMSgt with 26 years service versus what it would be if you retired as a Captain, after serving the required 10 years as an officer, I'll bet you'd make $200 more a month if you retired as a Captain."

"You think so?" I asked.

"I know so." Mert Baker confidently told me, that night in Donny Anderson's bar.

When I arrived home from that inspection trip, I announced to my wife: "Guess what? I'm going to be an officer!"

My biggest supporter jumped with joy and told me, "I know you can do it. I've said so all along."

I don't want to oversimplify it. By then, I had completed two years of college. I needed my degree before I could be commissioned as an officer and I wasn't getting any younger. With the incomparable drive that burned inside me, I proceeded to attend San Antonio college, five nights a week, took every correspondence course available from the University of Maryland, fried fish on Saturday nights at Hot Shots on Lake McQueeney for a friend who had a heart attack, and studied until the early hours of the morning every night, besides fulfilling my military duties in the daytime. The competition for the few Bootstrap Commissioning slots was fierce. Selection was primarily based on the applicants' Grade Point Average (GPA). NO, was not an option for me.

I was selected to attend Park College under the Bootstrap Commissioning Program. There would be no holding me back now. In December 1970, three months after our twin daughters were born, I graduated magna-cum-laude from Park College, in Parkville, Missouri, with dual degrees in Economics and Business Administration. On January 7, 1971, I began my first day as an Officer Candidate at Officer Training School, at Lackland AFB, Texas. Eleven weeks later, I graduated from OTS, with honors, placing first academically in my Squadron, and third overall in a graduating class of 1,200 cadets.

My one stipulation when I chose to become an officer was to remain in the Procurement field. While the "Godfather" wanted me to come back to Headquarters ATC, I convinced him I needed a little more "grass roots" experience before I returned to the Headquarters. My next two years were spent as the Chief, Contract Administration, at Mather AFB, California . . . my old stomping grounds, where I had previously served in Personnel as an NCO. It was like old homecoming week when I returned to Mather. During my tenure there, the Mather Procurement Division received an Excellent rating from the ATC Inspector General and was selected as the ATC Outstanding Procurement Office of the Year. By the end of the first year, the "Godfather" was calling me to return to the Headquarters.

"C'mon, I need you here. You've been out there long enough," he pleaded.

After the fourth phone call, he quit mincing words and flat out told me, "Listen, damn it Novak, if you don't come now, I'll send your ass to Laredo or some other hole in the wall."

"Yes, sir, I'm on my way!"

Shortly after I returned to Randolph AFB, the "Godfather," Colonel Wilkinson, retired.

However, I have no regrets of returning to the Headquarters. It was after I returned that I had one of the most fascinating jobs in my entire career. Because of my Base Procurement experience, and good old NCO knowledge, I was considered an "expert" on settling construction contract claims. For nearly three years, I traveled all over the Command, at the request of the Command Director of Engineering, to negotiate construction claims. I practically worked around the clock, digging into the facts of each claim, arriving at a settlement position, and negotiating with lawyers and overzealous contractors. Again, rank never fazed me. When I arrived at a base, it was step aside and just be honest with me so I can achieve the best settlement for both parties. I became so consumed with that job, I actually forgot my way home one night and ended up giving the cab driver directions to a former house.

The week before I was promoted to Captain, I received a telephone call from a Colonel Perkins, the Commander, 3750th Resource Management Group, Sheppard AFB, Texas. He recalled a claim I settled at his base and my out-briefing at the conclusion. He was so impressed by my drive and knowledge, he wanted me to be his next Base Procurement Officer.

I reminded him, "Sir, that's one of the largest Procurement Offices in the country. As I recall, it's a Lieutenant Colonel position. Are you sure you want me?"

His response was, "Listen, I'm so damn sure you're the right man for the job, General Fox is making me put it in writing. That's how damn sure I know I want you."

Flattery will get you everything! In July 1975, I took over the assignment of Chief, Procurement Division, Sheppard AFB, Texas. With 55 military and civilian employees under my direction, it was one of the largest Procurement offices in the entire Air Force. In my three years at the helm, that office, out it the barren plains of west Texas, won the coveted ATC Outstanding Procurement Office of the Year for two consecutive years. I was selected as the ATC Outstanding Procurement Officer of the Year, competing against some 80 other officers in the Command, not once, but twice. In my final year at Sheppard, my Procurement Division was selected as the second runner-up for the Outstanding Procurement Office in the entire Air Force, in competition with over 200 bases. Those three years were the most memorable and rewarding years of my military career. I also managed to earn a Master's degree in Public Administration from the University of Oklahoma, while stationed at Sheppard Air Force Base.

From there, I was selected to attend the Air Force Institute of Technology's eleven month Education With Industry Program at Lockheed Missiles & Space Company in Sunnyvale, California, in the summer of 1978. After eleven months in civilian clothes,

I was itching to get back to work on my next assignment as the Contracting Officer for all Navy programs at the Boeing Plant in Seattle, Washington.

After two year's as the Contracting Officer on the Navy Hydrofoil program, I reached a period in my life when I had to decide whether to continue my military career or ply my trade on the contractor side of the business. As much as I loved the Air Force, once I achieved my 10 years as a commissioned officer, I elected to retire from the Air Force. The very day I applied for retirement, I received three job offers.

Do I regret not staying in the Air Force for 30 years? Yes, only because of my unending appreciation and gratitude for the opportunities it gave me. It will always be my "family." When I chose to retire, it was like making the decision to leave St. Joseph's after the eighth grade. Something deep inside compels you to make a change. I had received a phone call from one of the Director's at Lockheed in Sunnyvale who told me about a big shipbuilding contract Lockheed had recently won in Seattle. That was my impetus to move on.

Lockheed Shipbuilding had just been awarded a multi-million dollar Cost Reimbursable contract to build three Landing Dock Ships (LSD's) for the Navy. For over two years, I averaged working at least ten hours a day, rarely went out to lunch, and took work home or worked in the office on Saturdays. At one time, I had 97 people working for me. The competition in Government contracting on major procurements is fierce. When the Navy awarded the follow-on contract to an East Coast shipyard, I elected to find another job. Influenced by my family's desire to live in Texas, when Lockheed opened a new Division in Austin, I saw my opportunity to leave the shipbuilding business and return to Texas.

I was able to land a supervisory position at the newly formed Lockheed-Austin Division. Armed with enthusiasm, the new Division of Lockheed was assigned responsibility for overseeing the Army's "Aquilla" program, which was chartered with developing unmanned drones. At Lockheed-Austin, I was promoted to a new position as the Manager, Subcontractor Management, on the Aquilla program. It was a new team approach to managing subcontractors. Under my direction, my manager's coordinated the efforts of various disciplines, such as, Quality Control, Engineering, Finance, Testing, and whatever disciplines were necessary to manage the subcontractors.

Due to a lack of Government funding, the future of the Aquila program and the Lockheed-Austin Division was jeopardized and eventually the Division was disbanded. However, an old Air Force cohort called me one day and encouraged me to accept a position as the Director of Subcontracts at the Aerojet Corporation in Downey, California. In view of the circumstances in Austin, it was the best option for me at the time. I enjoyed my assignment at Aerojet and was being considered for a promotion to Vice-President when a twist of fate occurred.

Bob Leonard, the Materiel Director of the Aeronautical Division of Lockheed, called one day and offered me an exciting job opportunity in Houston, Texas, to work on the International Space Station program. Bob Leonard was a man I trusted. With the prospect of a brighter future, I completed my year obligation with Aerojet and returned to Texas and Lockheed in 1991.

I was in charge of the Procurement operation for Lockheed Missiles & Space Company on the International Space Station for nearly four years until I retired in 1995. Essentially, I was their man in Houston. Plagued by funding restrictions on the Space Station, NASA terminated their contract with Lockheed and awarded complete oversight responsibility to the Boeing Company. Whether it was fortuitous or not, I decided it was time to hang it up and be the boy I never had a chance to be growing up in Laconia.

On May 1, 1995, I drove through the Eisenhower tunnel of Interstate 70 in a blinding spring snowstorm. What a relief it was to be retired at the early retirement age of 55, to pursue my next goal of becoming the best skier I could possibly be. Armed with a car full of clothes, and my traveling companion—my cat Elvis by my side, we ambled down the winding mountain to our new home in Silverthorne, Colorado.

I can't even conjure up the right words to express the joy I felt sitting on the floor by the lighted fireplace in our empty townhouse, watching the snow fall outside our window, that first night in Silverthorne, Colorado. It was another unforgettable moment, when my whole body succumbed to the joy of my fateful decision to leave the corporate rat race to live the life I had only dreamt about for far too long. At last, I had the means to support myself in a comfortable lifestyle doing whatever I chose to do. I was only envious of myself!

It was a good life until one ill-fated day in January, 2000, when my life was sucked out of me while helicopter skiing outside Revelstoke, Canada. I was following the guide down a steep pitch in an unknown forest on an overcast morning when it happened. Midway down a chute of snow, I felt the ground tremble under my feet. I was headed for a large tree directly in front of me and knew I had to turn before I encountered a head on collision with said tree. I briefly turned to witness a cascade of snow surging toward me. Before my dry mouth could release the word, "HELP," I swallowed a mouth full of snow and was knocked backwards to the ground by the passing avalanche. I was pinned under a sea of snow, buried alive. Yes, I have succumbed to a near death experience . . . and lived to tell about it. Perhaps, that's food for another tale?

The boy who loved the mountain, lived to ski, jumped off cliffs, became a ski guide and instructor, was suddenly drained of the passion that had so occupied a huge part of his life. I lost it that day in an avalanche in a foreign country. I was never able to rekindle the fire that fueled the thrill and excitement within me when I was on skis. Looking back, I have no regrets. I gave the sport my all, and have countless fond memories of many days skiing in far away places all over the world.

The following year, I spent the winter in Sierra Vista, Arizona, trying to adopt a new passion. Golf simply wasn't the same for me. The love of sport simply wasn't there. In the spring of 2001, Elvis and I packed our belongings and moved back to Laconia, New Hampshire.

What promise did my childhood home hold? None. I was told you can never go back. For me, it held true. All hopes of rekindling old childhood friendships never materialized. I was a stranger in my own hometown. It was flattering to hear old acquaintances say, "Hey, I heard you've done real well in life." Which was generally punctuated by the following sentence which begged the question: "What to hell are you doing back here?"

On a blind date in early January, 2002, I met my beautiful wife, Denise, at the former Laconia train station. We've been inseparable from the day we met. I warned her of my lust for travel.

It was on one of those return trips from our winter home in Florida to our summer home in New Hampshire, when I suggested we should check out Hilton Head, South Carolina, to add to our list of travels. My, what a pleasant surprise. We both immediately fell in love with the area, and especially Bluffton. Life is short enough. When you discover a place that brings you joy and comfort, I learned long ago to not let opportunity pass you by.

Despite the declining home prices in the never-ending recession our country embarked upon in 2008, we sold both homes and moved to our final (hopefully) home in Bluffton, South Carolina, in August, 2009.

Oddly enough, about a year ago an old friend and I got around to talking about our working days, when he asked the question, "What do you consider your greatest achievement in life?"

Without hesitation and forethought, I answered, "It was the ability to be in a position to help other people succeed and reach their goals. I was happiest when I was able to help other deserving people." Those words poured out of my mouth like honey flowing from a glass jar.

It wasn't long after when I began to write the memoirs of my very difficult youth with the faint hope that perhaps, just perhaps, there may be a message in there to inspire a disheartened, lost soul, searching for a glimmer of hope, to never give up, to believe in yourself against all odds, and to approach every day with the thought that it's another day forward to a much brighter future. In the wise words of Dean Karnazes: *"If you can't run, then walk. And if you can't walk, then crawl. Just keep moving forward and never, ever give up."* And if by chance we meet, that would be beautiful.

CPSIA information can be obtained at www.ICGtesting.com
Printed in the USA
LVOW13s1116131013

356698LV00014B/538/P